Exporting Transnational Education

Vangelis Tsiligiris • William Lawton
Editors

Exporting Transnational Education

Institutional Practice, Policy and National Goals

Editors
Vangelis Tsiligiris
Nottingham Business School
Nottingham Trent University
Nottingham, UK

William Lawton
Higher Education Consultant
London, UK

ISBN 978-3-319-74738-5   ISBN 978-3-319-74739-2   (eBook)
https://doi.org/10.1007/978-3-319-74739-2

Library of Congress Control Number: 2018943738

© The Editor(s) (if applicable) and The Author(s) 2018
This work is subject to copyright. All rights are solely and exclusively licensed by the Publisher, whether the whole or part of the material is concerned, specifically the rights of translation, reprinting, reuse of illustrations, recitation, broadcasting, reproduction on microfilms or in any other physical way, and transmission or information storage and retrieval, electronic adaptation, computer software, or by similar or dissimilar methodology now known or hereafter developed.
The use of general descriptive names, registered names, trademarks, service marks, etc. in this publication does not imply, even in the absence of a specific statement, that such names are exempt from the relevant protective laws and regulations and therefore free for general use.
The publisher, the authors and the editors are safe to assume that the advice and information in this book are believed to be true and accurate at the date of publication. Neither the publisher nor the authors or the editors give a warranty, express or implied, with respect to the material contained herein or for any errors or omissions that may have been made. The publisher remains neutral with regard to jurisdictional claims in published maps and institutional affiliations.

Cover illustration: © elenabs / Getty

Printed on acid-free paper

This Palgrave Macmillan imprint is published by the registered company Springer International Publishing AG part of Springer Nature.
The registered company address is: Gewerbestrasse 11, 6330 Cham, Switzerland

Foreword

The demand for higher education has been growing strongly in the recent decades, with the global number of tertiary enrolments rising from 50 million in 1980 to over 200 million by 2015. Increasing economic prosperity, population growth, the use of English as a *lingua franca* and the changing labour market needs of a post-industrial 'knowledge economy' have fuelled an explosion in the numbers entering universities and colleges around the world.

The tendency of demand to outstrip the supply of places in higher education institutions has been most pronounced in fast-growing developing countries like China and India. High rates of economic growth boost the willingness and ability to pay for tertiary education, but it takes years to build and staff high-quality institutions. Some of the excess demand in such countries ends up on campuses in the USA, Australia and the UK. Between 1980 and 2015, the number of students enrolled outside their own countries grew from 0.5 million to 4.5 million. In Australia and the UK, the market leaders in international student recruitment, approximately one in five students, come from overseas.

However, the percentage of tertiary students prepared to cross borders to study has remained stubbornly low, at just over 2% of global enrolments. This suggests that the overwhelming majority of students prefer to study at home, whether for financial, family, religious or cultural reasons. In the last 15–20 years, many of the same US, Australian and UK universities that pioneered international student recruitment have begun to shift from 'export education' (bringing students to their home campuses) to 'transnational education' (TNE) (taking education to foreign students in their own countries). For UK universities, transnational enrolments (those studying offshore) now dwarf the number of international students on their home campuses.

TNE embraces a range of delivery modes, from distance learning, double and joint degrees to franchising and validation (allowing foreign partners to deliver a university's qualifications) and the establishment of 'international branch campuses'. In turn, these modes of delivery raise a raft of issues and challenges.

What is the best way of setting up and providing educational services in a third market? How should a joint venture be structured to minimise financial and reputational risk? How should learning and teaching strategies be adapted to meet the needs of a very different group of students, who are accustomed to different pedagogies and face employers with different expectations of a graduate? How should locally hired staff be supported so that they can deliver an alien curriculum? How can the quality of in-country provision be maintained, and should the learning outcomes be the same as, or simply equivalent to, similar programmes on the home campus? How can the demands of home and host quality assurance agencies and regulatory bodies be balanced? How do Western universities mitigate the risk that TNE is perceived as commercially exploitative or, even worse, academic neo-colonialism?

These are all pressing issues for the growing number of universities involved in TNE. As the sector has grown, and the diversity and complexity of the various partnership arrangements have increased, there has been a parallel growth in the number of seminars, conferences, special interest groups' specialist consultancy firms and articles and government reports on TNE. However, most of this work is practitioner-oriented and, for the most part, atheoretical in nature. As a broad generalisation, the practice- and policy-based work on TNE has been isolated from the small but growing body of academic research devoted to cross-border delivery of educational services.

The collection of essays in this book represents an important step towards bridging the gap between academic researchers and practitioners and policymakers in TNE. It arises from a symposium in June 2016 at Nottingham Trent University that was organised by the editors and hosted by Vangelis Tsiligiris and myself. The aim of the symposium was to begin a conversation between researchers and practitioners, so that the former can better influence the evolution and performance of the sector and the latter can ensure that the right research questions are being framed.

The symposium also saw the launch of the TNE-Hub (www.tnehub.org), based at Nottingham Trent University, but with an expanding global reach. The TNE-Hub is an international community of researchers and practitioners who have joined forces to facilitate the exchange of good practice and research evidence and support the development of efficient and effective strategies and activities in TNE. As one of the most far-flung members of the TNE-Hub now based in Fiji, I look forward to its influence and prestige spreading as its members focus attention on this fascinating and innovative dimension of higher education.

Fiji National University, Suva, Fiji   Nigel Healey

Contents

1   TNE 2.0: Informing Practice Through Research   1
Vangelis Tsiligiris and William Lawton

Part I   Models and Strategic Considerations   7

2   Exploring Germany's Contribution to Global Activity in Transnational Higher Education   9
Stephan Geifes and Susanne Kammueller

3   Shaping Transnational Education in the Netherlands: National Policy Directions   27
Rosa Becker

4   The Design of International Dual Degree Programmes as Effective Transnational Education Experiences   45
Ofelia A. Palermo, Angelo P. Bisignano, and Simon Mercado

Part II Organisational Culture — 67

5 Intercultural Competence Development for All Students in Theory and Practice — 69
Albina Szeles

6 Collaborating Across Organisational Cultures: Lessons from a Study of International Branch Campuses — 89
Vicky Lewis

Part III Managing Quality — 109

7 The Challenges of Providing a Truly International Education: The Malaysia Nottingham Doctoral Programme — 111
Christopher Hill

8 Strengthening Cross-border Cooperation in the Quality Assurance of TNE: A QAA Perspective — 129
Fabrizio Trifiro'

Part IV Student Experience — 149

9 Chalk and Talk? Teaching Practice and Innovation in Transnational Education — 151
David Cockayne and Heather Cockayne

10 Designing a Successful International Course: What Can We Learn from Students' Experiences on an Erasmus Intensive Programme? — 177
Gill Richards, Simoni Symeonidou, and Eleni Livaniou

11 Images of Student Experiences on Social Media: The Case
    of International Branch Campuses in Dubai   197
    Ummesalma Mujtaba Husein

12 The Future of TNE   217
    William Lawton and Vangelis Tsiligiris

Index   227

Notes on Contributors

Rosa Becker works as a senior researcher in the Knowledge and Innovation Department at Nuffic, the Netherlands. Holding a Master's degree in Education (University of Groningen) and PhD in Comparative Education (University of London), she previously worked as a researcher at the Institute of Education University of London and the Observatory on Borderless Higher Education. Her main interest is in higher education and internationalisation policy and practices, and transnational education.

Angelo P. Bisignano is Principal Lecturer in Strategic Management and International Business at Nottingham Trent University with responsibilities on Academic Partnerships and Progression Agreements. His pedagogic research focuses on how students relate to issues of sustainability and how higher education institutions promote enterprising attitudes amongst graduates. Angelo actively promotes the implementation of the PRME principles and of the sustainable development goals in the curriculum.

David Cockayne is a senior lecturer at the University of Liverpool School of Management (Marketing & Operations) and is also a Fellow of the China Policy Institute at the University of Nottingham. David has over 10 years' experience in higher education, much of which has involved transnational education partnerships. David's research contributes to the growing 'marketing as practice' field and organisational studies.

Heather Cockayne has over 10 years' experience within UK higher education and is completing her PhD at the University of Manchester. Having previously worked on transnational provisions in China, her research focuses on the internationalisation of higher education with specific interests in higher education policy, transnational education and student experiences.

Stephan Geifes heads the Division 'Transnational Education and Cooperation Programmes' of the German Academic Exchange Service—DAAD. His prior career included postings as Scientific Coordinator of the German Historical Institute, Paris, Secretary General of Deutsch-Französische Hochschule (DFH) and Director of DAAD France in Paris. He holds a master's degree from Bielefeld University, a Diplôme d'administration publique from the Ecole nationale d'administration (ENA) Paris and a PhD in history from Ruhr-Universität Bochum. He has published widely on international exchange in higher education (HE).

Christopher Hill is an associate professor in Faculty of Education and Director of the Doctoral Training Centre at The British University in Dubai. Hill has worked in the field of international higher education since 2008 and held senior university leadership positions in Asia and the Middle East. Hill is an HEA Fellow and works on transnational education and its impact on host nations and the development and management of international education.

Susanne Kammueller is Senior Expert for Transnational Education with the German Academic Exchange Service—DAAD. She authored and co-authored various articles and is DAAD project manager in an ongoing collaboration with the British Council on transnational education (TNE), which to date has resulted in three major reports. Before her present post, she held various positions in the DAAD regional sections for South/Southeast Asia. Susanne studied English Literature, Indology and Political Sciences and holds a Magister degree of Bonn University.

William Lawton is a higher education consultant who was Director of the Observatory on Borderless Higher Education and a founding member of Universities UK International. He has authored reports for HEFCE, Jisc, the British Council and several other organisations. His interests are in transnational education (TNE), mobility, digital learning and government policy. He was a university lecturer in the 1990s and political analyst at the Canadian High Commission in London.

Vicky Lewis is a higher education consultant specialising in international strategy development and marketing planning. She founded Vicky Lewis Consulting in 2013 and has carried out diverse projects for higher education providers at different stages of the internationalisation process. Her research and consultancy interests include transnational education and translating institutional drivers for internationalisation into practical plans. She draws on 20 years' experience within UK universities, including Director of International Relations and Director of Marketing roles.

Eleni Livaniou is an educational psychologist with a PhD in Educational Psychology from Sussex University, where she was in the Department of Cognitive Psychology research team. Now living in Athens, she is Head of the Learning Difficulties Department at the non-profit multidisciplinary diagnostic, research and treatment unit 'Spyros Doxiadis'. Eleni regularly presents her research and publications at international conferences and is President of the Greek Dyslexia Association and a member of the European Dyslexia Association.

Simon Mercado is the Dean of the London Campus of ESCP Europe Business School. Simon has worked as a visiting professor for accredited EFMD member business schools and serves at Steering/Advisory Committee level for the EFMD and AACSB. His primary research interest is in the internationalisation of higher education and commercial services and he has published widely on issues related to international management and management education. He is a regular speaker and commentator on education management issues presenting and convening at major international events and conferences under the auspices of the AACSB, ABS, EFMD, APAIE and EAIE.

Ummesalma Mujtaba Husein is a higher education strategist, specialist in transnational higher education. With over a decade and half rich experience in transnational education (TNE), she has number of scholarly publications that are both pragmatic and empirical in nature. Her other research areas include tourism, pilgrimage and Islamic management.

Ofelia A. Palermo is Principal Lecturer in Management and Academic Director of the MSc International Business suite of programmes at Nottingham Business School, Nottingham Trent University (NTU). Her research expertise relates to the areas of identity, control, resistance, gender and ethics in leadership. Ofelia is involved in the design and review of academic programmes and is a member of the Academic Development and Quality Committee of the university, participating in the review of programmes and international partnerships.

Gill Richards is Emeritus Professor of Special Education, Equity and Inclusion at Nottingham Trent University (NTU). She originally trained as a teacher, working for 21 years in mainstream and special education before joining NTU as Director of Professional Development. Since joining NTU, she has led government SEN projects in UK schools and a European Erasmus project in Greece with teachers. Her research, publications and international conference presentations focus on issues of equity and inclusive education practice.

Simoni Symeonidou is Assistant Professor of Inclusive Education at the Department of Education, the University of Cyprus. She has published widely on inclusive education issues including teacher education, curriculum development, disability politics, policy and practice. She is actively involved in networks and organisations promoting inclusive education and is the scientific co-ordinator of the research project 'Tesserae of Knowledge' (www.ucy.ac.cy/psifidesgnosis), a project promoting teachers' professional development through the usage of disability arts and narratives.

Albina Szeles is Deputy Director at the Centre for Global Engagement, Coventry University, UK, overseeing a broad range of internationalisation activities including international student and staff mobility, internationalisation of the curriculum agenda and Online International Learning across the university. She has previously served as an Intercultural Engagement Manager where she was responsible for intercultural education programmes for both students and staff. Szeles is a strong advocate of intercultural preparation, digitalisation and internationalisation of higher education.

Fabrizio Trifiro' is an international manager at the Quality Assurance Agency for Higher Education in the UK, where he leads on the quality assurance of transnational education, strategic engagement with counter-part agencies overseas and the international student experience. He holds a PhD in Political Philosophy, an MA in Human Rights and an MSc in Social Research Methods, and has previously undertaken research, taught and published on the interconnections between globalisation, democracy and epistemology.

Vangelis Tsiligiris is a principal lecturer at Nottingham Business School, Nottingham Trent University, UK. He has had broad experience in transnational education, having developed and managed the overseas partnerships of several European universities. He is an active researcher with publications in academic journals and organisations such as the British Council. He has acted as advisor to the Greek and Maltese governments and in 2016 he founded the TNE-Hub, an international community of researchers and practitioners in TNE.

List of Figures

Fig. 2.1	Classification of German TNE activity. Source: DAAD/DZHW (2017)	13
Fig. 2.2	TNE activities of German universities 2017: Locations. Source: DAAD/DZHW (2017)	14
Fig. 4.1	The WHEEL framework	53
Fig. 8.1	The geographical scope of UK TNE	131
Fig. 8.2	TNE as the main area of growth for UK HE	132
Fig. 8.3	The top 5 host countries for UK TNE	133
Fig. 8.4	The QACHE vicious circle	137
Fig. 8.5	The QACHE virtuous circle	137
Fig. 9.1	Practice field of teaching in TNE institutions in China	171
Fig. 9.2	Practice-based process model of innovation in teaching	172

List of Tables

Table 4.1	The IDD MSc programme at Nottingham Business School—Structure	50
Table 4.2	The IDD MSc programme at Nottingham Business School—Partners and complementary programmes	51
Table 4.3	Action points suggested for managing the 'Weigh the Partnership' process	56
Table 4.4	Action points suggested for managing the 'Heed Practices and Customs' process	58
Table 4.5	Action points suggested for managing the 'Evaluate Quality Assurance Processes'	59
Table 4.6	Action points suggested for managing the 'Establish Completion Requirements' process	61
Table 4.7	Action points suggested for managing the 'Lay-down the Programme Management Plan' process	62
Table 11.1	Evaluating the seven dimensions	211

1

TNE 2.0: Informing Practice Through Research

Vangelis Tsiligiris and William Lawton

The idea for this book emerged during planning for a research symposium titled *Bridging the gap: Research and practice in transnational education*, which was the inaugural event of the TNE-Hub in June 2016. The TNE-Hub is a community of researchers and practitioners in transnational education (TNE) created in an effort to bring together those of who work, research, and have a wider interest in the area of TNE.

Over the past 20 or so years, there have been significant developments in the field of TNE. This does not refer only to the organic growth of TNE (e.g. number of students enrolled) but also to the range of TNE delivery arrangements and the countries involved. The major exporting countries are still the UK, Australia, the USA, Germany, and the Netherlands, while the main importing countries are China, Malaysia, Singapore, Hong Kong, and many others. However, in recent years we

---

V. Tsiligiris (✉)
Nottingham Trent University, Nottingham, UK
e-mail: vangelis.tsiligiris@ntu.ac.uk

W. Lawton
Higher Education Consultant, London, UK

have witnessed a disruption to this taxonomy of TNE importing and exporting countries. For example, countries like India and China have started exporting their higher education (HE) programmes to other countries through international branch campuses. This trend, of TNE being offered by non-western institutions, will continue to grow as economic activity and demographic trends shift in favour of non-western countries.

The rise of new players in the global higher education market has accelerated the negative impact in the flow of international students, a process which is further worsened by the rise of protectionist policies at national level (e.g. the UK) aiming to reduce the number of international students. Overall, TNE has become a central mode of international higher education, allowing access to higher education for hundreds of thousands of students, in most countries around the world, while at the same time, competition in the global TNE market is intensifying.

Despite this significant growth and the fundamental challenges faced by higher education institutions (HEIs) and national governments, TNE continues to be sidelined as a subject for research and scholarly activity. Often, we refer to TNE researchers as "lone wolfs" who struggle to find support and resources within their academic departments for their TNE research. As result, TNE researchers find themselves in a situation where, while they strive to conduct research in such a dynamic field, they have to work in isolation, thus missing out vital opportunities for collaboration.

At the same time, following a range of developments in exporting countries (e.g. Brexit in the UK) and importing countries (e.g. HE capacity development in Southeast Asia), TNE has been under the spotlight of governments and HEIs. Thus, TNE has been identified as a cure for all ills by several HEIs and government bodies that belatedly discovered it.

However, despite the recent hype in TNE, there is still an absence of systematic market research and accurate data—a well-known and persistent problem of TNE. This is partly caused by the disregard of TNE as an area of HE strategy and policy that deserves its own space in the research agenda of HEIs and government bodies.

This lack of systematic research and accurate data creates a range of challenges for those who engage in TNE activities. Intense competition—now emerging from non-traditional TNE exporting, and previously importing, countries such as China and India—requires careful planning and swift implementation of TNE projects. This requires comprehensive market analysis, use of accurate data, and careful evaluation of institutional resources before embarking on any TNE project. Additionally, TNE activities vary in resource requirements, timescale, risk, and institutional strategic commitment. As such, TNE should be carefully considered in the context of the institutional capabilities and wider strategic aspirations. However, the reality is that TNE projects continue to be a result of individual initiatives, usually emerging as result of personal connections of academics, administrators, and researchers. As result, TNE projects often lack the necessary strategic alignment with the institutional wider strategic objectives, which then affects their success and sustainability.

By providing a selection of chapters on different areas of TNE (strategy, quality, organisational culture, and student experience), this book aims to capture some valuable "lessons learnt" that can be useful to TNE practitioners and researchers. For practitioners, we believe that there is the need to use an evidence-based approach to plan and manage sustainable TNE projects. Using research and experiential evidence is the best way to manage risk and avoid failure in TNE activities.

This evidence-based approach should be supported by those who conduct research in TNE. Considering that TNE is primarily a business and policy-related activity and less of a theoretical field, TNE researchers should aim to highlight the practical applications of their research findings in a way that supports the evidence-based approach required to plan and manage sustainable TNE projects. As such we believe that research and practice in TNE should be considered as inseparable, and the chapters of this book aim to present how this might look like.

We have had the privilege to work with a superb group of authors who represent a diverse set of roles within the wider TNE world. The diversity of our authors' background allows to provide valuable inputs from a range of different areas and perspectives, which is a key strength of this book.

This book is organised in four parts: (A) models and strategic considerations; (B) organisational culture; (C) managing quality; and (D) student experience.

Part A starts with Chap. 2 where Stephan Geifes and Sussane Kammükker, from DAAD in Germany, outline the recent developments of German TNE and explain the fundamental differences it has in comparison to UK and Australian TNE. This chapter provides a valuable and rich source of information to the German TNE model which, as the authors explain, is a result of a national strategy aiming to strengthen the internationalisation of German HE and to boost regional and bilateral cooperation of a wider scale.

In Chap. 3, Rosa Becker from EP-Nuffic writes about the TNE policy evolution in the Netherlands in the recent years. TNE in the Netherlands is a rather dynamic area which has been at the centre of the HE policy debate. It is indicative of the dynamic nature of TNE in the Netherlands that the author has been updating this chapter until the last minute before the book manuscript submission.

Part A concludes with Chap. 4, where Ofelia Palermo and Angelo Bisigiano from Nottingham Business School and Simon Mercado from ESCP London share their experience on designing and managing dual degree programmes. Considering the increasing popularity of dual degree programmes—especially amongst traditional HEIs that have been reluctant to embark on TNE activities—this chapter provides a valuable insight on how to build and manage sustainable arrangements of this type.

Part B begins with Chap. 5 where Albina Szeles from Coventry University explains how the Online International Learning (OIL) model is used as a tool for connecting domestic and TNE students and empowering them to become global graduates. Also, this chapter unpacks the concept of intercultural competence as an integral part of internationalisation process for all students.

In Chap. 6, Vicky Lewis, founder of Vicky Lewis Consulting, reports the findings from an interview-based study of international branch campus (IBC) marketing. The study provides insights on the challenges and potential solutions at each stage of the IBC development process. Specifically, this chapter explains how differences in organisational culture, stage of development, and operating context must be recognised in order to optimise relationships and outcomes in an IBC context.

Part C consists of two chapters providing alternative viewpoints on TNE quality management. In Chap. 7, Christopher Hill, from the British University in Dubai, presents that the challenges and opportunities of creating an international research degree programme. The author employs a case study approach using the Malaysia Nottingham Doctoral Programme—a dual PhD programme between Nottingham UK and nine public Malaysian universities. In his chapter, Christopher Hill outlines the value and rationale of partnership programmes and discusses the lessons learned throughout the initial and development stages. This chapter provides insight into key factors to consider and explores the opportunities for institutional growth and development as a result of external activity.

In Chap. 8, Fabrizio Trifiro', from the UK Quality Assurance Agency (QAA), analyses the Agency's approach to TNE, focusing specifically on its strategies to strengthen cooperation with host countries' quality assurance agencies to ensure the efficiency and effectiveness of its oversight of UK TNE. This chapter emphasises the importance for quality assurance agencies to engage with governments, cross-border providers, and TNE students to develop international approaches that are capable of fully harnessing the benefits of TNE for societies while avoiding regulatory gaps and overlaps.

The fourth and final part of this book contains three chapters on TNE student experience. Part D begins with Chap. 9 where David Cockayne, from the University of Liverpool, and Heather Cockayne, from the University of Manchester's Institute of Education, explore the nature of teaching innovation in TNE. Rather than seeing innovation as stimulated by management, the authors utilise a practice-based approach and argue that teaching innovation is derived from the day-to-day activities of teaching staff. They identify three broad practices evidenced by TNE staff: interacting, exploring, and exploiting. These practices are constantly being (re)shaped through micro-level activities introduced by staff as a result of their environment. Over time these activities are legitimised and normalised, or rejected. Teaching innovation is therefore constantly evolving as the result of staff performativity.

In Chap. 10, Gill Richards from Nottingham Trent University, Simoni Symeonidou from the University of Cyprus, and Eleni Livaniou explore the experiences of a group of mature students from three European countries who participated in an Erasmus Intensive Programme, studying for an additional qualification, during a university summer vacation. The "intensive programme" context exacerbated anxieties and situations that would usually take longer to surface and involve longer-term strategies to resolve. The authors reflect on the student-centred issues for universities to consider when planning and delivering international courses, which can be also extended to TNE provision.

In Chap. 11, Ummesalma Mujtaba, an independent academic scholar and TNE consultant, analyses the student experience at international branch campuses as portrayed on social media, and whether the depicted experience reflects student development. This chapter aligns the social media postings of the seven primary aspects that present the determinants of students' perceptions of quality and experience of study at international branch campuses and explores their implications on student development. This analysis provides international branch campuses with an opportunity to evaluate their social media postings against the student experience criteria.

Our book concludes with Chap. 12, where we provide our views on the future course of TNE. Reflecting on the most recent developments, research findings, and the expected future trends in the wider area of global higher education, we explain that TNE is becoming increasingly integral part of high education provision. Additionally, we explain why we believe that the import-export approach to international higher education, which is still the main prevailing approach in exporting countries like the UK, does no longer meet the aspirations of prospective partners in other countries. On the Brexit debate, we challenge the appropriateness of UK HEIs using branch campuses to overcome the potential negative implications. Instead, we highlight the need for UK HEIs to consider the imminent impact of Brexit on existing TNE arrangements in the EU area. Across this chapter we highlight the critical role of TNE in the evolving transition from the campus-centred university to the "metanational" university.

Part I

Models and Strategic Considerations

2

Exploring Germany's Contribution to Global Activity in Transnational Higher Education

Stephan Geifes and Susanne Kammueller

Until not very long ago, transnational education (TNE) used to be almost exclusively perceived as an Anglo-Saxon phenomenon. Australian, British, and American universities were the first to export and market their higher education (HE) programmes on a larger scale and have been active in this field for several decades. Consequently, analytical discourse on TNE for a long time centred mainly on examples from these sending countries.

German universities started to make an appearance on the TNE scene only after the turn of the new millennium. After some 15 years of TNE engagement of German higher education institutions (HEIs), their study offers abroad currently number more than 31,000 enrolled students worldwide, not including distance learning programmes. Compared to an estimated 195,000 students in comparable British (HE Global 2016) or 96,000 students in Australian (Research Snapshot 2016) university projects, the number might not appear too high.

S. Geifes (✉) • S. Kammueller
DAAD German Academic Exchange Service, Bonn, Germany
e-mail: geifes@daad.de; kammueller@daad.de

Nonetheless, TNE "made in Germany", often strongly associated with institutions known as "binational universities", is of some interest for exploring the phenomenon of worldwide TNE because it shows some marked difference in practice and policies from the approaches associated with the majority of provision. The TNE activities of British, Australian, and US universities are primarily driven by institutional needs and practices and in general involve a strong element of institutional economic interest, especially in times of decreasing government funds allocated to HE. German TNE activities, too, are based on the commitment of German HEI but are characterised to a strong degree by a partnership approach stressing cooperation with universities in TNE host countries and, for the most part, receive financial support from the German Academic Exchange Service (DAAD). In this sense, Germany has a national strategy for TNE which can be summarised as follows: Strengthening the internationalisation of the German HE system through TNE activities of German universities and at the same time employing TNE as an instrument of regional or bilateral cooperation beyond mere HE policy, for science diplomacy, development cooperation, and so on.

National strategies for TNE can develop in different forms and derive from a broad range of conditions and motivations. Just as in other countries, the context in which TNE activity and strategy evolved in Germany is defined by globalisation and internationalisation. The engagement of German universities as TNE providers and the national perspective on the role of TNE, however, have been shaped by a number of specific factors including the German system of public HE funding (no tuition fees), the federal government's internationalisation strategy for HE (active funding policy), and a mix of different political objectives which form the basis for the involvement of the German government and DAAD in supporting cross-border activities of German HEIs. These determinants made themselves felt from the beginning and have resulted in a strategic national focus on broader political over economic aspects in TNE.

This chapter will analyse the transformation of German TNE from an experimental playground for universities into a strategic tool for national HE, foreign cultural and development policy and outline some research activity accompanying and ensuing from this development. In the absence of a generally accepted definition, it is first appropriate to define how the term TNE is interpreted and understood in Germany, where TNE translates into German as "Transnationale Bildung" or TNB. The next section will give an overview of German TNE in the year 2016/17. From here, the third section will discuss how German TNE got to its present shape. The fourth part will depict the main lessons learnt on the operational level. The analysis of German TNE activity will conclude with a description of TNE as part of a broader national strategy.

The Concept of TNE in Germany

In accordance with a 2013 DAAD position paper, TNE is understood here as a form of HE involving an HEI from a "sending" country which bears fundamental academic responsibility for study programmes that are offered at an HEI in another, the "host" country, and specifically target potential students in the "host" country or region.

As a consistent international TNE terminology and categorisation is missing to date, an in-depth comparison of TNE activity between different providing countries remains a challenge waiting to be tackled. The same applies to overall comparison of TNE activity between various host countries. A recently published classification framework for TNE, developed as part of a joint study project of the DAAD and the British Council, proposes an approach towards the creation of international standards for TNE statistics. The framework is based on the principal distinction between academically collaborative TNE forms, which are offered jointly by a university from a providing country and a local university in the country where the programme is delivered, and stand-alone or independent TNE offerings delivered under the sole responsibility of a providing foreign university. Within these two fundamental categories, a further distinction is made between TNE forms on the level of study programmes (i.e. franchise models versus joint study courses) and of entire TNE institutions (branch campus versus joint university). Distance learning is classified as a third distinctive level with collaborative and independent modes (Knight and McNamara 2017).

A first application of the final version of the framework to data on German TNE collected by DAAD shows that by far the major part of German TNE falls under the category of "collaborative TNE provision". Of all TNE programmes recorded, 93 per cent were either degree courses jointly offered by a German university with a local university partner at the partner institution or programmes offered at joint institutions, also referred to as "German binational universities". Together, these programmes and institutions enrolled 96 per cent of students in German TNE. Only 7 per cent of study programmes with 4 per cent of students are classified as "independent" (DAAD/DZHW 2017). A prototype of the TNE classification framework was earlier used by Bernard Ramanantsoa et Quentin Delpeche in an extensive analysis of French TNE activity. (France Strategy 2016)

German TNE Provision 2016/17

At the beginning of the academic year 2016/17, the number of students registering for German TNE courses had increased to 31,330. The enrolment numbers bear witness to the continuation of a steady growth trend observed over the last years, with regular annual increases of approximately 10 per cent (DAAD/DZHW 2014, 2015, 2016).

As shown in the map below, German universities are represented with TNE programmes on four continents, in 34 countries and at over 60 locations worldwide, offering a total of 274 undergraduate and postgraduate courses. The DAAD currently supports or supported in an earlier phase of establishment more than 80 German TNE projects (see Figs. 2.1 and 2.2).

The Wissenschaft Weltoffen data on German TNE is based on reports submitted to the DAAD by German HEIs which maintain TNE projects supported under a number of various schemes from funds provided by the Federal Ministry of Education and Research (BMBF) and the Federal Foreign Office (AA). As the HE statistics of the German federal and state governments do not capture TNE data as yet, no comprehensive data is available on activities without any DAAD support. The TNE data presented in Wissenschaft Weltoffen therefore cannot be considered complete, but

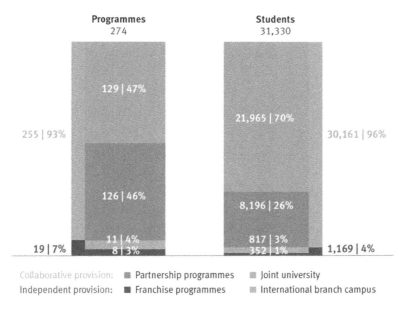

Fig. 2.1 Classification of German TNE activity. Source: DAAD/DZHW (2017)

it is safe to assume that they cover the statistically verified majority of all German TNE activities.

With regard to regional distribution and student numbers, the data highlights the significance of "binational universities" for Germany's TNE profile. The five largest German TNE locations feature four binational universities, namely the German University in Cairo (GUC), the German Jordanian University in Amman, the Vietnamese German University (VGU) in Ho Chi Minh City, and the German University of Technology in Muscat, Oman. 64 per cent of the TNE students surveyed are enrolled at these four institutions.

China has the third largest group of TNE students after Egypt and Jordan. With regard to the mode of TNE delivery, the picture here is different, however, because the 3728, or 12 per cent of students, in German TNE in China are distributed over several small- and medium-sized projects. A tendency towards regional concentration can be observed in

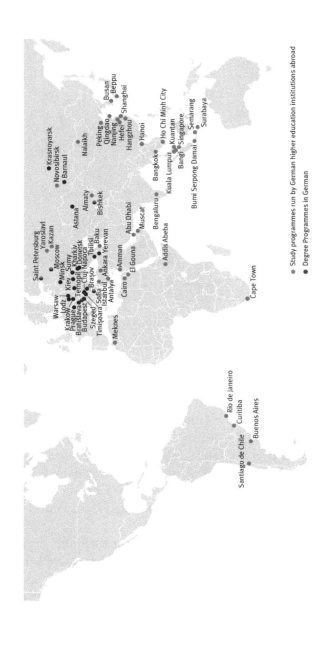

Fig. 2.2 TNE activities of German universities 2017: Locations. Source: DAAD/DZHW (2017)

China too. Shanghai, base of several German TNE offers including the Chinese-German College for Postgraduate Studies (CDHK) and the Chinese-German University of Applied Sciences at Tongji University, is the study location of 63 per cent of Chinese TNE students. Another 28 per cent study at the Chinese-German Technology College in Quingdao.

A look at the study fields of students registered in German TNE reveals a marked and increasing preference for engineering subjects, with 56 per cent of student enrolment. More than three-quarters of enrolments (77 per cent) are in degree programmes on bachelor's level. The share of students in engineering as well as in undergraduate studies in TNE is considerably higher than the corresponding shares of international students in Germany, that is, students with a foreign university entrance examination. The high proportion of bachelor students in TNE gives rise to expectations that graduates might choose German postgraduate programmes offered in Germany or abroad to continue their academic education.

Not surveyed in the data is a large majority of the approximately 650 double and joint degree courses offered by German universities with foreign partners recorded as of 2016 in the database of the German Rectors' Conference at www.hochschulkompass.de. Germany's overall internationalisation strategy for HE, besides promoting the international mobility of German HE providers and programmes and international student mobility to Germany, includes high aims for a further enhancement of the level of international experience, intercultural competence, and language skills of students and graduates in Germany through study-related stays abroad for 50 per cent and extended study-abroad stays of one semester or more for at least 30 per cent of its students by 2020. By far the greater number of double and joint degree programmes of German universities therefore are based on the principle of reciprocal student exchange (BMBF 2016).

How Did Germany Get There?

From what was basically a scholarship organisation, the DAAD from the 1990 developed into a national agency for the internationalisation of the German HE system with a much broader remit. A first action plan for the internationalisation of Germany as a study destination was presented in 1996.

The aim was to increase the number of international students in Germany. By the year 2000, 175,000 international students studied in Germany, among them 65 per cent "Bildungsauslaender" who had gained their university entrance qualification in another country. By 2016, the numbers had risen to 340,000 international students including 74 per cent "Bildungsauslaender" (Wissenschaft Weltoffen 2017). The DAAD strategy published in 2013 set the goal to attract a minimum of 350,000 international students to German HEI by 2020 (DAAD 2013a). The federal government adopted this target in its internationalisation strategy for education, science and research (BMBF 2016).

It is within this context of a deliberate policy to internationalise German HE that TNE became a subject of debate and action in the early years of the new millennium. The increasingly felt necessity to intensify the integration of German HE with the evolving global HE market in order to keep in touch with international developments was the main driving force and triggered further steps to deepen the internationalisation of the domestic HE system, while public funding of HE in Germany remained unquestioned. TNE appeared as a means to enhance the international reputation of German HE through stronger visibility, serving national motivations to market Germany as a leading location for study, research, and innovation as well as institutional strategies to raise international standing.

For German universities, the main stimulus to engage in TNE derived from academic rather than economic motivations. TNE opened additional possibilities to make contact with new partners for cooperation in teaching and research, get access to additional groups of potential students, and enhance the international experience of domestic academic staff through assignments abroad. It also offered new opportunities to develop and test innovations in curricula design and teaching methods. In this spirit, TNE after the turn of the millennium began to be seen in Germany as an experimental ground for new models of teaching and international engagement, leading the DAAD to offer funding schemes that enable German HEIs to set up study programmes abroad from 2001 onwards.

The move was not entirely without precedent, as there had been encouraging experience with TNE "avant la lettre" already in the 1990s. Examples include an initiative of the German AA after the end of the cold war to support the installation of degree courses of all fields taught in German at universities in middle and eastern European countries from 1993 onwards ("Deutschsprachige Studiengänge") and the establishment of German faculties of engineering at Technical University (TU) Sofia from 1990 and at Tongji University in Shanghai (CDHK) from 1998 onwards.

A new era for TNE started in Germany with the "Future Initiative for Knowledge" ("Zukunftsinitiative Wissen") launched by the BMBF in 2001. It included funds which enabled the DAAD to issue a first call for applications to German universities offering three years financial support for the development and testing of new structures abroad. Among the first recipients of TNE funding was the University of Ulm to support their engagement at the GUC, founded in 2002 by polymer physicist Professor Ashraf Mansour, who in the 1990s obtained his doctorate and habilitation from Ulm.

Beginning in 2003, the DAAD developed the pilot call into a dedicated funding scheme for TNE with regular calls for applications and streamlined funding objectives focusing on support for the establishment of full degree courses (BA or MA) offered abroad by German universities. Over the years, the funding scheme underwent several adjustments based on insights gained from systematic evaluation and experience with funded projects. The principal idea, however, has remained the same: The DAAD supports German HEIs engaging in TNE while cooperating with foreign universities. Although the medium of instruction in German TNE programmes is mainly English, the overwhelming majority of students acquire German language skills preparing them for study periods or industry internships in Germany. The curricula are German ones, adapted to local needs and requirements. More than 50 per cent of degree programmes offer German degrees, either as a stand-alone qualification or in the form of a double or joint degree. The award of a double or joint degree in most cases requires a study stay at the German home university of one semester or more. The majority of programmes leading exclusively to local degrees of the host country, for example those of the GUC, are accredited in Germany in compliance with the standards and requirements applying to programmes offered at German universities in Germany. In contrast, the VGU in Ho Chi Minh City offers exclusively German degrees to all of its students.

The success of the first binational universities in the Arabic world made this model a popular instrument for Germany's international cooperation. New institutions were founded in Turkey (2008/13), Vietnam (2008), Russia (2014), Mongolia (2014), and Indonesia (2015). In 2017, there are ongoing negotiations about the establishment of two further binational universities in Tunisia and Kenya.

Lessons Learnt: Key Success Factors for German TNE Projects

While smaller ventures for the establishment of individual study programmes at partner universities invariably arise bottom-up from initiatives coming from German HEIs, often as a result of previous institute-level collaborations in research or student exchange, bigger projects in some cases are driven top-down by government interest. However, the impulse has to be endorsed by German universities or networks of German universities and in order to develop successfully, the project like any other TNE engagement must be aligned to their institutional interest. This can be said to be one of the key lessons learnt from German TNE engagement so far.

Referring to the level of operations, the DAAD from its experience of supporting German HE projects abroad defined ten crucial points as determinant for the success or failure of TNE projects. The ten points were included in a position paper on TNE to serve as initial guidelines for universities considering active engagement in TNE (DAAD 2014). While the relevance of each point for any TNE endeavour is unquestionable, the weight assigned to each point may vary depending on the type and focus of the project under consideration. The following is a slightly revised version of the list published in 2012.

1. Knowledge of the surrounding general conditions

As a major commitment, a decision to enter into a TNE project requires a balanced, fact-based decision. This involves thorough market analysis investigating the need and potential demand for the planned study offer as well as an in-depth examination of the regulatory framework and legal conditions at the host location, a regional analysis of the surrounding educational system and culture, and, last but not least, a critical assessment of the providing institutions' resources in terms of staff, finance, and organisational infrastructure.

2. Integration at the home institution

For a TNE venture to become successful and sustainable, the commitment to establish and maintain a study offer abroad needs to be borne not only by individual project leaders, institutes, or university management, but by the entire institution. Hence, any TNE engagement needs to be aligned to the home university's general strategic focus as well as its strategy for internationalisation and to be integrated into its structures and processes, including the application of standard quality assurance measures and standard administrative support regarding staffing, admission, legal issues, and so on.

3. Professional project management

Allocation of experienced staff or training of existing academic personnel to manage the TNE programme with clearly defined tasks and procedures is a necessary requirement. The appointed management must be competent to perform, monitor, and when necessary adjust solid financial planning, to define tasks and milestones of the project, and to implement and enforce appropriate procedures.

4. Securing financial sustainability

Apart from taking into account specific operational costs, incurred, for example, by necessary international money transfer or risk factors like fluctuating exchange rates, solid financial planning from the very beginning requires dedicated efforts to build an independent financial base to replace declining and ultimately expiring DAAD funding, for example through tuition fees or procurement of third-party funding. At any point, it must be absolutely guaranteed that students who have taken up their studies can complete their programme and take their degree within appropriate time even if the TNE study programme should be discontinued.

5. Clear and transparent agreements with the local partner

A cooperation agreement which clearly states the respective rights and responsibilities of all partners involved is essential. In addition to a clear definition of each party's tasks and obligations, including the use of logos, observance of intellectual property rights, and the minimum academic and administrative standards among other things, the agreement in particular needs to lay down the financial obligations of each side and provisions for the use and distribution of income, for example, through tuition fees and also for a potential premature cessation of the cooperation by either party. Adequate governance structures guaranteeing an appropriate level of representation and decision-making powers of the German partner are indispensable.

6. Quality of the TNE programme

It is the responsibility of each HEI providing a TNE offer to ensure that the quality of the programme offered abroad to the greatest possible extent corresponds to that of comparable programmes delivered at the HEI in Germany. This refers to admission requirements, curricula, and study conditions as well as to the selection and performance of teaching staff. Questions to be considered include the language of tuition as well as the permanent instalment of German staff at the TNE location. External quality assurance must comply with the respective requirements of the host location; however, accreditation of programmes and degrees according to recognised German or European standards is strongly recommended.

7. Quality assurance

Study programmes delivered abroad should be subject to the same quality assurance and management procedures as programmes at the university in Germany.

8. Provision of information to students and parents

Any HEI offering a TNE programme abroad should be well aware of and unhesitant in taking responsibility for providing clear, transparent, and accessible information on curricular contents and requirements, study conditions, awarded degrees, admission regulations, and any fees incurred by students. In view of the different information background of potential students abroad, particular emphasis should be given to the provision of information that allows an assessment of the quality of the offered programme, such as accreditation, status of the providing university, and recognition of degrees.

9. Sustainable staffing

A critical element affecting the success of any TNE project is the lasting willingness of academic staff from the providing university to teach abroad. Especially with TNE programmes initiated by individual professors and relying on their personal commitment, there is a risk that the withdrawal of this key person, for example, at retirement, endangers the continuation of the programme abroad. Therefore, appropriate financial and legal arrangements for staff who accept assignments abroad should be worked out from an early stage in cooperation with the university's legal and human resources departments to be able to offer acceptable solutions to all staff involved. At the same time, it is vital to ensure that the TNE offer abroad remains connected to and institutionally integrated at the department of the providing university. Constant involvement of faculty at the partner institution from an early stage, too, contributes to sustainability in terms of staffing. In most cases this will require capacity building and qualification for teaching staff at the partner HEI.

10. Visibility of the connection with Germany

Independent of the awarded degree, the TNE programme should be clearly recognisable as a course of a German university. There are a number of ways to achieve this, beginning with course contents and typical features or models of German HE, such as linking of teaching and research, the practice orientation of the German universities of applied sciences, or student participation in decision-making processes of the university, down to study visits and internships in Germany or using German as a language of instruction. The choice of appropriate measures to demonstrate and strengthen the connection with Germany will among other things depend on the strategic goals to be achieved with the project. If students are to be educated for the specific demands of a local labour market, for example, practice-related training might be more useful than learning German. If the programme aims at qualifying or recruiting students for postgraduate studies or research in Germany after the completion of an undergraduate TNE course, advanced German language skills might be taught.

Towards a National German TNE Strategy

As shown above, the shape of German TNE provision today results from a mixture of national goals which have been and continue to be pursued through government funding encouraging certain activities on the one hand and supporting strategic institutional goals of HEI, or parts of HEI as departments or faculties, on the other hand. Without public funding, very few German universities would have entered into TNE at all and those who did would almost certainly have chosen other forms than the collaborative modes of engagement now typical for German TNE.

The motivations of universities to accept the opportunities opened by the government funds offered through the DAAD have been examined above. The definition of a national strategy requires an analysis of the rationales inducing the federal government to offer incentives for HEIs to engage abroad. While all TNE projects surveyed in the German TNE data receive funding from the DAAD, a closer look at the funding schemes used for realising them reveals differences with regard to the focus of interest and primary goals underlying the funding offers. These depend on the government departments providing the financial means for the DAAD to support different purposes. Three federal ministries are involved, whose broader political motives are analysed here in chronological order of the departments' appearance as active supporters of TNE.

The AA has been engaged in the field since the 1990s through their support for TNE projects "avant la lettre". Until today, the AA provides funds for individual binational faculties (in Bulgaria and China) and universities (German-Kazakh University; upcoming binational institution in Kenia). As instruments of foreign policy, these projects serve goals related to cultural and knowledge diplomacy: They are to convey an image of Germany as a modern and innovative country and also to promote and foster the knowledge and use of German as a foreign language. This is also the main reason why the AA since 2006 has financed scholarship schemes to support (non-German) students enrolled in German TNE projects, who might receive bursaries for their studies at the TNE location or for study periods in Germany.

The main motivation of the BMBF, whose groundbreaking role for the development of TNE in Germany has been outlined above, targets the HE system in Germany and its internationalisation. Engagement in TNE provision is expected to enhance the international competitiveness of German HE and is seen, among other functions, as an instrument for marketing German HE and research abroad. Recruiting talent for Germany's research and industry sectors has a role to play in this context, too, since universities use their TNE programmes to identify highly qualified graduates for master's and doctoral studies and research in Germany, whose prior education allows them to come to Germany better equipped for success than many other international students.

For the third relevant government sponsor, the Federal Ministry for Economic Cooperation and Development, TNE is mainly an instrument for competence and capacity building within a broader context of cooperation with developing and emerging countries. Examples for this political approach are the establishment of the German-Mongolian Institute of Resources and Technology and or the funding scheme "Higher Education

Excellence in Development Cooperation—exceed" to support the development of competence centres in specific disciplines through close networks of German universities and their partners in developing countries. These centres are expected to make valuable contributions for the solution of major development challenges.

Notwithstanding their differences in political focus and specific goals, all three ministries found TNE a suitable instrument to pursue their objectives. At the same time these very goals favour and more often as not absolutely require collaborative forms of TNE. At this point, political and institutional interests meet in a domestic system based on state-funded HE not relying on tuition fees.

From the perspective of HEIs, the collaborative approach described here forms an essential aspect of their international relations and dealings, which found expression in the "Code of conduct for German Higher Education Projects abroad" (2013), jointly initiated and adopted by the German Rectors' Conference (HRK) and the DAAD as the two major national associations and representations of German universities. The Code of Conduct defines TNE projects as an "important element of the internationalisation of German universities" and highlights the focus on collaborative relations with academic partners in its preamble and its very first point. On this basis, the code demands for the main principles guiding German HE in Germany to be applied also in cooperative ventures and study programmes offered abroad: Academic freedom in research and teaching and non-discriminatory access to education, research, and teaching. It further defines a set of academic, administrative, and ethical standards for German TNE activities, including a demand to charge tuition fees abroad "only to the extent required and appropriate to ensure the continuity of the course" (DAAD/HRK 2013).

As the discussion above has shown, there is a shared awareness at the federal government, the leadership of German universities as represented in the HRK, and the DAAD that the success of German HE projects abroad rests primarily on the consideration given to the interests of all parties concerned, the commitment of all active partners, and the involvement of all stakeholders in Germany and the partner countries. It is this awareness which from the beginning has shaped the development of the international engagement considered as TNE in Germany today.

References

Australian Government, Department of Education and Training (2016) Research Snapshot October 2016: Transnational education in the higher education sector.
Bundesministerium für Bildung und Forschung/BMBF (2016) Internationalisation of education, science and research. Strategy of the Federal Government, p. 31. Available at: https://www.bmbf.de/pub/Internationalization_Strategy.pdf
DAAD (2013a) Strategy DAAD 2020, p. 26.
DAAD (2013b) Transnational education in Germany—DAAD position paper.
DAAD (2014) Transnational education in Germany—DAAD position paper. Available at: www.daad.de/der-daad/analysen-und-studien/de/43093-transnationale-bildung-tnb-praxishandbuch-und-weitere-studien/
DAAD/DZHW: Wissenschaft weltoffen 2014, 2015, 2016. Available at: www.wissenschaft-weltoffen.de
DAAD/DZHW (2017) Wissenschaft weltoffen 2017, p. 34f. Available at: www.wissenschaft-weltoffen.de
DAAD HRK (2013) Code of conduct for German higher education projects abroad. English version available at: https://www.daad.de/medien/der-daad/unsere-mission/standpunkte/daad_standpunkte_kodex_hochschulprojekte_ausland_englisch.pdf
France Stratègie (2016) L'enseignement supérieur Francais par-delà les frontières: L'urgence d'une stratégie. Auteurs: Bernard Ramanantsoa et Quentin Delpech.
HE Global (2016) The scale and scope of UK transnational education.
Knight, J. and McNamara, J. (2017): Transnational education: A classification framework and data collection guidelines for International Programme and Provider Mobility (IPPM). Ed. British Council and DAAD.
Wissenschaft Weltoffen (2017) 1.1—Studierende insgesamt, Deutsche und ausländische Studierende, Bildungsausländer, Bildungsinländer, insgesamt und weiblich, WS47/48-WS15/16. Available at: www.wissenschaft-weltoffen.de

3

Shaping Transnational Education in the Netherlands: National Policy Directions

Rosa Becker

This chapter aims to provide an understanding of current national policy directions on transnational education (TNE) in the Netherlands. It looks at the TNE debate at the national policy level and recent changes in national legislation to facilitate TNE development. The chapter shows that after an initial reluctance to stimulate TNE – out of fear that commercial interests would harm educational quality and the international reputation of Dutch higher education – in recent years, the Dutch government has been looking carefully into ways to encourage the development of TNE programmes based on the academic benefits TNE would bring to Dutch higher education, and with emphasis on international collaboration.

In this chapter, the national TNE debate and policy directions are analysed through two contradictions, namely between commerce and community (section 1), and between policy and vision (section 2). The conclusion is offered in section 3. Section 4 identifies the lessons learned.

R. Becker (✉)
Nuffic, The Hague, Netherlands
e-mail: rbecker@nuffic.nl

© The Author(s) 2018
V. Tsiligiris, W. Lawton (eds.), *Exporting Transnational Education*,
https://doi.org/10.1007/978-3-319-74739-2_3

Commerce and Community

This section suggests that in the Dutch national TNE policy debate and policy directions, there is a contradiction between 'commerce' and 'community'. 'Commerce' here refers to offering TNE programmes in foreign markets with the motive to generate income or other trade benefits, for instance, through attracting more fee-paying foreign students. The notion of 'community' here refers to a belief in – and adoption of – equal collaborative partnership, working together as one group, based on shared norms and towards a common goal. This contradiction between commerce and community is visible in (i) current Dutch TNE practices, (ii) the national policy debate on TNE, and (iii) elements in the new Dutch TNE legislation.

Current Dutch TNE Practices

At the institutional level, the reasons for TNE development appear to be a mix of academic, economic, and development collaboration aims. While not all Dutch higher education institutions are interested in TNE development, those who do, view TNE as an interesting way to promote and market Dutch higher education abroad in specific niche areas, to intensify international collaborations and encourage international student exchange.

Dutch institutions have developed several kinds of TNE activities. There are no nationally collected data, but we do know that the Dutch research universities offer approximately 20 joint degree and over 220 double- or multiple-degree programmes, with more in development, with at least one foreign partner university. These joint programme initiatives often build on existing student exchange arrangements with strategic partners. The Dutch universities of applied sciences currently offer an estimated total of eight double-degree programmes with a foreign partner, and their interest in international joint programme development is also growing.

Several research universities offer Massive Online Open Courses (MOOCs; approximately ten in total, leading to certificates rather than degrees) that attract tens of thousands of students from around the world and increase the international visibility of Dutch higher education. Some institutions offer pathway programmes to prepare foreign students for enrolling in a Dutch degree programme in the Netherlands.

International branch campus activity is limited. Stenden University of Applied Sciences is the only publicly funded Dutch institution that runs international branch campuses (established between 2000 and 2009). It operates four campuses, in South Africa, Qatar, Thailand, and Indonesia, with an estimated total of 600 degree students enrolled at the four branch campuses, plus 500 studying at one of the campuses via 'intercampus' mobility. Stenden has defined its TNE activities as central to its institutional mission. Following an invitation from the Chinese authorities, the University of Groningen has been planning to establish a branch campus in China, pending Dutch government approval to do so. The university intended to offer four bachelor and two master degree programmes in chemistry, engineering, and science and technology. In early 2018, however, the university announced that it would not proceed with its branch campus plan since its University Council did not give the necessary approval to do so. Without consent of the University Council (that in the Netherlands has a legal right to co-decide), the branch campus plan could not be considered for approval by the Dutch education ministry. The main objections expressed by the University Council were (i) a lack of confidence in the academic benefits the branch campus would bring to Dutch students, including a fear that Dutch professors would spend more time teaching abroad than at the home campus, leading to a potential loss of educational quality at home, (ii) a fear that international students would be recruited to generate fee income, and (iii) concerns about academic freedom, including the necessary appointment of a Chinese party secretary in the branch campus council. The university is currently considering ways to offer degree programmes abroad in a more collaborative form. This development is illustrative of the community notion (along with concerns over educational quality) taking precedence over commerce.

Overall, the main form of Dutch TNE practice consists of joint and double/multiple-degree programmes. It is exactly this form of TNE that is strongly based on a notion of community, since joint programmes are characterised by a sense of international collaboration and joint curriculum development, aimed at equal mutual benefit. Joint programmes are not based on a notion of commerce: they are unlikely to bring financial profit as operating costs are comparatively high due to the physical mobility periods involved and the relatively small group of students they cater for.

The TNE Policy Debate at the National Level

The contradiction between commerce and community is also visible in the TNE debate at the national policy level. Until recently, there was very little national strategic TNE planning and regulation in the Netherlands. Broad TNE development was not encouraged. In the past couple of years, however, TNE has taken a more central role in the Dutch government's policy on internationalisation of higher education. The main Dutch policy debate on TNE has focused on the development of international joint and double/multiple-degree programmes, and it is only since recently that the broader term 'TNE' is being used, which the Dutch government uses to refer to full-degree programmes offered abroad.

The national TNE policy debate in the Netherlands began around 2008, and has been informed by a series of research and policy papers, several of which were published by the Association of Dutch Universities (VSNU), one of the main driving forces behind the debate. In 2008, the Ministry of Education, Culture and Science published an internationalisation agenda for higher education with four key aims, namely (i) to increase the international mobility of Dutch students, (ii) to strengthen the international orientation of Dutch higher education, (iii) to increase the international 'brain circulation' of academic and research staff, and (iv) to improve the conditions for attracting foreign research institutes (Ministerie van Onderwijs, Cultuur en Wetenschap 2008).

The development of international joint and double-degree programmes was seen as one way to reach these aims, and in 2010, it became legally possible for Dutch higher education institutions to offer an international joint degree programme with one or more foreign partner institutions. The VSNU successfully lobbied with the education ministry for a government-allocated incentive fund for the development of international joint degree programmes with a €7 million budget over 2010–2014 (Vereniging van Universiteiten 2009), the only form of Dutch government funding for TNE development to date.

This legal possibility and funding helped the Dutch research universities to develop joint degree programmes with foreign partners, but in practice, the institutions continued to face difficulties that hindered joint degree development. The research universities asked for changes to national legislation, and this gave the VSNU, as their representative organisation, an instrumental role in lobbying for national legislative changes that would further encourage joint programme development. The main legislative difficulties faced by the universities are analysed here through identifying four 'hindrances'.

The first hindrance to joint programme development was the fact that Dutch legislation required universities to register all students on international joint degree programmes at the Dutch university for the full duration of their course programme. This meant that foreign students on joint degree programmes were required to pay Dutch tuition fees for the full course programme, while they were often also required to pay tuition fees at their home institution, thus paying double. Similarly, Dutch students would have to pay tuition fees in the Netherlands for the full duration of their course programme, even though they would study abroad for a year or so.

The second hindrance to international joint degree development was the legal stipulation that all students on international joint degree programmes and Dutch degree programmes abroad were required to spend at least a quarter of their course programme in the Netherlands. This formed a major problem for students from countries like Indonesia, who were keen to enrol in a Dutch-Indonesian joint degree programme, but would not have the funds or practical opportunity to leave their family responsibilities at home to undertake a quarter of their degree programme on Dutch soil.

Third, Dutch legislation stated that a master degree programme should comprise 60 ECTS credits, whereas other countries often adopt a standard of 120 ECTS. This made it difficult for universities to convert an existing Dutch master degree programme into an international joint degree programme. Fourth, accreditation and recognition procedures were seen as cumbersome, with international joint degree programmes required to undergo separate accreditation and recognition procedures in each participating country with programme accreditation – sometimes with accreditation requirements that were not in line with, or even contradictory to, each other. In reaction to this, the Dutch government is supporting the implementation of the single European Approach for Quality Assurance of Joint Programmes.

These hindrances to joint programme development dominated the national TNE debate for nearly five years. With the allocation of the four-year government incentive fund for the development of international joint degree programmes in 2010, the VSNU was tasked with monitoring joint programme development. It set up a national network to exchange good practices between the universities, and published a mid-term and a final review that promoted international joint degree programmes as an important instrument in the Dutch internationalisation strategy to attract foreign 'knowledge workers' – highly educated staff instrumental in strengthening the knowledge economy – to increase international student mobility, to internationalise the curriculum, and to improve the international reputation of Dutch higher education (VSNU 2012, 2015). Both reports argued that national legislation should remove obstacles to international joint degree programme development. This argument was supported by University of Twente researchers who called on the education ministry to give Dutch higher education institutions more flexibility to meet the legal stipulations of partner countries (Kolster and Vossensteyn 2013).

The VSNU and the Association of the Dutch Universities of Applied Sciences then joined forces. Recognising a rise in international higher education collaboration and a perceived need to strengthen the Dutch position in the international higher education market, they argued that a growth in international joint degree programmes should be instrumental in realising this. Thus, in their view, joint degree programme development is based on both a notion of community and a notion of commerce.

In 2014, the two representative organisations published a joint vision paper on the internationalisation of higher education pointing to the crucial role of internationalisation in acquiring knowledge and professional competences, and in contributing to students' personal development (Vereniging Hogescholen and VSNU 2014). The vision paper called for more flexible national legislation to encourage international joint programme development, particularly simplified accreditation and recognition procedures, clarity on funding conditions, and simpler tuition fee arrangements.

In response to this vision, the then Dutch education minister expressed her clear intention to help achieve these ambitions. She announced plans to eliminate legal obstacles to joint programme development. In her own 'vision letter', the minister also introduced the broader theme of TNE to the national debate, referring to full Dutch degree programmes to be offered abroad (Ministerie van Onderwijs, Cultuur en Wetenschap 2016). This theme was introduced partly in response to the wishes of some Dutch universities to start offering full-degree programmes abroad as a means to intensify existing international partnerships and enter new markets (Ministerie van OCW 2014b). The overall policy debate led to the development of new TNE legislation (details are given in the next section).

Looking at this national policy debate, it can be concluded that TNE development by Dutch institutions is based on both the conflicting notions of community and commerce, with the emphasis on commerce added more recently. The emphasis on community is expressed in the government argument to establish long-term international partnerships and high-quality TNE programmes, rather than encouraging TNE as a commodity focused on income generation. The requirement in previous legislation (2010–2017) that all students registered in international joint degree programmes and Dutch degree programmes abroad had to study within the Netherlands for at least a quarter of their degree programme was in line with this. This requirement intended to prevent TNE to be undertaken out of commercial motives and it helped to increase international knowledge circulation through incoming and outgoing student mobility within joint programmes and Dutch programmes offered abroad. This helped to create – at least to an extent – an international student community where Dutch and foreign students would discuss and collaborate.

The importance attached to commerce is seen in the arguments by the higher education institutions' representative organisations, which see joint degree programme development as a way to strengthen the Dutch knowledge economy, to increase the Dutch position in the international higher education market, and to improve the international reputation of Dutch higher education (e.g. to attract more students – and partnerships). This element of partnerships is interesting in that they are based on the notion of community, whereas the partnerships themselves can also be adopted as a means to strengthen the commercial position of Dutch higher education.

TNE Legislation

The contradiction between commerce and community is also visible in the new TNE legislation. To show this, this section will first illustrate the legislative details.

The national policy debate led to the development of two strands of legislation, namely (i) to facilitate the further development of international joint and double/multiple-degree programmes and (ii) to allow Dutch higher education institutions to offer full and accredited Dutch degree programmes abroad (Becker 2017). The new legislation does not address other forms of TNE, such as validation and articulation agreements, and franchises of Dutch course programmes to institutions abroad. Dutch universities are allowed to offer a course programme in collaboration with a foreign partner, but in case of a franchise, the Dutch institution is legally required to offer the course programme itself (this task cannot be delegated to the foreign partner institution). The new TNE legislation does not regulate online programmes since the government believes that regulation might hinder the dynamic development of new forms of open and online education. Incoming TNE is not addressed either.

The new legislation on international joint programmes came into force in January 2018 and includes five main points (Government of the Netherlands 2017a, b). First, Dutch higher education institutions are allowed to offer a joint programme with one or more foreign institutions, which may lead to a joint, double, or other type of multiple degree. Until then, legislation did not address double/multiple-degree programmes.

Second, Dutch institutions are required to enter into a formal agreement with the foreign partner institution(s). This agreement must state (i) the content of the joint programme, (ii) the division of course module responsibilities between the institutions involved, (iii) the degree(s) awarded, and the ways in which these degree(s) are awarded, (iv) student registration procedures, and (v) tuition fee arrangements.

Third, Dutch institutions are allowed to require students enrolled in international joint programmes to register at the Dutch institution for the full duration of their studies. This is to reduce the administrative burden for Dutch institutions, since several universities required staff to register, de-register, and re-register Dutch students enrolled in a joint degree programme every time they moved to study abroad and returned to their home institution.

Fourth, Dutch institutions are allowed to remove or lower the (nationally set minimum) tuition fee for students enrolled in an international joint programme. This allows for reciprocity, with students paying full fees at their home institution, and no fees at all at the foreign partner institution, and *vice versa*, thus preventing students from paying double fees. Previous law required all students registered at a Dutch institution to pay tuition fees at home, even when they studied abroad as part of an international joint programme.

Fifth, the law introduced the 'PhD' degree, which is common in many countries, but until then did not formally exist in the Netherlands. Only the 'Doctor' (Dr) degree existed, which made it legally impossible to combine the PhD and Dr degrees into a joint 'PhD' degree.

The second strand of legislation, expected to go into force in the Summer of 2018, will for the first time allow Dutch higher education institutions to offer full Dutch degree programmes abroad. To do so, institutions need to guarantee educational quality and academic freedom. They are not allowed to spend public funding on education offered abroad, and institutions are required to ask the education minister for advance permission to start offering a full Dutch degree programme or a branch campus abroad. Thus, the education minister can refuse or withdraw permission to offer a degree programme abroad. Permission is refused when the degree programme to be offered abroad is not also offered within the Netherlands. Other grounds for refusal or withdrawal of a programme are the following (Government of the Netherlands 2017a):

1. The accreditation status of the degree programme that is offered within the Netherlands (e.g. conditional or unconditional),
2. The way in which programme quality will be assured in the host country,
3. The financial position of the institution asking for permission to offer a degree programme abroad, and the ways in which financial risks will be reduced,

4. The actions that the institution will take to prevent the use of public funding for TNE development,
5. The scale of the TNE initiative, with special attention to prospective student numbers,
6. The ways in which the sustainability of the TNE programme is assured within the Netherlands,
7. The safety and rights of staff involved in offering the TNE programme in the host country,
8. The nature of the Dutch-foreign diplomatic relations in the host country (a TNE programme may not damage these relations),
9. The ways in which the host country deals with human rights and social relations,
10. Where applicable, the ways in which collaboration with partner organisations will be organised,
11. The views of official government organisations in the host country on the proposed TNE programme,
12. The proposed exit strategy, namely the ways in which the institution will deal with finances, staff, and students in case the TNE programme will cease to exist, and
13. The ways in which any potential income generated from the TNE programme in the host country is spent, and the degree to which these funds benefit the quality of higher education delivered in the Netherlands.

Clearly, the grounds for refusal and withdrawal of a TNE programme leave room for interpretation. Once institutions have been given permission to offer a degree programme abroad, it is possible that—at some point—this permission is withdrawn. It remains to be seen how these grounds will be evaluated and at what point they have consequences. Also, the list of criteria is long. Every worry and risk politicians could think of has been translated into a requirement or ground for refusal. On the other hand, prudent institutions will likely take into account most of these points in their TNE planning in any case. What remains somewhat unclear is the degree of flexibility that Dutch institutions will have to meet host country stipulations, which are at least as important as domestic legislation and may be subject to change in ways that can be difficult to anticipate.

The contradiction between commerce and community is visible in three elements in the new TNE law. First, it is visible between the two strands of new legislation. The part allowing full Dutch degree programmes offered abroad is based on a notion of commerce: it is a form of trade where education is primarily sold abroad as a commodity, for instance, to attract more students to make up for a declining student population at home. The other part of legislation, facilitating joint programme development, is based on a government focus on establishing long-term and equal international partnerships, rather than encouraging TNE as a commodity focused on income generation.

Second, new legislation states that in its assessment of new Dutch degree programmes to be offered abroad, the Dutch government will critically look at the ways in which the institutions organise collaboration with (foreign) partner organisations. The commerce-community contradiction is visible in this criterion since it is about evaluating the relevant partnership arrangements within the more commercial form of TNE.

Third, the legal possibility for Dutch institutions to lower or cancel the minimum required tuition fees for students registered in international joint programmes gives institutions more flexibility. At the same time, it also indicates that joint programme development is not about generating additional tuition income, but about realising international student and staff exchange and collaboration in joint curriculum development—in other words, a notion of an education community.

In this section, it was suggested that in the Dutch national policy debate and policy directions, there is a contradiction between commerce and community. It is concluded that the emphasis on international joint and double/multiple-degree programmes – in current TNE practice, half of the policy debate, and four new legislative elements – has been due to a strong government focus on a notion of a community, equal international partnerships, and joint curriculum development, rather than on a notion of commerce, where TNE is encouraged as a commodity focused on income generation. At the same time, however, new policy makes it possible to offer full Dutch degree programmes abroad, and this form of TNE is more strongly based on a notion of commerce.

Policy and Vision

This section suggests that there is a contradiction between the Dutch government's vision of adopting TNE as a means to bring about academic benefit to Dutch higher education at home rather than focus on economic aims, and some policy regulations that are aimed at realising economic gain. This contradiction is illustrated in the next sections that discuss the government's TNE vision and strategic aims, the main points of resistance to core themes in the government policy debate, and elements in the new legislative policy framework.

Vision

The Dutch government's strategic aims for TNE development are threefold, namely (i) to increase international student and staff mobility, (ii) to encourage long-term international higher education partnerships, and (iii) to strengthen the international visibility and positioning of Dutch higher education (Government of the Netherlands 2017a).

In her 2014 vision letter, and in line with higher education institutions' views, the then[1] education minister also considered TNE as having a clear added value in selling Dutch higher education abroad (Ministerie van OCW 2014a). This vision is based on the recognition that knowledge is a valuable export product and that TNE is a commodity to be sold. In the political struggles that characterised the legislative development process, her stance on the idea of TNE as an export product was softened in order to pass the whole package of TNE legislation through Parliament. In consequence, and importantly, the government vision is that academic aims must be more important in TNE development than economic ones. In other words, TNE is not to be used as a prime instrument to generate additional tuition fee income.

Points of Resistance

In this section, the legislative development debate is analysed through identifying five 'points of resistance' in the political struggles over the main TNE policy themes. These points of resistance focused on the added value of TNE, quality assurance, academic freedom, the potential use of public funding, and financial risks involved.

In a first point of resistance, several political parties objected to the TNE Bill because they did not consider TNE to have any added value over already existing forms of internationalisation of higher education, such as international research collaboration and student exchange. In response, the minister of education pointed out that TNE would be an additional means to bring innovative curriculum approaches to host countries, increase the international visibility of Dutch institutions in niche areas, and strengthen international education and research networks. The leading government party added that TNE would boost international interest in studying in the Netherlands, and lead to financial and academic benefits to the country. These responses thus saw TNE as having added value in realising a combination of academic benefits (to both home and host country) and economic gain (to the home country).

Quality assurance was a second point of resistance in the Parliamentary debate, with several parties fearing that the best Dutch university staff would spend more time teaching abroad than at home, potentially leading to a decline in the quality of education at home. To prevent this, these parties insisted that the new TNE law should ensure that TNE would lead to academic benefits in the Netherlands.

Third, political parties expressed major concerns about academic freedom. If a host country would require students enrolled in Dutch programmes to undergo military training, or would impose limited freedom of speech or limited access to internet data, it was argued that Dutch institutions should not offer TNE there. In response, the education minister indicated that academic freedom in Dutch TNE programmes would be evaluated and guaranteed.

Fourth, Dutch political parties asked the government to ensure that no public funding would be spent on any kind of TNE activity, including accreditation of full Dutch degree programmes to be offered abroad. The fifth concern related to the need to eliminate financial risk, particularly in the case of international branch campus establishment, with the education minister promising to consider any potential financial risk carefully in advance.

These points of resistance, expressed in the Parliamentary policy debate, led to various amendments in the TNE Bill and the long list of grounds for refusal and withdrawal of TNE initiatives.

The Legislative Policy Framework

The new elements in joint programme legislation, described earlier, are in line with the Dutch government's vision on TNE. The fact that to offer full-degree programmes abroad Dutch institutions need to guarantee in advance that their programmes have a high quality, are based on full academic freedom, and entirely focused on the academic benefits that they bring to the home institution also supports the government vision. As indicated, institutions are required to ask the education minister for advance permission to start offering a full Dutch degree programme or a branch campus abroad. The aims of this request for permission – and form of advance quality assurance – are threefold, namely (i) to guarantee higher education quality and consider any potential risks beforehand, (ii) to prevent Dutch publicly funded higher education institutions to compete with each other abroad, and (iii) to prevent TNE development out of commercial interests. The advance ministerial permission necessary to start a new TNE initiative is an interesting requirement in that it is based on an effort to guarantee beforehand a full risk management of all potential risks that may turn up. It also is a sign of the strong government interest in guaranteeing a continued high-quality brand name of Dutch higher education.

Also supporting the government's vision on TNE is the stipulation that the Dutch education minister can refuse or withdraw permission to offer a degree programme abroad if an institution provides insufficient advance evidence on the ways in which potential income generated from the TNE programme in the host country is spent, and the degree to which these funds benefit the quality of higher education delivered within the Netherlands. What was not discussed in the legislative development process was the fact that TNE activities are unlikely to bring financial profit, and as institutions are not allowed to invest public funding in their overseas TNE activities, tuition fee income for TNE programmes will likely be needed to assure the quality of the TNE programme itself and cover parts of its operational costs. Furthermore, host countries may also require tuition fee income to be re-invested in the TNE programme.

There is a contradiction, however, between the Dutch government vision that TNE may not be directed to commercial interests and must fully lead to increased educational quality and academic benefit to Dutch higher education at home – and two legislative policies that are aimed at realising economic benefits.

First, new policy allows institutions to offer full Dutch degree programmes abroad, but this activity may not be commercial. However, the main principle of this form of TNE is that of trade (education to be sold abroad) and economic benefit (e.g. tuition fee income, making up for a declining student population at home, gaining access to new sources of knowledge and funding). In the government vision, TNE is not to be used as a prime instrument to generate additional funds, even though Dutch tuition fees are market oriented, with full-fee non-EU student recruitment. It seems that as long as TNE has a high quality and is focused on bringing academic benefits, attracting additional income to increase 'education quality' may be an added advantage. Furthermore, offering programmes abroad can be a means to attract high-quality foreign students from TNE to master and doctoral courses within the Netherlands, which may in turn increase education quality at Dutch institutions. However, this policy in practice adopts academic aims next to – and not above – economic ones.

Second, new policy has removed the legal requirement that students on Dutch TNE programmes should spend at least a quarter of their degree programme within the Netherlands. While this was done at the universities' request and will enable them to recruit students who do not study in the Netherlands itself (potentially bringing economic gain), the requirement guaranteed incoming student mobility to the Netherlands through TNE, which helped internationalise the home curriculum, potentially enhancing the quality of Dutch education at home. Of course, universities can organise mobility between their home and TNE programmes/campuses, but the removal of this requirement does not automatically encourage increased education quality through student mobility.

Conclusion

This chapter showed that after an initial reluctance, the Dutch government has now introduced legislation to encourage TNE development. In the government vision, TNE may not be directed to commercial interests, and must fully lead to increased educational quality and other academic benefits to higher education in the Netherlands. The new policy framework includes regulations that support this vision: the new law gives Dutch institutions more flexibility in developing jointly developed degree programmes, and the ways in which TNE initiatives bring academic benefit to higher education in the Netherlands are evaluated.

However, there is a contradiction between policy and vision. The new policy for the first time allows universities to offer full Dutch degree programmes abroad, a form of TNE whose main principle is based on trade: using education as a commodity to be sold and bring economic benefit. At the same time, both vision and policy state that this TNE activity may not be commercial. So, if academic benefits are clear and demonstrated, may TNE be geared to commercial interests as well, and what consequences may that have?

There is also a contradiction in Dutch TNE policies between commerce and community. Current Dutch TNE practice is dominated by joint and double/multiple-degree programmes and strongly based on a notion of community and a partnership model, rather than on a notion of commerce. This community model is encouraged in the new policy framework. However, with the law now allowing full-degree programmes to be offered abroad, another form of TNE is being facilitated that, in principle, is primarily based on commercial interests than on a notion of community and partnership.

It is promising that these concerns on education quality, academic benefits, and commercial interests are debated broadly at the national level, and that concerns have been taken into account in the policy-making process. To date, the partnership model between Dutch institutions and those in host countries is clearly dominating. Many host countries are interested in international student and staff exchange, good educational quality, and sustainable education and research partnerships. The Dutch partnership model, focused on high educational quality and equal partnerships, is promising in that it may fit well to meet those host country aims while also encouraging international knowledge circulation and curriculum innovation.

Lessons Learned

Three lessons can be learned from the Dutch TNE policy-making process.

- First, there is value in well thought-through policy-making. While the drafting of TNE legislation has taken two to three years, careful legislative development with broad consultation with higher education stakeholders and cautious consideration of potential risks is a better strategy than jumping in the TNE market without having done proper homework. In the Netherlands, throughout the process of policy-making and legislative development, major concerns – such as the potential 'leaking away' of public funds to foreign ventures – were taken into account and regulatory approaches were carefully sought.
- Second, a strong TNE emphasis on community and partnership models is meaningful since they are based on equal partnerships with shared responsibility and co-creation of degree programmes. Equal partnerships are more likely to lead to mutual understanding, mutual benefits, and more sustainable partnerships. In the community and partnership model, education programmes are not so much 'transferred' from one country to another and adapted in time, but they are co-created through joint curriculum development and joint adaptation.
- Third, a strong emphasis in TNE development on educational quality and academic benefits to both the home institution and the host country is key to good quality – and thus sustainable – partnerships, and the international reputation of the providing institution(s).

Notes

1. In October 2017, a new government coalition took office, and the new education minister is expected to set out her vision on internationalisation of higher education in June 2018.

References

Becker, R.F.J. (2017) *Perspectives and prospects as long-awaited TNE Bill is approved in the Netherlands.* The Observatory on Borderless Higher Education.

Government of the Netherlands (2017a) *Wet van 7 juni 2017 tot wijziging van onder meer de Wet op het hoger onderwijs en wetenschappelijk onderzoek (Wet bevordering internationalisering hoger onderwijs en wetenschappelijk onderzoek)*, no. 306.

Government of the Netherlands (2017b) *Besluit van 19 augustus 2017, houdende vaststelling van de tijdstippen van de gedeeltelijke inwerkingtreding van de Wet van 7 juni 2017 (Wet bevordering internationalisering hoger onderwijs en wetenschappelijk onderzoek)*, no. 319.

Kolster, R. and Vossensteyn, H. (2013) *Internationale quick scan naar wettelijke verankering van joint programmes. Op zoek naar bevorderende maatregelen.* Centre for Higher Education Policy Studies, University of Twente.

Ministerie van Onderwijs, Cultuur en Wetenschap (2008) *Grenzeloos Goed: internationaliseringsagenda hoger onderwijs-, onderzoeks- en wetenschapsbeleid.* Den Haag: Ministerie van OCW.

Ministerie van Onderwijs, Cultuur en Wetenschap (2014a) *De wereld in: visiebrief internationale dimensie van ho en mbo.* Den Haag: Ministerie van OCW. Visiebrief 15 July.

Ministerie van Onderwijs, Cultuur en Wetenschap (2014b) *Open en online hoger onderwijs.* Den Haag: Ministerie van OCW. Kamerbrief 8 January.

Ministerie van Onderwijs, Cultuur en Wetenschap (2016) *De waarde(n) van de wereld—Voortgangsbrief over de internationale dimensie van ho en mbo.* Den Haag: Ministerie van OCW. Voortgangsbrief 19 September.

Vereniging Hogescholen & Vereniging van Universiteiten (2014) *Gezamenlijke visie internationaal.* Vereniging Hogescholen & VSNU.

Vereniging van Universiteiten (2009) *Notitie Stimuleringsmiddelen joint degrees.* VSNU.

Vereniging van Universiteiten (2012) *Internationale joint programmes bij Nederlandse universiteiten. Tussenrapportage project stimulering joint degrees 2012.* VSNU.

Vereniging van Universiteiten (2015) *Internationale joint programmes bij Nederlandse universiteiten. Eindrapportage project stimulering joint degrees 2014.* VSNU.

4

The Design of International Dual Degree Programmes as Effective Transnational Education Experiences

Ofelia A. Palermo, Angelo P. Bisignano, and Simon Mercado

Introduction

Competition dynamics in the higher education (HE) sector require institutions to develop the ability not only to respond quickly to global changes, but also to anticipate and drive them. In a global context, HE institutions cope with the global environment developing novel internationalization strategies, enhancing the internationalization of curricula, and fostering the mobility of staff and students. Mobility is an especially pragmatic way for valuing multiculturalism and transnational education (TNE) (HEGlobal 2016). Furthermore, it facilitates reflection on global citizenship as a key educational value relevant not only for personal development, but also for professional practice.

O. A. Palermo (✉) • A. P. Bisignano
Nottingham Trent University, Nottingham, UK
e-mail: ofelia.palermo@ntu.ac.uk; angelo.bisignano@ntu.ac.uk

S. Mercado
ESCP, London, UK
e-mail: smercardo@escpeurope.eu

In this context, collaborative degree programmes can facilitate TNE by complementing provisions at equivalent levels in different countries (Gallicchio 2007). International Dual Degree (IDD) programmes recently emerged as an especially effective TNE opportunity for both prospective students and HE Institutions (Chevallier 2013).

A decade ago, IDD programmes promised to be the future of TNE (Gutierrez et al. 2008). They surely appear to offer numerous advantages. Students can experience the chosen disciplines in different education systems, increase their employability, access a variety of facilities, and develop transnational professional networks (Carlin 2008; Crossman and Clarke 2010). HE institutions, in turn, can increase their portfolio of pedagogic offer and develop stronger international academic partnerships. Such collaborations especially allow educational institutions to share financial, marketing, and operational resources. Moreover, they also seem to facilitate the exchange of best practices in teaching and learning approaches, research collaborations, and quality assurance processes (Carlin 2008; Culver et al. 2011).

Moreover, IDD programmes redesigned the geopolitical global balance in TNE (HEGlobal 2016). Current approaches to TNE have been mostly one-way oriented, with universities from one educational system transferring solutions, practices, and awarding powers to institutions in another educational system (Healey and Bordogna 2014). A common critique of TNE is that some solutions (licensing, franchising, offshore presence, validation agreements especially) favour the encroachment of one education system into another, leading to a homogenization of educational approaches (Egege and Kutieleh 2008). Some authors take this further by interpreting the dominant role of American, British, and Australian universities in TNE as a form of academic imperialism (see Healey and Bordogna 2014 for a review). In this perspective, TNE experiences need to embed solutions that enhance context-sensitive measures (Pyvis 2011). IDD programmes can represent an opportunity for rebalancing the contribution of different educational systems in the international student experience. With their focus on dual-way knowledge transfer, IDD programmes could essentially democratize relationships in strategic international partnerships.

In spite of these promises, IDD programmes seem to remain marginal in terms of both the number of students and income generated (HEGlobal 2016). This chapter discusses the strategic role of this type of programmes in the portfolio of TNE activities in the HE sector. Building on the evidence of a case study, the chapter also offers a useful framework for supporting the design of effective IDD programmes.

The fast-growing interest in the internationalization of the HE sector, the rapid increase in worldwide TNE experiences, and the variety of TNE solutions available to HE institutions all imply a lack of consensus amongst actors with regard to the notions used. This is especially relevant as definitions vary across countries (Culver et al. 2011).

In this context, we define IDD programmes as those TNE experiences where two (or more) HE institutions collaborate to offer to prospective students the participation in two separate programmes in different countries and the possibility to achieve two distinct award qualifications at an equivalent level upon completion (Michael and Balraj 2003; Kuder and Obst 2009; Asgary and Robbert 2010).

IDD programmes differ from simple dual awards as in these a student can obtain two separate degrees in two distinct subjects within the same institution (Michael and Balraj 2003; Kuder and Obst 2009). IDD programmes also differ from joint degrees as in these two international institutions collaborate to share the delivery of one programme in a process of TNE and the student is awarded one single title upon completion (Michael and Balraj 2003; Asgary and Robbert 2010).

The Strategic Role of International Dual Degrees

The literature has traditionally agreed on the role of IDD programmes in developing and strengthening international collaborations (Carlin 2008; Asgary and Robbert 2010). Besides, IDD programmes cement the organization's commitment to an internationalization process and increase the variety of options, facilities, and academic faculty offered to students (Carlin 2008).

Nevertheless, such programmes remain marginal even in innovative and internationally oriented markets. In the UK, IDDs account for 11% of the total population of students experiencing some form of TNE and for 9% of the programmes (HEGlobal 2016). Although the trend shows absolute growth (from 8% and 6%, respectively, in 2014), the number of students per programme is in fact shrinking (HEGlobal 2016). This trend should not be surprising. Even authors who predicted IDD as an area of growth have argued this with attention to their strategic role rather than to their potential for numbers (Gutierrez et al. 2008).

IDD programmes attract high achievers with innate adaptation abilities and with either a strong international background or a strong cultural sensitivity (Delisle 2011). Prospective students need to be able to adapt at a very fast pace to different environments, teaching methods, subject areas, and potentially languages and cultures (Collins and Davidson 2002). In addition, the complexity of the management of IDD programmes requires a higher ratio of staff (both academic and administrative) per student (Tobenkin 2008). IDD programmes are hence more suitable to a relatively small number of students (Kuder et al. 2013).

However, a recent survey of UK universities indicates the desire to increase student numbers and the target of income generation as the main drivers for pursuing IDD programmes (HEGlobal 2016). Other aspects such as the increase of reputation/status and the strengthening of strategic partnerships appear to be marginal in the decision-making process.

This misalignment of expectations can partially explain the frustration of several HE institutions in evaluating the impact of IDD programmes in their strategic portfolio. Especially in the UK, IDD programmes are often interpreted as an opportunity to re-balance numbers in terms of student exchanges between existing partners. HE institutions hence underestimate the importance these programmes have in increasing the international reputation and in strengthening existing partnerships (Carlin 2008). This leads to a casual approach in designing and implementing IDD programmes that has, in turn, generated few cases of best practice. The next section will propose a framework to support the design and development of IDD programmes building on a reflective case study based on research conducted at Nottingham Business School (NBS).

Designing Effective International Dual Degree Programmes: The WHEEL Framework

IDD programmes are the most intimate form of collaboration between HE institutions. Different organizations have to open up to the scrutiny of external stakeholders and perhaps challenge some of their traditional methods of working (Griffiths 2003). This solution is hence more suitable for partner organizations that have already been working together and know their respective processes, culture, and ethos (Culver et al. 2011). Therefore, IDD programmes are often the results of other internationalization activities (Michael and Balraj 2003). IDD programmes usually stem from ad hoc intra-organizational collaborations, such as a coordinated research symposium or conference; the participation in international networks (e.g. EFMD, AACSB); or the participation in governmental promotional activities such as trade missions, twinning events, and shared funding bids (Asgary and Robbert 2010). The action of individual members of staff can also promote the decision to engage in IDD programmes. Cooperation on specific research projects, personal connections, or previous appointments in the partner institution can all have a role in starting up such collaborations (Michael and Balraj 2003).

These examples show that an array of international activities can contribute to the diffusion of IDD programmes. On the other hand, they evidence how HE institutions too often leave the decision-making process regarding IDD programmes to chance or opportunity. Instead, the design and implementation of IDD programmes can be laborious, and requires specific competences and skills (Griffiths 2003; Tobenkin 2008).

IDD programmes present major challenges such as the *definition of completion requirements*, the *alignment of regulations and customs*, the *assurance of quality processes*, and the programme's *management and delivery* (Michael and Balraj 2003; Asgary and Robbert 2010; Culver et al. 2011). In spite of the growing interest in IDD programmes, the literature offered limited attention to these issues and failed to provide HE managers with frameworks to support their decision-making. This section proposes a framework to fill this gap.

The framework emerges from the empirical evidence experienced in the design and implementation of the IDD MSc programme at NBS.

Although we have chosen this case mainly because of access to the data, its relevance for research is important. In the British HE sector, 40% of TNE activities take the form of local delivery partnerships (HEGlobal 2016). Although these also include franchised programmes, validated or 'quality assurance' programmes, joint and top-up programmes, IDDs are the only category recording growth. In addition, while business and management programmes still represent the vast majority at 36% of the total (42% in terms of students), TNE experiences across disciplines remain novel with relatively few cases of success (HEGlobal 2016).

The IDD MSc Programme at NBS is based on an innovative structure of TNE. The programme is 15 months long over four semesters. Students attend the first semester in the MSc International Business Programme at NBS, whilst the second semester in a different programme at one of the partner institutions. The third semester is dedicated to work placement. During this period, students begin a research method module as a work-based learning experience, with online support. Finally, students eventually return to NBS to conclude the research method module and to produce and defend a Master dissertation. Table 4.1 summarizes the structure of the IDD MSc Programme, whilst Table 4.2 introduces the partners and the complementary programmes students can attend in each location.

The case study is based on both secondary and primary data. The former refer to archival data such as quality-process documentation and minutes of decision-making meetings. The research team collected primary data using two focus groups, interviews, and participant observation. One focus group included students at the end of the course, whilst the other comprised students at the beginning of their experience. Focus

Table 4.1 The IDD MSc programme at Nottingham Business School—Structure

	Institution—Country	Programme(s)
Term 1	Nottingham Business School—UK	MSc International Business
Term 2	See Table 4.2 (one to choose)	See Table 4.2
Term 3	Work placement	
Term 4	Nottingham Business School—UK	Research methods Dissertation

Table 4.2 The IDD MSc programme at Nottingham Business School—Partners and complementary programmes

Partner University	Country	Programme(s)
ESC Clermont—Graduate School of Management	France	MSc Project Management MSc International Business Development
KEDGE Business School—Marseille	France	MSc International Finance and Organizational Management MSc Luxury and Brand Management MSc Sports and Events Management
University of Brescia	Italy	MSc International Management
ISCTE Business School	Portugal	MSc International Management
National Sun Yat-sen	Taiwan	MBA Global Human Resources Management

groups took place in informal settings (i.e. cafés) in order to facilitate the flow of conversation amongst students, and between students and researchers. This arrangement was critical as researchers were part of the faculty and the aim was to minimize 'scripted' responses from the students.

In addition, the research team conducted interviews with the programme management team, faculty members, and decision-makers in partner institutions. Interviews were open ended and were conducted in informal settings. Again, the main rationale for this decision was to overcome potential 'double hermeneutics' issues where interviewees produce the accounts they anticipate the interviewer might expect (Giddens 1991).

The research team asked these stakeholders to identify the main processes that characterized the decision-making in designing and implementing the programme and to discuss the main challenges to the success of the student experience.

The analysis of the primary data highlighted four central themes in the accounts of both students and staff. The themes emerged as the key issues these stakeholders associated to the effectiveness of the design of the IDD programme. The themes were *clarity*, *priority*, *measure*, and *dependence*.

First, *clarity* included polysemic situations where stakeholders attributed different meanings to words, signs, and procedures. This variety seemed to be negatively associated with the effectiveness of the programme. For example, partners from diverse educational systems or working within different accreditation frameworks struggled to understand the terminology used for procedures or their relevance within the wider strategy for each school. Similarly, students had to cope with adjustment periods in their transitions from a system to the other. Notions such as 'attendance', 'authority', and 'independent study' embodied different meanings in different institutions. This increased the challenges of transition and hence the chance of academic achievement for these students.

Second, the theme *priority* referred to how HE institutions ranked the importance of actions, requirements, policies, and resources. This seems to affect the overall perceived commitment of each institution to the project or to internationalization in general. For example, the time and effort offered to support international students during transition varied sensibly amongst partners. If this diversity is indeed the appealing aspect of TNE programmes, it might also be an indicator of the level of success of each collaborative venture.

The third theme, *measure*, comprised references to the variety of assessments, completion requirements, timings, and institutional performance achievements. Data showed how stakeholders linked an increase in variety in the IDD programme to higher complexity. This shaped the decision-making processes as the higher the perceived complexity, the higher the associated difficulties to engage with the programme.

The final theme, *dependency*, encompassed aspects of both consequentiality and causality where decisions are shaped by previous actions, policies, timings, and projects. The data showed how the stakeholders have difficulty in coping with misaligned dependency being this, for example, an administrative issue such as recognition of credits or a strategic issue such as the attainment of an international accreditation.

Taking into consideration these four themes, this chapter proposes a framework to support the decision-making processes in designing and implementing IDD programmes.

The WHEEL framework identifies five processes that can drive effectively the design and the implementation of IDD programmes. The acronym reflects the processes that stakeholders of the IDD MSc Programme at NBS identified as critical to supporting the development of a successful programme. They widely reflect what previously identified in the literature (Michael and Balraj 2003).

Weigh the Partnership
Heed Practices and Customs
Evaluate Quality Assurance Processes
Establish Completion Requirements
Lay Down the Programme Management Plan

For each process, the framework proposes four action points, each addressing one of the themes identified as critical in the primary research. Figure 4.1 presents the WHEEL framework.

Decision-makers should consider the WHEEL framework when evaluating the feasibility of an IDD programme. However, the action points highlighted in the WHEEL framework are not a normative checklist. They are more alike to signposts that invite decision-makers to reflect on the nature of their choices. Besides, the aim is not to ensure similarity between the two partners, but to make sure that the two partners can identify bottlenecks and the emergence of potential issues *ex ante* at the time of setting up the IDD programme.

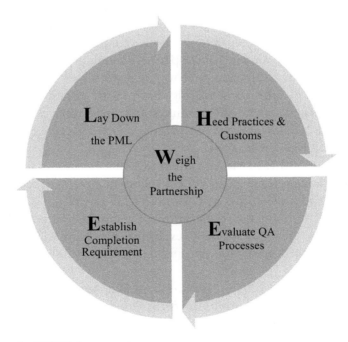

Fig. 4.1 The WHEEL framework

Weigh the Partnership

True to its name, the WHEEL framework presents a central hub and four spokes. The central aspect is indeed the identification, evaluation, and management of the partner institution. Just as the hub of a wheel holds the spokes in place and allows a continuous turning movement, the processes of identification, evaluation, and management of the partner are critical to the development of a successful IDD programme.

Collaboration projects such as dual and joint degree are often the result of the effort of individual members of faculty who have been previously collaborating with another university. Previous studies identified collaborations such as joint research projects, the organization of conferences, previous appointments, and staff exchanges as likely experiences to form the basis for IDD programmes (Michael and Balraj 2003).

Such previous joint experiences do not only offer a chance opportunity to have a 'ready-to-go' partner institution. They indeed represent an excellent opportunity to know and evaluate the partner especially with regard to issues such as trustworthiness, professionalism, work ethics, and approach to education (Asgary and Robbert 2010). Nevertheless, such previous joint experiences can represent inaccurate heuristics that replace a more structured evaluation of the partner's suitability for the IDD programme. Such heuristics can lead to cognitive biases in the decision-making process. This is especially likely with regard to issues of representativeness, where shortcomings and opportunism in decision-making can lead to an underestimation of the probability of events (Tversky and Kahneman 1974).

This is indeed true in the case observed. Three of the five partnerships emerged from previous extended collaboration between faculty members. As is common in the experience of IDD programmes, NBS nurtured the relationships with these partners for a number of years. Previous collaborations involved student exchange programmes, progression agreements, organization of summer schools and study tours, and research collaborations.

The creation of an IDD programme appeared therefore to be a natural progression of the relationship. Partners trusted each other and assumed that success in a previous experience was an adequate indicator of positive outcomes in the design of the IDD programme.

The evaluation of the previous experience led decision-makers to a classical conjunction fallacy, where a particular situation (i.e. excellent relationship in one field) was associated with the probability that success in more than one field was likely. The experience, however, did not yet replicate the same success as other collaboration opportunities. Issues such as the student experience, the integration of the programmes, and the smooth proceeding of the quality processes did not always live to the expectations of the partners.

Interviews with faculty members in both partners highlighted how the previous relationship shaped expectations in terms of speed of processes, requirements, and full commitment from the entire institution.

Although personal relationships are an excellent indicator of the effort, commitment, and understanding that the two partners will include in the process, HE institutions that decide to pursue the TNE route of IDD programmes should consider how other aspects come into play. Just like in a wheel, the hub only supports the momentum of the turning, but the spokes have to provide acceleration and velocity in order for the vehicle to move steadily and without faltering. The global strategic management literature reminds us that organizations that want to structure global alliances need to select partners primarily because of cultural similitude and sharing of strategic intents (Frynas and Mellahi 2015). For example, two universities with a similar strategic positioning would better suit the recruitment of students who will likely choose either in their career path. Moreover, managers and decision-makers would more easily share values and cultural understandings. Similarly, two HE institutions with processes aligned to an international accreditation (e.g. AACSB) will have an easier understanding of processes and requirements. This was indeed the case for the two other partnerships in the IDD programme. The entire organizations, prospective students, validators, and external bodies found easier to see the strategic fit, the future potential, and the processes required. Organizations evolve over time and their missions, expectations, and priorities change. The processes of partner identification and management need therefore to be consciously monitored and updated. Table 4.3 below indicates actions for decision-makers that would support their continuous evaluation of the relationship with the partner.

Table 4.3 Action points suggested for managing the 'Weigh the Partnership' process

Theme	Action	Aim
Clarity	Compare mission statements and clearly position the IDD programme in both portfolios.	Ensure both partners share the same strategic intent and that the IDD programme will have a clear similar positioning in the portfolio of international activities.
Priority	Create visual artefacts and examples that represent the culture of each organization.	Ensure both partners share values and cultural understandings as these will guide the prioritization of activities and resources allocations.
Measure	Produce a comparative five-year budget of committed resources.	Ensure both partners fully commit sustainable resources, with particular attention to financial assets and support staff.
Dependence	Indicate wider institutional endorsement and individual responsibilities and covers.	Ensure both partners are committed at an organizational level and not only with selected members of staff.

Heed Practices and Customs

The literature widely discussed the importance of managing cultural aspects in shaping TNE experiences (Knight 2008; Kim 2009, Pyvis 2011). Heffernan et al. (2010) argued that decision-makers should focus more on areas such as the variety of students' learning styles. Similarly, Kim (2009) invited to consider the challenges and opportunities that the different teaching styles of international faculty members offer to TNE experiences. McBurnie and Ziguras (2007) recognized the importance of these aspects as well as the need to assess the cultural relevance of educational material and learning resources. A careful evaluation of such cultural elements appears critical in undertaking TNE projects for two main reasons. First, decision-makers need to minimize the risk to impose the mark of one cultural system over the other (Egege and Kutieleh 2008; Healey and Bordogna 2014). Second, HE institutions need to prepare students to the cultural challenges they would experience during TNE experiences (Teichler 2009; Heffernan et al. 2010). With regard to the former, IDD programmes represent an ideal format of TNE. The opportunity for prospective students to experience an appropriate balance between two different education systems is in fact one of the unique selling points of such education offerings. On the other hand, there is a considerable variety in the sector in terms of cultural support offered to outgoing students (Teichler 2009). Some HE institutions have a structured approach to the preparation of their outgoing students (Leask 2001; McBurnie and Ziguras 2007). However, this is especially common in TNE projects such as student exchanges and in areas such as language support (Collins and Davidson 2002). However, there is little attention to the preparation of students in terms of getting used to other regulations and customs more specific to the educational system. In particular, students in TNE projects experience different methods of teaching and learning, different levels of support from academic staff, different administrative support systems, and different workloads. Tobenkin (2008) identified these issues as key limitations for the establishment of effective IDD programmes. The required pace of adjustment to different expectations, although an intrinsic characteristic of IDD, is especially highlighted as a critical determinant of student satisfaction in accelerated international programmes (Knight 2013). The focus group with students in the IDD MSc programme evidenced this cultural misalignment to be a key determinant of student satisfaction.

In addition, these issues seem not only to affect the organization of the programmes and the student satisfaction, but they also increase the level of stress amongst academic and support staff (Kuder and Obst 2009). The role of educators and support staff varies in different educational systems (McBurnie and Ziguras 2007). For example, the staff-hours dedicated to pastoral care, the type of access (e.g. face-to-face versus digital), the availability of staff on campus, and formalization of the relationship can all vary sensibly between educational systems. Interviews with faculty members supported these insights and confirmed how cultural misalignment can be a source of stress to educators.

The data showed how both students and staff also experienced issues of 'cultural re-adjustment'. This refers to the processes of cultural re-adjustment students in IDD programmes experience when they returned to the home institution for the final part of their project. In the IDD MSc programme, students re-engage with NBS for the final dissertation after their periods in the partner HE institution and in the work placement. Students, academic faculty, and subject administrators in the home institution struggled to re-adapt to the system after having adjusted to that of the host institution. Table 4.4 summarizes the actions HE institutions can take to inform their decision-making when setting up the programme.

An evaluation of these cultural factors will also inform communication to students. Universities will hence be able to anticipate and manage the expectations of outgoing students. In addition, the evaluation will form the basis for short programmes to prepare outgoing students to the new educational environment. Finally, HE institutions can use such knowledge to provide professional development opportunities to faculty staff on different education systems and on international students' expectations.

Table 4.4 Action points suggested for managing the 'Heed Practices and Customs' process

Theme	Action	Aim
Clarity	Disclose details of the cultural relationship between staff and students.	Facilitate student transition and minimize sources of conflict and dissatisfaction.
Priority	Evidence students' support provisions (e.g. facilities, staff hours).	Manage students' expectations and anticipate issues of fitness to study.
Measure	Publish assessment schedules that highlight expectations and administrative burdens for both students and staff.	Manage both students' and faculty's expectations. Facilitate resource planning. Assure measurements of learning.
Dependence	Detail the structure of teaching and learning. Present the balance of contact time (e.g. seminars/workshops, lectures); independent study; and directed learning.	Manage students' expectations and anticipate issues of pedagogic alignment during the transition.

Evaluate Quality Assurance Processes

Quality assurance processes are a critical element in shaping the design of IDD programmes (Asgary and Robbert 2010). The importance of these processes pervades the dynamics of the IDD programme from the inception (e.g. the formulation of a memorandum of understanding) through the day-to-day administrative operations (Gallicchio 2007). Traditionally, partner institutions focus their attention on quality assurance processes at the time of designing the programme and signing off the agreement. However, a misalignment of quality assurance processes between the two partners can delay or altogether halt the implementation of the process (Kuder and Obst 2009). HE institutions therefore need to introduce design elements that would facilitate a continuous monitoring of the changes in quality assurance processes (Altbach and Knight 2007). The WHEEL framework proposes to conduct four actions during the evaluation process of the IDD programme that would eventually support the monitoring of quality activities during its implementation. Table 4.5 below summarizes these actions.

In the case, the main difficulties between partners emerged when a partner failed to understand the rationale behind sudden requests from another

Table 4.5 Action points suggested for managing the 'Evaluate Quality Assurance Processes'

Theme	Action	Aim
Clarity	Produce and circulate a glossary of quality assurance terms for both partners (integrated with a *frequently asked questions* factsheet).	Familiarize partners with each other vocabulary and quality requirements.
Priority	Include in the evaluation process at least a person familiar with the partner's national and institutional framework.	Simplify the comprehension of quality requirements. Understand between-the-lines issues.
Measure	Present road maps to international accreditations and relevant expected commitments and measurements.	Anticipate stress points and prepare staff in both institutions to extra workload.
Dependence	Draw and compare flow charts of quality assurance procedures for both partners.	Familiarize partners with each other procedures and requirements for change.

partner. Interviews highlighted how this situation 'strained relationships' and required for staff 'enormous efforts and a lot of patience [...] I don't know if others would have done it'. Accreditation processes in one or more institutions especially exacerbated these difficulties. Sudden requests for documentation were not considered a priority for partners with less familiarity with the process. In some cases, partners considered some requests as a 'violation' of privacy or independence.

The difficulty for staff to capture the importance of steps or procedures in one partner's institutional governance or state bureaucracy increased faculty resistance (Michael and Balraj 2003). Both academic and administrative staff interpreted some requirements as unjustified extra workload. This was mainly due to the absence in one's institutional and national framework of an immediate infrastructure to use as a point of reference (Griffiths 2003). In the case, the presence in the programme team of members of staff familiar with quality processes in different countries facilitated communication and promotion of activities amongst colleagues.

In addition, quality assurance procedures are different not only in terms of decision-making centres, but also in terms of independence and timing. In the case, changes to the programme were difficult to implement timely as partners could not recognize the need for tight turnaround of documentation or could not identify in time equivalent bodies of governance across institutional frameworks. Creating visual artefacts (e.g. maps, flow charts) that clarify meanings and processes ensures that partner HE institutions have an immediate and clear understanding of each other's quality requirements. They can hence anticipate procedural bottlenecks more easily and share quality requirements imposed by an accreditation process.

Establish Completion Requirements

A key challenge to the development of both joint and dual degree programmes is the definition of the completion requirements (Kuder et al. 2013). The primary issue of concern is the difficulty in understanding the terms of equivalence of credits (Obst et al. 2011). However, the presence of different grading systems also makes credit recognition difficult (Tobenkin 2008). Besides, other factors are widely underestimated. So, for example, some contexts strongly enforce prerequisites, whilst others consider them as only advisory. Similarly, the required capstone performance to complete a programme varies between countries as well as between subject disciplines (Baird 1997). The traditional dissertation seems to evaporate from the curricula in several countries, whereas others remain anchored to this defining requirement. The situation regarding completion requirements is also complicated because of the different levels of autonomy that HE institutions experience in various countries (Kuder et al. 2013). For example, institutions in Germany see their efforts often frustrated from the national limitations to title-awarding powers, especially in regimes of joint degree (Tarazona 2013).

The case of the IDD MSc programme confirmed the difficulties partner institutions encounter with regard to the different requirements in terms of capstone requirements for the completion of individual awards. For example, in the IDD MSc programme, a key aspect was the expectation from European partners that students would need to complete a structured dissertation. NBS had previously abandoned this form of assignment in *lieu* of a consultancy project students completed with a company. This choice reflects the mission to be a Business School that links theory and practice. However, this choice did not align with the expectations of the partner universities on the IDD Programme. For them, the completion of a dissertation in the form of a monograph remains an essential feature of Masters Programmes. Table 4.6 summarizes the actions to support the evaluation of completion requirements between institutional partners.

Table 4.6 Action points suggested for managing the 'Establish Completion Requirements' process

Theme	Action	Aim
Clarity	Pre-valuate and map credits and equivalences of modules/experiences.	Consider diversity as richness. Facilitate credits mapping and conversions.
Priority	Identify requirements at programme, institutional, professional, and national levels.	Anticipate issues of completion linked to requirements outside control of the team.
Measure	Identify details for capstone projects (e.g. work experience, dissertation, and projects).	Anticipate issues of completion linked to specific requirements.
Dependence	Define alternatives to completion (credit recognition and exit awards).	Account for special cases or issues of achievement and completion.

Table 4.7 Action points suggested for managing the 'Lay-down the Programme Management Plan' process

Theme	Action	Aim
Clarity	Share the programmes' calendars (e.g. term starts; exam timetables).	Facilitate students' and staff's workload planning.
Priority	Represent visually administrative responsibilities at each stage.	Pre-empt risks of vacuum in decision-making and student support.
Measure	Plan the balance between students' engagement and independent work.	Manage expectations and prepare students for transition in TNE.
Dependence	Determine the exact requirement of weeks in each programme for students.	Ensure movement between institutions is smooth and it does not impact tuitions.

Lay Down the Programme Management Plan

Often underestimated in the design and implementation of TNE programmes are timing issues such as the programme's calendar (Kuder and Obst 2009). While some research exists with regard to other TNE practices such as student exchange, there is little evidence regarding the experience of integrating two different programmes in different universities and relative education systems (Asgary and Robbert 2010). The programme team of the IDD MSc programme at NBS experienced this issue as each partner has a different starting date of the second semester. For example, one partner institution normally starts its second semester in the early days of January, whereas other partners start the second semester in late January or at the beginning of February. In this case, a lot of flexibility was required for students and staff to adjust to different timetables. In addition, IDD programmes often have unique calendars that differ from the ones of other academic provisions (Griffiths 2003). This is problematic as student support services are often geared towards standard programmes. In this case, students on the IDD programme experienced difficulties in registering for accommodation and for language classes at all partner institutions.

Especially in the presence of multiple partner organizations on a single IDD project, the coordination of the different project timescales becomes critical to ensuring student satisfaction, workload planning for faculty, and adequate support from agencies such as a university's student accommodation service. Administrators and support services traditionally highlight as a considerable source of stress the lack of clarity surrounding the timings of the programmes and the associated responsibilities (Kuder and Obst 2009). In the case explored, these issues emerged strongly from the interviews with staff members. Student support services often strived to accommodate the needs of a programme that did not necessarily follow the traditional academic calendar. Support staff duly supported the team, nevertheless, but referred to actions related to the IDD MSc programme as 'favours', 'one-off', and 'goodwill'.

Gallicchio (2007) identified the key role played by administrative support and advocacy in ensuring the establishment of an effective IDD programme. The alignment of administrative support is especially important as it contributes to minimise disruption and to increase student satisfaction. The focus groups confirmed this critical aspect as students often compared the level of support received (across all partner institutions) with the one accessible to other students in more traditionally structured programmes.

Finally, laying down a programme management plan also effectively supports the programme teams in sharing best practices between organizations, in setting clear responsibilities, and in reducing the dependency on each other's actions (Griffiths 2003). The plan becomes an effective tool of coordination, reduces duplication activities across universities, and minimizes the risk of students being caught in a 'no man's land' between the decision-making systems of two organizations. The actions proposed in the WHEEL framework highlight these issues to anticipate possible bottlenecks and organizational issues.

Conclusion

This chapter reflected on the strategic role of IDD Programmes and introduced a framework to design and implement them effectively. The considerations on expectations and practice invite policy makers and HE managers to review the role of these programmes in the portfolio of educational offer. These programmes are not mere means to increase student numbers, but opportunities to strengthen international partnerships, to increase reputation, and to reflect on the organization's approach to TNE.

The chapter also presented the research-based case study of the IDD MSc programme at NBS. The evidence from the primary research conducted with both students and staff suggested to consider four areas of attention: *clarity, priority, measure,* and *dependence*. Combining these issues with the processes identified in the literature, the chapter proposed the WHEEL framework. This is intended to be a management tool for international educators and for decision-makers in HE institutions.

The framework discusses the role of key institutional processes in supporting the feasibility assessment of IDD programmes and their continuous monitoring. It highlights the strategic issues of partner identification, evaluation, and selection in light of operational decisions such as practices and customs, quality assurance processes, completion requirements, and programme management plans.

The evidence from the case shows, however, how it is not possible to decouple these processes from the dynamics of design and implementation of the dual degree programme. Aspects that might look more operational in nature are in reality also relevant at a strategic level. The WHEEL framework hence moves them more centrally to the decision-making process of partner selection and engagement.

The WHEEL framework's action points are not exhaustive and could be adapted to the specific requirements of each institution. Besides, they do not represent a normative checklist aimed at aligning the two partners. They should represent the basis for an ongoing reflection on the status of the programme so as to identify bottlenecks and the emergence of potential issues timely. In this perspective, the IDD programme can fulfil its strategic role and maximize both students' and staff's satisfaction.

References

Altbach, P.G. and Knight, J. (2007) The internationalization of higher education: Motivations and realities. *Journal of Studies in International Education*, 11(3–4), 290–305.

Asgary, N. and Robbert, M.A. (2010) A cost-benefit analysis of an international dual degree programme. *Journal of Higher Education Policy and Management*, 32(3), 317–325.

Baird, L.L. (1997) Completing the dissertation: Theory, research, and practice. *New Directions for Higher Education*, Autumn (99), 99–105.

Carlin, D.B. (2008) Engaging globally through joint and dual degrees: The graduate experience. *Global Higher Education*. Available at: https://globalhighered.wordpress.com/2008/02/23/engaging-globally-through-joint-and-dual-degrees-the-graduate-experience/. Last accessed 5 April 2018.

Chevallier, A. (2013) *A process for screening and authorizing joint and double degree programs a briefing paper*. New York, NY: Institute of International Education.

Collins, N.F. and Davidson, D.E. (2002) From the margin to the mainstream: Innovative approaches to internationalizing education for a new century. *Change: The Magazine of Higher Learning*, 34(50), 50–58.

Crossman, J.E. and Clarke, M. (2010) International experience and graduate employability: Stakeholder perceptions on the connection. *High Education*, 59, 599–613.

Culver, S.M., Puri, I.K., Spinelli, G., DePauw, K.P.K. and Dooley, J.E. (2011) Collaborative dual-degree programs and value added for students: Lessons learned through the evaluate-E project. *Journal of Studies in International Education*, 20(10), 1–22.

Delisle, P. (2011) Rationales and strategies behind double degrees: A transatlantic approach. In D. Obst and M. Kuder (eds.) *Joint and double degree programs: An emerging model for transatlantic exchange*. New York, NY: Institute of International Education.

Egege, S. and Kutieleh, S. (2008) Dimming down difference. In Lee Dunn and Michelle Wallace (eds.) *Teaching in transnational higher education* (pp. 67–76). New York: Routledge.

Gallicchio, V. S. (2007) Administration of an innovative programme of international cooperation: Success across the pond. *Journal of Research Administration*, 38(2), 78–86.

Giddens, A. (1991) *Modernity and self-identity. Self and society in the late modern age*. Cambridge: Polity Press.

Griffith, V. (2003) A degree that bridges the world. *Financial Times*, March 10, p. 13.

Gutierrez, R., Bhandari, R. and Obst, D. (2008) *Exploring host country capacity for increasing US study abroad*. IIE Study Abroad White Paper Series, Issue No. 2. New York, NY: Institute of International Education.

Healey, N. M. and Bordogna, C. (2014) From transnational to multinational education: Emerging trends in international higher education. *Internationalisation of Higher Education*, 3, 33–53. Available at: www.handbook-internationalisation.com

Heffernan, T., Morrison, M., Basu, P. and Sweeney, A. (2010) Cultural differences, learning styles and transnational education. *Journal of Higher Education Policy and Management*, 32(1), 27–39.

HEGlobal (2016) *The scale and scope of UK higher education transnational education*. Available at: www.heglobal.international.ac.uk. Last accessed 30 November 2016.

Kim, T. (2009) Transnational academic mobility, internationalization and interculturality in higher education, *Intercultural Education*, 20(5), 395–405.

Knight, J. (2008) The internationalisation of higher education: Are we on the right track? The Global University—Issue of Academic Matters. *The Journal of Higher Education*, October/November. Available at: http://www.academicmatters.ca/current_issue.article.gk?catalog_item_id=1234&category=/issues/OCT2008

Knight, J. (2013) Joint, double, and consecutive degree programs: Definition, doubts, and dilemmas. In M. Kuder, N. Lemmens, and D. Obst (eds.) *Global perspectives on international joint and double degree programs*. New York, NY: Institute of International Education.

Kuder, M., Lemmens, N. and Obst, D. (2013) *Global perspectives on international joint and double degree programs*. New York, NY: Institute of International Education.

Kuder, M. and Obst, D. (2009) *Joint and double degree programs in the transatlantic context—A survey report*. New York, NY: Institute of International Education.

Leask, B. (2001) Bridging the gap: Internationalizing university curricula. *Journal of Studies in International Education*, 5(2), 100–115.

McBurnie, G. and Ziguras, C. (2007) *Transnational education: Issues and trends in offshore higher education*. London: Routledge.

Michael, S.O. and Balraj, L. (2003) Higher education institutional collaborations: An analysis of models of joint degree programs. *Journal of Higher Education Policy and Management*, 25(2), 131–145.

Obst, D., Kuder, M. and Banks, C. (2011) *Joint and double degree programs in the global context: A report on an international survey*. New York, NY: Institute of International Education.

Pyvis, D. (2011) The need for context sensitive measures of educational quality in transnational higher education. *Teaching in Higher Education*, 16(6), 733–744.

Tarazona, M. (2013) Influences on the sustainability of joint and double degree programs: Empirical findings from programs with German participation. In M. Kuder, N. Lemmens, and D. Obst (eds.) *Global perspectives on international joint and double degree programs*. New York, NY: Institute of International Education.

Teichler, U. (2009) Internationalisation of higher education: European experiences. *Asia Pacific Education Review*, 10(1), 93–106.

Tobenkin, D. (2008) Degrees of success. *NAFSA: International Educator*, May/June, pp. 36–46.

Tversky, A. and Kahneman, D. (1974) Judgment under uncertainty: Heuristics and biases. *Science, New Series*, 185(4157), 1124–1131.

Part II

Organisational Culture

5

Intercultural Competence Development for All Students in Theory and Practice

Albina Szeles

Introduction

Internationalisation has become a priority for many higher education (HE) institutions located worldwide (Knight 2006; Middlehurst and Woodfield 2007; Leask 2014; Hudzik 2017). Internationalisation activities have spread rapidly in recent decades, pulling institutions in a number of directions. These activities include mainly campus-based internationalisation initiatives such as recruitment of international students, study abroad exchanges, foreign language instruction, and curriculum internationalisation through comparative perspectives.

International education is considered a powerful force that can facilitate intercultural dialogue and inclusion. However, is this potential being recognised in all pursuits of global universities? As global demand for higher education grows and many universities engage in profitgenerating activities, transnational education (TNE) tends to run as separate

A. Szeles (✉)
Coventry University, Coventry, UK
e-mail: ab1244@coventry.ac.uk

agenda to campus internationalisation. In a new global economy, demand for a globally agile and interculturally competent workforce is rising. It is universally recognised that the diversity which cross-border activity brings can be a valuable asset. With this in mind, institutions are responding to the changing environment by infusing both formal and informal curriculum with a range of activities, preparing students to live and work globally.

While those actions are firmly embedded for students studying within home campuses, there is relatively little evidence of how students on fast growing TNE programmes benefit from this form of internationalisation. For the first time since 2010–12, the number of students enrolled on the UK TNE programmes abroad has been higher than those on the UK-based courses. The Higher Education Statistics Agency's Aggregate Offshore Record (HESA AOR) data for 2015–16 shows that the gap has significantly increased with 201,860 more students being enrolled abroad than in the UK (International Facts and Figures 2017; British Council Education Intelligence 2017). UK qualifications are now delivered in 213 countries and territories outside the UK. What is striking is that the predictions show that in the next five years two-thirds of students will study overseas towards the UK degree (Van-Cauter 2017). The UK already has more graduates from TNE programmes than those who studied at 'home' being ambassadors for many universities worldwide. However, are we certain that all graduates had been given the opportunity to become 'global ready'?

This chapter introduces transnational HE from a diverse sociocultural perspective, providing frameworks for creativity and transformative teaching and learning. Drawing on existing literature and examples of initiatives developed at Coventry University, this chapter outlines tools and ideas for the development of intercultural competencies among students on TNE provision. It explores the association between virtual mobility as a part of internationalisation at home (IaH) and internationalisation of the curriculum (IoC) and intercultural competence development, evaluating the relevance of extending the practice to all learning environments.

Intercultural Competence Development Approaches at Home and Abroad

Intercultural competence should be a primary outcome of international education. However, it appears to be a vague concept to many educators. Intercultural competence is widely defined as 'the ability to communicate effectively and appropriately in intercultural situations based on one's intercultural knowledge, skills and attitudes' (Deardorff 2006: 247). Intercultural competence relates to capabilities such as openness, respect (attitudes), active listening, ability to evaluate (skills), self-awareness, and cultural awareness of other cultures (knowledge). Lantz and Davies (2015: 43) suggest that 'Intercultural development (e.g. Bennett 1986) involves advancing cognitive complexity, which relates directly to fostering critical thinking skills, arguably an important outcome for university students.'

Even though it is developmental in nature, learning about other cultures or even having contact with people from other cultures does not automatically contribute to growth. Facilitation of intercultural learning is a challenge and requires a shift beyond traditional teaching and learning. Self-awareness and reflexive and critical analyses of assumptions can be developed only with student-centred and experiential approaches. The way in which institutions prioritise internationalisation interventions aimed at intercultural competence development varies across the sector. As university leaders assume unintentional development, bottom-up approaches tend to precede the policies.

From the perspective of TNE, increasing exportation of the UK HE abroad has contributed to the impression of this mode as a product and the perception of students as customers. The economic impact of TNE for providers has been emphasised more often than its value to students and societies at large. In 2014, the British Council, in collaboration with DAAD German Academic Exchange service, published a study on the impact of TNE on host countries. The research revealed interesting findings from the intercultural perspective, showing increased international outlook to be the most significant benefit of TNE, and intercultural awareness being ranked as the third benefit providing clear evidence of the need. Despite that, the research found that cross-cultural learning does not meet student expectations with the skill being ranked as the seventh most developed skill (British Council and DAAD 2014).

Consequently, as Jean-François et al. (2016) pointed out, the application of TNE programmes may not always support the 'glocal' symbiosis that is required to address negative conceptions of internationalisation and sustain the development of innovative pedagogies and interculturally sensitive practices.

The United Nations Educational Scientific and Cultural Organisation (UNESCO) advocates intercultural dialogues through education. Gabriela Ramos, OECD Chief of Staff and Sherpa to the G20 cited in the OECD (2016) report, has highlighted that

> Reinforcing global competencies is vital for individuals to thrive in a rapidly changing world and for societies to progress without leaving anyone behind. Against a context in which we all have much to gain from growing openness and connectivity, and much to lose from rising inequalities and radicalism, citizens need not only the skills to be competitive and ready for a new world of work, but more importantly they also need to develop the capacity to analyse and understand global and intercultural issues. The development of social and emotional skills, as well as values like tolerance, self-confidence and a sense of belonging, are of the utmost importance to create opportunities for all and advance a shared respect for human dignity.

According to the British Council and DAAD study (2014), 76% of HE experts believe that TNE has a positive impact on intercultural relations within the country. What is more, non-TNE students and non-TNE staff perceive TNE undergraduates as better equipped than locally educated students. That is an encouraging sign, but whether the skillset of TNE graduates matches the global acumen of students on home programmes and how TNE contributes to intercultural dialogue worldwide needs further verification.

It seems to be clear that TNE is a part of internationalisation but is internationalisation an integral part of TNE? Recognising the need and expectations of students, providers should reflect on the meaning of internationalisation and implications on TNE.

The understanding and definitions of 'internationalisation' as a term have been debated for a number of years. With the world of education becoming increasingly interconnected, new terms and definitions are being constantly introduced. Thus, with internationalisation at its momentum, it is important that the concept is understood clearly and followed by practice that benefits all students equally.

One of the most popular definitions proposed by Jane Knight (2015) describes internationalisation as 'the process of integrating an international, intercultural, or global dimension into the purpose, functions or delivery of postsecondary education' which attempts to provide a universal definition appropriate to different cultural and educational contexts. Although it does point out the ongoing nature of it, as with many other definitions, it does not specify the variety of activities and methods.

An alternative definition proposed by Hans De Wit et al. (2015: 29) adds purpose to the concept describing internationalisation as 'the intentional process of integrating an international, intercultural or global dimension into the purpose, functions and delivery of post-secondary education, in order to enhance the quality of education and research for all students and staff, and to make a meaningful contribution to society'.

The rationale for internationalisation is very often connected to the idea of preparing graduates to live in a globalised world. 'Global Graduates' and 'Global citizens' are the new buzz words in the sector. It has been critically applauded that HE institutions have a duty to produce graduates who are able to work and live in a global world effectively.

Many universities have visionary statements focused on global attributes, but how exactly this intention is implemented and connected to student learning is not often explicit. Marginson and Sawir (2011: 6) argue that 'international education promises to integrate nations more closely and open up institutions to the world, so local and international students experience life-changing learning. Is it working out? No, it is not.' While many institutions concentrate their efforts on physical mobility, focusing on sending students abroad for short- and long-term trips and exchanges, this is happening using mainly an infused approach and rarely including necessary cross-cultural preparation.

Owing to initiatives like Erasmus, the largest mobility programme in the world, millions of students have participated in exchanges. The benefits of outward mobility have been widely acclaimed. For example, the impact study of the Erasmus programme reports that mobile students are more likely to attain managerial positions in their future career (Brandenburg et al. 2015). Celebrating its 30th year in operation, the European Erasmus programme is now serving as a case study for ASEAN Student Mobility Forum wishing to create their intra-regional scheme (Chipperfield 2017). Whereas there seems to be consensus on the general benefits of mobility, there is a need for more evidence specific to intercultural development. Despite 49% of TNE students having studied abroad as a part of their programme, intercultural competence was ranked only as the seventh most enhanced skill (British Council and DAAD 2014).

On the other hand, even if mobility could be a solution for the development of intercultural competence, at some universities it is still considered to be unavailable to the vast majority (Jones and Killick 2013). Coventry University has been leading in the provision of mobility for their campus students for the past couple of years (Hesa.ac.uk 2017); however, the challenge to ensure all students have an opportunity to undertake an overseas field trip or exchange experience at some point of their studies is recognised. In addition, in the context of TNE where students chose a foreign degree provided locally in order to stay closer to home (Validated or Franchise arrangements), mobility may not be an option. With this in mind, more inclusive approaches to internationalisation should be considered.

The term 'intercultural' is also incorporated in definitions of other concepts such as IoC or IaH that have grown in significance particularly in Australia and Europe.

Leask (2009: 209) defines IoC as 'the incorporation of an international and intercultural dimension into the content of the curriculum as well as the teaching, learning, and assessment arrangements and support services of a program of study.' Consequently, internationalised curriculum through changes in pedagogy aims to develop intercultural competence (skills, knowledge, and attitudes) of all students.

Is TNE curriculum internationalised? Much of the criticism relates to the approach to TNE curriculum that is very often viewed as a homogenised product. Ziguras (2008: 44) raises a series of relevant issues such as:

Should an international branch campus of an Anglophone university insist that its students speak only English on campus? Should lecturers travelling overseas to teach in transnational programs be required to undertake cultural awareness training? Should Western universities teach in Asia the same way they would in their home country, or as Asian universities do?

An emerging discourse points out the complexity of the transnational pedagogy. So far the discussion about the challenge of navigating multicultural classrooms and responding to different learning cultures has been mainly connected to the growing influx of international students to the UK. In this respect, the TNE classroom environment where students and teachers come from different cultures and discipline contexts poses unique challenges for both groups alike. With an increase of TNE, the role of academic staff is becoming more demanding than ever, requiring high levels of self-awareness and intercultural knowledge (Galvin 2004). Nevertheless, in spite of growing domination of TNE as a mode of delivery, there is still a relatively small body of research concerned with stakeholders' expectations, cultural values, norms, and behavioural patterns.

One criticism of much of the literature on TNE is oscillating around the use of 'western' curriculum that fails to adapt its content, delivery, and assessment to the context. Some research calls for decolonisation of education to create internationally minded collaborative communities (Wallace and Dunn 2008).

However, the centre of the current debate tends to show that the approach of simply 'transplanting' programmes is shifting towards more contextualised approaches. Crabtree and Sapp (2004) under the intriguing title 'Your Culture, My Classroom, Whose Pedagogy?' provide their perspective on teaching in different cultural contexts. Drawing on their experience, they emphasise the value of understanding intercultural communication theory and practice and the need for adaptation to the context. It can be argued that any curriculum whether at home or abroad should be made transnational from the inception.

More recent attention has focused on the internationalisation of the learning outcomes as an essential part of IoC process. Deardorff (2015) holds a view that internationalisation of learning outcomes is fundamental to effective teaching and assessment for diverse populations. The primary concern is to design curriculum systematically informed by a broad range of international and intercultural research and practice including non-dominant perspectives. Well-defined, communicated, and assessed internationalised learning outcomes provide flexibility for educators to contextualise the learning experience to the needs of the programme and students alike without losing sight of core curriculum requirements. With the alignment of learning outcomes, the emphasis is put on the importance of multiple perspectives through not only content and materials but also creating learning environments which enable multicultural interaction and critical reflection and organising appropriate assessment.

In the same vein, Carroll (2015) is building a picture of effective teaching, learning, and assessment practice in the globally interconnected world for Anglo-western teachers. In her book 'Tools for teaching in educational mobile world', she proposes a definition of 'mobile students' which also encompasses those on transnational programmes and does not distinguish between home and international student cohorts. This book examines challenges and offers ideas and methods for adjusting teaching approaches highlighting not only the need for a change of content and materials but also teaching and learning strategies and methods.

Overall, these studies highlight the complexity of teaching in HE not only in diverse home campuses but also in overlooked tertiary classrooms. In a world where programmes, teachers, and students move, these topics become of great concern to educators, and they deserve ongoing attention in both research and practice.

The concept of IaH proposes another way of looking at internationalisation. While IaH is highly overlapping with IoC, it does not include the mobility aspect. Despite the substantial growth and clear benefits, universities recognise that international experiences should also be provided to the non-mobile student body.

IaH is defined as 'the purposeful integration of international and intercultural dimensions into the formal and informal curriculum for all students, within domestic learning environments' (Beelen and Jones 2015: 69). It emphasises the role of internationalisation for all students, including the non-mobile, with an intention to offer international and intercultural perspectives at 'home'. But then again discussing 'home' and 'domestic learning environments' causes a misunderstanding that internationalisation should apply to home campus students. Internationalisation is an imperative and should not only impact all of campus life but the institution as a whole including partnerships and relations.

As universities in the UK become more entrepreneurial, income generation tends to be the major driver behind the international development (Levidow 2002). With the changing landscape and focus on economic viability, institutions regard TNE as an opportunity to increase revenues (Tian and Lowe 2009; Turner and Robson 2007), whereas internationalisation, in general, is considered to be an investment of time and resources.

Over the past decade, agendas have matured and are very often linked to the educational strategies and corporate plans setting directions for both academic and professional staff. The premises are commonly connected to growing international student numbers at home and developing TNE or enhancing the range of international activities within universities. However,

> the main benefits of globalisation of higher education are not financial (as valuable as that may be) but intellectual and cultural. The coming together of people from different parts of the world to study has the potential to form creative global communities that learn and interact and collaborate in new and previously incomprehensible ways. Such is the dynamism of life in the 'global village. (Pillay 2006: 1)

There is a consensus among practitioners with the grounds of the above definitions. However, the implementation strategies and application tend to vary considerably. Although a range of studies has investigated intercultural competence in general, few studies have attempted to present valuable, but cost-effective tools and services offered to students within HE and the impact of such programmes on students' intercultural competencies.

While UK universities have always been engaged in the internationalisation of some sort, as more universities embark on the journey of capitalising on the increasingly diverse student populations at home and abroad, the actions should reflect the discourse.

Internationalisation Through Virtual Mobility

Digitalisation is transforming teaching and learning. Information technology has reformed each part of the sector and offered providers the opportunity to deliver TNE online. Until recently, discussions on connecting home courses with offshore programmes have rarely focused on the potential for virtual mobility to assist with other initiatives such as exchanges and summer schools. As the digital revolution made its way into our lives, a slower burning digital transformation is forcing its way into classrooms. Technological advancements are now revolutionising the 'internationalisation landscape' with the addition of virtual mobility as means for a meaningful international experience.

The term 'virtual mobility' has been popularised by the European Commission particularly in Europe. According to the elearningeuropa cited in Virtual Mobility Best-Practice Manual (Bijnens et al. 2006: 25), 'virtual mobility means the use of information and communication technologies to obtain the same benefits as one would have with physical mobility but without the need for travel.' Alternative terms have been introduced in the United States as Collaborative Online International Learning (COIL) and in the UK as Online International Learning (OIL) developed by Coventry University.

> Online International Learning (OIL) is the term that we use to refer to 'virtual mobility' experiences that are incorporated into the formal curriculum and provide students with an opportunity to interact with peers at international universities and professionals, so they can develop intercultural competencies and digital skills while working together on subject-specific learning tasks or activities. (Online International Learning 2017)

Virtual mobility aims to integrate international and intercultural dimension into the functions of the curriculum. With the desire to focus on all students, including those who are not mobile, OIL forms an integral part of the IaH and IoC agenda.

What makes virtual mobility a viable 'alternative' to physical mobility? Villar-Onrubia and Rajpal (2015: 82) have reported that

> virtual mobility initiatives such as OIL are one of the most flexible, versatile and inclusive approaches to the provision of experiential learning opportunities aimed at facilitating students' intercultural competence development. While forms of IoC that involve travelling abroad exclude a considerable segment of the student population at most universities, virtual mobility can help increase the number of students who benefit from collaborative work with peers at universities around the globe.

With increasing competition and submerging funds, institutions need to look at innovative and cost-effective ways to ensure internationalisation for all and consequently produce global graduates regardless of the location of study. At Coventry University, transnational engagement through virtual mobility is bringing much-needed innovation to the student experience. OIL projects have the potential to greatly expand TNE students' exposure to 'home' campus and equally campus students to their peers located worldwide.

Information and communication technology (ICT) can contribute to diminishing physical proximity and building learning communities in a dispersed learning provision. The anecdotal evidence suggests that collaborative activity between host and provider deepens the relationship and partnership and contributes to academic dialogue and solidarity among teachers.

OIL has a unique role in reshaping student learning and consequently when used creatively has the potential to give all students the opportunity to become global graduates. As a result, Coventry University contends that OIL should be one of the fundamental tools supporting the development of twenty-first-century skills. The main advantages of OIL are that students have an opportunity to:

- Interact, engage, and collaborate with peers they would have not otherwise had the chance to work with.
- Share understanding of one another's societies, ways of living, and perspectives to develop valuable intercultural skills and mutual understanding.
- Observe, listen, and learn about differences in communication style, non-verbal cues, and body language, increasing their intercultural communication capacity for understanding and managing interactions in diverse, complex, and novel scenarios.
- Experience, interact, and gain insight into cultural differences in human relationships, behaviour, and communication that are relevant to their discipline, enhancing their ability to effectively manage and appropriately respond to diverse opinions, beliefs, and values that might be different to their own.
- Develop digital skills that are key to life in the twenty-first century, especially those that will enable them to participate in teamwork involving networks of geographically dispersed professionals (Online International Learning 2017).

What is important to note is that OIL is not as simple as having webinars and the so-called Skype calls. The OIL definition is followed by four key principles that any projects must meet:

- It involves a cross-border collaboration or interaction with people from different backgrounds and cultures.
- Students must engage in some sort of online interaction, whether it is asynchronous or synchronous.
- It must be driven by a set of internationalised learning outcomes aimed at developing global perspectives and/or fostering students' intercultural competencies.
- There must be a reflective component that helps students think critically about such interactions (Online International Learning 2017).

Previous studies demonstrated that exposure to diversity does not guarantee intercultural competence development (Harrison and Peacock

2010; Maguth and Hilburn 2015; Volet and Ang 1998). Through OIL, teaching and learning facilitate and reward intercultural interaction, teach students how to work in cross-cultural groups/teams, and enable reflection. This model professes an active and transformative learning process where enhancement of cross-cultural understanding and knowledge transfer is the main purpose. Ultimately, the goal is to prepare students for unknown futures with the focus on lifelong learning. It also enables students to be more effective and appropriate in any given situation through the enhancement of culture-specific and culture-general knowledge, intercultural skills, and forming ethnorelative attitudes.

The mechanics of virtual mobility differs across projects. Beyond the above requirements, there is no one-size-fits-all approach. Poly-people interaction across the internet allowing students to show or share different views and perspectives can happen synchronously or asynchronously, using one platform or multiple, with only one partner or many. Successful and sustainable initiatives are those that are developed to meet the needs of all students and participating institutions. In other words, successful OIL is a mutually beneficial relationship between international peers that carry on from year to year (Villar-Onrubia and Rajpal 2015; Op de Beeck and Van Petergem n.d.; Poulová et al. 2009).

Here are some snapshot examples of OIL projects[1] at Coventry University with TNE partners.

Building a Global Graduate Experience, Skills, and Knowledge—Understanding the Viewpoints of Kazakhstan and UK Students

In today's competitive global market, employers are looking for the graduates with not only subject-specific skills and a good degree qualification but also the ability to effectively work across various countries and with people from different cultural backgrounds. Such graduates are considered promising in driving the business strategies and growth on a global scale. Both universities place a heavy emphasis on providing our students all the exciting opportunities to gain cross-cultural and global perspectives, hence making them more employable. In this OIL project, the students will be involved in the online collaborative information exchange and knowledge building on understanding which experiences, skills, and knowledge are highly desirable in the global job market. The perspectives and career prospects

> from Kazakhstan and UK students will be explored through online interaction during eight days. This way, they will be able to understand different cultural contexts and viewpoints in relation to becoming a global graduate. They will also develop the respect for the students with various cultural and career orientations and perspectives.
> Country: Kazakhstan
> Communication: Asynchronous and Synchronous
> Tools: Email, Facebook, Skype

> **International Business: Challenges and Drivers**
> International business is a broad and vibrant area of study and offers many players in the business environment an opportunity to grow and increase their scale of operation. This OIL project aims to offer an introduction to the challenges and drivers for companies deciding to do business internationally. The OIL project comprises five activities/interactions on a mutual, shared digital platform. Students from both universities are asked to work, present, and discuss case studies critically. The whole online experience aims to provide students with a new perspective on student interaction, student experience, and student learning in HE.
> Country: Malaysia
> Communication: Asynchronous
> Tools: Email, Facebook, Google Docs

Although above examples constitute full-virtual projects, virtual and physical mobility do not have to be considered as alternative approaches. They should be treated as complementary tools that can also be blended to reinforce and reconstruct learning.

OIL design can have many objectives, use various interaction methods and instruments, and can offer diverse discipline benefits. Through OIL, project teams can collaboratively introduce an international and intercultural dimension into the content, teaching arrangements, and learning support systems both at home and offshore courses as a part of ongoing pedagogical development. However, ownership of the internationalisation by the faculty and a proactive approach are paramount for transformative internationalisation for all students. Institutional buy in, strategic approach, or target-oriented culture also tends to be favourable and has been crucial to Coventry University's remarkable development (Villar-Onrubia and Rajpal 2015; Evans and Wilson 2016) however are not necessary for early stages of implementation.

The reflective nature of OIL models supports the development of not only students but also staff and intuitional practice. Rethinking how we teach in the globally interconnected and digital world should be a priority for all educators to prepare global-ready graduates. OIL, when used creatively, can serve as a sustainable, cost-effective, interactive, and reflexive model that can engage communities of teachers and learners across the world.

Conclusion

In short, as globalisation is changing the world, institutions engaged in TNE need to consider the global impact of its graduates and unintended reputational consequences. As more and more students graduate from UK courses abroad and become ambassadors for those institutions, equitable provision of intercultural competence and global citizenship development initiatives should be considered along with the disciplinary knowledge. Efforts need to be made through education to bring cultures together and contribute to intercultural dialogue.

In order to prepare students to be effective professionals and citizens in a globalised world, internationalisation should be tailored to the context of the different cultures and attitudes, knowledge, and skills required for successful operation in a discipline and a wider world for all students. Institutions wishing to engage or further develop their TNE provision should consider the holistic approach to their internationalisation strategy.

Whereas virtual mobility is not an only or a perfect method of internationalisation, it presents a practical option to institutions and students to enhance necessary knowledge and skills. OIL, in particular, can serve as a tool for transformative practice enabling institutions to become interculturally minded communities. As the findings warrant further investigation, we must continue to question how internationalisation can be meaningful for all, and pay attention to the unexploited potential of information and communication tools.

While further enquiry is pursued into student intercultural learning, the practice and research should not overlook those students on TNE programmes.

Notes

1. More about those and other examples can be found on www.onlineinternationallearning.org.

References

Beelen, J. and Jones, E. (2015) Redefining internationalisation at home. In A. Curaj, L. Matei, R. Pricopie, J. Salmi and P. Scott (eds.) *The European higher education area*. Cham: Springer.

Bennett, M. (1986) A developmental approach to training for intercultural sensitivity. *International Journal of Intercultural Relations*, 10(2), 179–196.

Bijnens, H., Boussemaere, M., Rajagopal, K., Op de Beeck, I. and Van Petegem, W. (2006) *Virtual mobility best-practice manual*. [ebook]. Heverlee: EuroPACE IVZW. Available at: http://www.virtualschoolsandcolleges.eu/images/9/9b/BM_handbook_final.pdf. Last accessed 10 July 2017.

Brandenburg, U., Taboadela, O. and Vancea, M. (2015) Mobility matters: The ERASMUS impact study. *International Higher Education*, 82, 5.

British Council and DAAD (2014) *Impacts of transnational education on host countries: Academic, cultural, economic and skills impacts and implications of programme and provider mobility*. [online] Available at: https://www.daad.de/medien/hochschulen/projekte/studienangebote/2014_e003_tne_study_final_web.pdf. Last accessed 7 June 2017.

British Council Education Intelligence (2017) *Transnational student trends from 2007 to 2016*. Partnership Access.

Carroll, J. (2015) *Tools for teaching in an educationally mobile world*. Oxon: Routledge.

Chipperfield, C. (2017) ASIA creating an Erasmus-style mobility scheme for ASEAN? *University World News*. [online] Available at: http://www.universityworldnews.com/article.php?story=20170628091116858. Last accessed 9 July 2017.

Crabtree, R. and Sapp, D. (2004). Your culture, my classroom, whose pedagogy? Negotiating effective teaching and learning in Brazil. *Journal of Studies in International Education*, 8(1), 105–132.

de Wit, H., Hunter, F., Howard, L. and Egron-Polak, E. (2015) Internationalisation of higher education. [ebook] Policy Department European Union. Available at: http://www.europarl.europa.eu/RegData/etudes/STUD/2015/540370/IPOL_STU(2015)540370_EN.pdf. Last accessed 6 July 2017.

Deardorff, D. (2006) Identification and assessment of intercultural competence as a student outcome of internationalization. *Journal of Studies in International Education*, 10(3), 241–266.

Deardorff, D. (2015). *Demystifying outcomes assessment for international educators*. Sterling, VA: Stylus.

Evans, A. and Wilson, C. (2016) Linking attainment to interculturalism and global citizenship. In G. Steventon, D. Cureton and L. Clouder (eds.) *Student attainment in higher education: Issues, controversies and debates*. Abingdon: Routledge, pp. 82–103.

Galvin, P. (2004) Success with offshore DBAs: Experience from Hong Kong and Thailand. *International Journal of Organisational Behavior*, 7(7), 431–439.

Harrison, N. and Peacock, N. (2010). Interactions in the intercultural classroom: The UK perspective. In: E. Jones (ed.) *Internationalisation and the student voice*. London: Routledge, pp. 125–142.

Hesa.ac.uk (2017) *HESA—Experts in higher education data and analysis*. [online] Available at: https://www.hesa.ac.uk/. Last accessed 10 July 2017.

Hudzik, J. (2017) *Comprehensive internationalization: From concept to action*. [ebook] Available at: http://www.nafsa.org/Shop/detail.aspx?id=116E. Last accessed 7 July 2017.

International Facts and Figures (2017) [ebook] Universities UK International. Available at: http://www.universitiesuk.ac.uk/policy-and-analysis/reports/Documents/International/International_Facts_and_Figures_2017.pdf. Last accessed 24 June 2017.

Jean-François, E., Avoseh, M. and Griswold, W. (2016). *Perspectives in transnational higher education*. Rotterdam: Sense Publishers.

Jones, E. and Killick, D. (2013). Graduate attributes and the internationalized curriculum. *Journal of Studies in International Education*, 17(2), 165–182.

Knight, J. (2006) *Internationalization of higher education: New directions, new challenges. 2005 IAU global survey report*. Paris, France: International Association of Universities, 172 pp.

Knight, J. (2015). Updated definition of internationalization. *International Higher Education*, 33, 2–3.

Lantz, C. and Davies, I. (2015). Global education in theory: The centrality of intercultural competence. In B. Maguth and J. Hilburn (eds.) *The state of global education: Learning with the world and its people*. New York: Routledge, pp. 41–61.

Leask, B. (2009). Using formal and informal curricula to improve interactions between home and international students. *Journal of Studies in International Education*, 13(2), 205–221.

Leask, B. (2014) *Internationalisation of the curriculum in context*. London: Routledge.

Levidow, L. (2002) Marketizing higher education: Neoliberal strategies and counter-strategies. In K. Robins and F. Webster (eds.) *The virtual university? Knowledge, markets and management*. Oxford: Oxford University Press, pp. 227–248.

Maguth, B. and Hilburn, J. (2015). *The state of global education: Learning with the world and its people*. Taylor & Francis.

Marginson, S. and Sawir, E. (2011). *Ideas for intercultural education*. New York: Palgrave Macmillan.

Middlehurst, R. and Woodfield, S. (2007) Responding to the internationalisation agenda: Implications for institutional strategy. [ebook] Available at: https://www.heacademy.ac.uk/system/files/web0582_responding_to_the_internationalisation_agenda.pdf. Last accessed 10 July 2017.

OECD (2016) *Global competency for an inclusive world*. [online] Available at: https://www.oecd.org/education/Global-competency-for-an-inclusive-world.pdf. Last accessed 13 July 2017.

Online International Learning (2017) *About OIL—Online International Learning*. [online] Available at: http://onlineinternationallearning.org/about/. Last accessed 10 July 2017.

Op de Beeck, I. and Van Petergem, W. (n.d.) *Virtual mobility: An alternative or complement to physical mobility?* [ebook] Available at: http://i2agora.odl.uni-miskolc.hu/i2agora_home/data/P3_D6_ERACON_Virtual%20mobility_paper.pdf. Last accessed 12 July 2017.

Pillay, G. (2006). Preface. In D. Bourn, A. Mckenzie and C. Sheil (eds.) *The global university: The role of the curriculum*. [online] London: Development Education Association. Available at: https://thinkglobal.org.uk/resource/the-global-university-the-role-of-the-curriculum/. Last accessed 10 July 2017.

Poulová, P., Svobodová, L. and Černá, M. (2009). University network—Efficiency of virtual mobility. [online] Available at: https://www.researchgate.net/publication/229001351_University_Network_Efficiency_of_Virtual_Mobility. Last accessed 12 July 2017.

The Shape of Global Higher Education (Volume 2) (n.d.) [ebook] British Council. Available at: https://www.britishcouncil.org/sites/default/files/initial_report_-_shape_of_global_he_vol_2_v2_pdf.pdf. Last accessed 7 July 2017.

Tian, M. and Lowe, J. (2009) Existentialist internationalisation and the Chinese student experience in English universities. *Compare: A Journal of Comparative and International Education*, 39(5), 659–676.

Turner, Y. and Robson, S. (2007) Competitive and cooperative impulses to internationalization: Reflecting on the interplay between management intentions and the experience of academics in a British university. *Education, Knowledge & Economy*, 1(1), 65–82.

Van-Cauter, K. (2017) The rise of transnational education, British Council. Technology in learning: Reshaping the educational landscape symposium. Held 4 July 2017 in Manchester.

Villar-Onrubia, D. and Rajpal, B. (2015) Online international learning: Internationalising the curriculum through virtual mobility at Coventry University. *Perspectives: Policy and Practice in Higher Education*, 20(2–3), 75–82.

Volet, S.E. and Ang, G. (1998) Culturally mixed groups on international campuses: An opportunity for intercultural learning. *Higher Education Research and Development*, 17(1), 5–23.

Wallace, M. and Dunn, L. (2008). *Teaching in transnational higher education*. Hoboken: Taylor and Francis.

Ziguras, C. (2008) The cultural politics of transnational education: Ideological and pedagogical issues for teaching staff. In L. Dunn and M. Wallace (eds.) *Teaching in transnational education: Enhancing learning for offshore international students*. London, UK: Routledge.

6

Collaborating Across Organisational Cultures: Lessons from a Study of International Branch Campuses

Vicky Lewis

Introduction

A key concern for those involved in transnational education (TNE) is how to collaborate effectively across organisational cultures. This comes to the fore in studies of collaborative, partnership-based TNE. However, it is also relevant for some independent TNE modes, as demonstrated in recent research on managing international branch campuses (IBCs) (Healey 2015) and coordinating functions such as marketing, which span both home and international campus (Lewis 2016a).

Differences in organisational culture between the home campus (a large organisation with established processes) and the IBC (a small, dynamic start-up operation in a new market) can be significant. It is difficult to escape the sense of having a senior and junior partner, often expressed in parent–child related metaphors.

This chapter arises from a study of international campus marketing which included interviews with eight UK and overseas-based senior managers at three UK universities with campuses in Malaysia. A key theme voiced in these interviews related to collaboration between the home and international campuses—and the challenges associated with them being different sorts of organisations, at different stages of development, and working within quite different contexts.

Participants tended to frame this challenge in terms of organisational culture difference. Just as establishing a traditional international partnership relies on collaboration across organisational cultures, so too does setting up an international campus. However, this dimension can be underestimated since the new campus is often not conceptualised as a separate institution. Differences in organisational culture, stage of development and operating context need to be better recognised in order to optimise relationships and outcomes.

The chapter starts by briefly positioning international campuses within the TNE landscape, and then explores existing research relating to the theme of collaboration between home and international campuses. It goes on to highlight relevant findings from the research study on international campus marketing.

These cluster around three key themes: shared understanding of vision, values and mission; development of a cross-boundary single-team ethos; clear allocation of responsibility and accountability. Two further threads emerge, highlighting the need for individual and organisational adaptation as both campuses evolve; and the need to harness diverse perspectives and use these as an asset.

These themes and threads have been developed into a checklist of guiding principles and key questions, which are designed to be of practical use to leaders and managers seeking effective collaboration between campuses based in different countries.

Since the ability to collaborate effectively across different organisational cultures is a critical success factor for many modes of TNE, it is anticipated that these guiding principles will also be relevant to those involved in establishing and managing other TNE ventures involving some form of partnership.

International Campuses: Scope, Scale and Research to Date

At the end of 2015, there were 249 IBCs worldwide, according to the latest Observatory on Borderless Higher Education (OBHE)/Cross-Border Education Research Team (C-BERT) report (Garrett et al. 2016). For the purpose of that report, the C-BERT definition of an IBC was used: 'an entity that is owned, at least in part, by a foreign education provider; operated in the name of the foreign education provider; and provides an entire academic program, substantially on site, leading to a degree awarded by the foreign education provider.'

The global rate of growth for IBCs has been high over the last decade, with 133 new campuses established between 2006 and 2015. Collectively IBCs now enrol an estimated 180,000 students. China and the United Arab Emirates host by far the largest numbers of campuses (32 each), followed by Singapore and Malaysia (12 each) and Qatar (11) (C-BERT 2017).

However, IBCs represent a high risk, high investment form of TNE. There have been 42 IBC closures to date and the literature suggests that 'there is a slowing pace in investment…, as institutions now better understand the challenges of setting up a branch campus, and host countries are also becoming more selective and ambitious in delivering TNE themselves' (HEGlobal 2016: 11).

IBCs are—and will remain—a minority pursuit. In the UK, which is the second largest exporter of IBCs after the USA, enrolments represent only 4 per cent of total UK TNE enrolments (Mellors-Bourne et al. 2014). Globally, only 4 per cent of universities have established a campus overseas (Garrett et al. 2016). However, IBCs attract both academic attention (Wilkins and Huisman 2011; Lawton and Kasomitros 2012; Wilkins 2013; Healey 2014, 2015; Redden 2014, 2015) and significant media interest, especially when matters go awry (Maslen 2015; Morgan 2015; Mangan 2015).

The literature on IBCs explores conditions for success. These include preparing and supporting IBC managers effectively (Healey 2015), and embedding marketing expertise into the development process (Lewis

2014, 2016a; Wilkins and Huisman 2011) in order to ensure the campus is established on the basis of a strong business case, with realistic enrolment targets and a deep understanding of local context. Research also exists on the challenges of managing staff, managing students, managing academic quality and managing the curriculum. Healey (2015) provides a helpful summary of this research (p. 3).

Less attention has been given to exploring the relationships and partnerships that IBCs need to establish and navigate in order to operate effectively—not least the relationship with the home campus.

International Campuses: Independent but by No Means Autonomous

Knight (2015) identifies the 'proliferation of TNE terms and mass confusion' resulting from the change in scope and scale of TNE over the last decade (p. 1). To help address this confusion, she proposes a common TNE framework of categories and definitions. This is based on there being two major categories of TNE provision: collaborative and independent.

She places IBCs into the 'independent (foreign) provision' category. The definition of this category is that the 'foreign sending provider operates without any formalised collaboration with local HEIs' (p. 6). It must 'meet host country regulations and policies but does not cooperate with local HEIs in terms of academic course design or delivery' (p. 6). The framework is consistent with that included in a report prepared for the British Council and the German Academic Exchange Service (DAAD) (McNamara and Knight 2015).

Although IBCs do not generally have academic partnerships with local higher education institutions (HEIs), this does not imply that they are wholly independent of local partners. Most IBCs are established 'as a private educational company in the host country, in which the home university normally shares an equity stake with one or more local joint venture (JV) partners' (Healey 2015: 7). Some may have a broader partnership with the host country government or its agencies. For example,

Newcastle University Medicine Malaysia identifies one of its success factors as 'partnering with Malaysia' (HEGlobal 2016: 69). They are also often subject to local quality assurance requirements and must forge positive relationships with regulatory bodies.

A further critical relationship is that with the home university. As Healey's (2015) study of the 'lived experience' of in-country senior managers of IBCs reveals, a fundamental challenge is 'balancing the competing demands of a range of internal and external stakeholders' (p. 1). Such stakeholders include colleagues at the home campus. 'You are always far more dependent on the home campus than they are on you' (interviewee comment cited on p. 8).

So, while IBCs may fall into the category of 'independent' TNE, they are anything but autonomous.

Collaborating across (Organisational) Cultures

The ability to build relationships across cultures is recognised as a key success factor for *collaborative* forms of TNE (Fielden 2011; British Council 2015; Brandenburg 2016; Hoey 2016; Lindsay and Antoniou 2016). This capacity is likely to become even more important as institutions develop more complex, multinational education modes (Healey and Bordogna 2014; Healey 2016).

Fielden (2011) describes three kinds of 'cultural' difference which can 'become conflated': those relating to personalities; those relating to national characteristics and customs; and those relating to institutional cultures. Fielden's study notes that 'some institutions are more bureaucratic than others so that complaints by one partner about the other's regulations or processes may not be due to national cultures' (p. 50). He notes frequent occasions when one side is 'frustrated by the slow speed of decision making or the ever changing processes in the other partner' and observes that 'this may well be due to the pioneering nature of a partnership and to the fact that both parties are nervous at going ahead when the ground rules are not well defined' (p. 50).

The current chapter contends that effectively managing *organisational* culture difference is a critical success factor not only in collaborative TNE partnerships, but also in TNE modes characterised as 'independent' such as IBCs. While those involved generally anticipate the need to adjust to a different national culture and different practices within local partner organisations, they may underestimate the differences in institutional culture that emerge between home and international campus—and the resulting challenges.

As one manager in Healey's (2015) study remarks: 'When I started this it was clear to me that the biggest challenge would be the [local] context, cultural differences. I couldn't have been more wrong. The biggest challenge from day one has been the UK campus' (p. 8).

How the 'Inter-campus Collaboration' Theme Emerged from a Study of International Campus Marketing

The primary purpose of the international campus marketing study was to generate a set of recommendations for HEIs looking to set up an effective marketing, communications and student recruitment operation to support a new international campus.

Insights were gathered via structured interviews, conducted between November 2014 and February 2015 with eight senior managers at three UK universities, all with campuses in Malaysia. Some staff were based in the UK, others in Malaysia. All had some degree of responsibility for marketing the international campus (whether as part of a broader oversight role such as Chief Executive Officer (CEO) or as their professional specialism). The campuses themselves were at different stages of maturity.

The research generated some marketing-specific recommendations (see Lewis 2016a). However, it also resulted in some broader observations on the theme of inter-campus collaboration. It is these that are the focus of this chapter.

Because the interviews involved managers based at both UK and Malaysian campuses, it was possible to detect differences in perspective which related to their physical and organisational location. This may be one reason why this theme emerged so starkly.

Metaphors: Family Relationships and Space Travel

The interviews reinforced previous research observations (e.g. Healey 2014) about the way home and international campuses perceive one another.

The home campus was sometimes regarded as risk-averse, set in its ways, slow and obstructive; a large, established operation in a stable, familiar environment, with a focus on delivering corporate strategy.

By contrast, the international campus could be perceived as rash, headstrong and eager to experiment; a small, dynamic start-up business entering a new, competitive marketplace, with a focus on meeting local needs.

The dominant metaphors used by interviewees to describe the relationship tended to revolve around family relationships (with frequent references to parent–child relationships and headstrong teenagers); or around space travel (with references to the mothership, satellites and comets).

These quotations give a flavour of what it felt like to some of those involved. In line with Healey's (2015) findings, one Malaysia-based interviewee suggested that negotiating the local market was easier than dealing with the home institution.

> *[The relationship is] closest to parent-child—where that child is a teenager wanting to do its own thing. At the outset I had assumed that all the problems would be in the local market. However, that's been predictable and manageable. The biggest difficulty is with the parent. There are constant issues.* [In-country manager, HEI A]

A UK-based interviewee described how they believed the home campus was viewed by the IBC. 'The perspective from [the international campus] was that anything coming from here was bureaucratic, an imposition, even a criticism' [Home-based manager, HEI A].

Another Malaysia-based interviewee noted that the home university is torn between wanting to get involved and having other pressing priorities to attend to closer to home. 'The home university wants to be involved—and that is genuine—but it is easy for other priorities at home to divert its attention' [In-country manager, HEI B]. When asked to characterise the operating relationship between the home and international campus, the same interviewee observed: 'It's like the mothership trying to land a piece of equipment on a comet! It cares about us *but* has lots of other stuff going on' [In-country manager, HEI B].

One in-country manager observed that the relationship between the two campuses changes over time and needs to be kept under constant review.

> *Our experience is that it's not linear. We started off wanting a quite egalitarian model, with the campuses fully integrated, not in a parent-child relationship at all. We saw no reason why a Head of School might not at some point in the future be based in Malaysia. We then realised at a relatively early stage that this might not work after all. The model became a bit more hub and spoke, with the UK campus as 'the mother ship'. However, we have recently started moving away from this again, more towards a network concept.* [In-country manager, HEI C]

The parent–child analogy is a familiar one, highlighted by Healey (2014) among others. Some institutions set out to develop much more egalitarian relationships from the outset, seeing the international campus as one member of a global network. However, it is inevitable that the younger campus will feel like a junior partner at the start. The relationship is firmly linked to the campus's stage of development, its maturity—and the 'age gap' should lessen over time. As Kratochvil and Karram (2014) point out, one measure of maturity is the extent to which administrative processes such as quality assurance are reciprocal, as opposed to the more familiar one-way supervisory approach designed to maintain institutional oversight from the home campus.

Healey's (2015) article on the 'lived experience' of in-country managers identified a thematic cluster described as 'self-determination', the desire for more independence than the 'parent' might like. 'This is the sense of a separate identity… Put simply, when managers are sent to lead IBCs, there is a natural tendency for them to seek greater autonomy' (Healey 2015: 10).

Going back to the parent–child analogy, it is important to note that having a child is something that changes the parent profoundly.

Establishing an international campus is not just about bringing up a child that becomes gradually more independent. It is also about recognising how the home campus needs to change and evolve throughout that process.

Interview Findings: Common Themes and Golden Threads

Given these initial power dynamics, it is important for those contemplating an IBC development to be clear from the outset about what is needed to make the relationship work.

Analysis of the interviews with senior managers revealed three themes on the topic of building a strong inter-campus relationship, along with what could be described as two 'golden threads'.

The themes resemble the key responsibilities outlined within a job description, while the golden threads are more like the personal attributes articulated in the related person specification.

The themes (responsibilities) are:

- Establish a shared understanding of vision, values and mission;
- Actively develop a cross-boundary single-team ethos;
- Clearly allocate responsibility and accountability.

The threads (attributes) running through the interviews are:

- Willingness to adapt—both individually and organisationally—as the campus evolves;
- Willingness to harness diverse perspectives and use them as an asset and a strength.

Theme 1: Shared Vision, Values and Mission

Establishing a shared understanding of vision, values and mission relies on the appropriate internal positioning of the international campus project at its very outset. If it is not presented by senior leaders as central to the institutional mission, it risks being perceived as subsidiary to the 'main' campus (a poor relation, remembered only as an afterthought) or, on occasion, as a pet project or whim of top management.

Some interviewees observed that treating such a major initiative as an experiment or test case is very unwise. Key stakeholders in the host country and at home (including staff, students, partner organisations, governors and potential supporters and advocates) will sense the half-heartedness and lose faith. One interviewee advised: 'Make your international campus a part of the corporate university, not a "spin-out". This will help to focus resource on building institutional reputation in the region' [Home-based manager, HEI A].

Home campus-based managers highlighted the need for unwavering commitment from senior management and clear contextualisation of the campus within wider institutional strategy.

> *Senior management have to show absolute commitment. They need to explain why the campus is being developed—in the context of the university strategy… Without that, an international campus can be a "woolly" concept.* [Home-based manager, HEI A]

They also stressed the importance of taking explicit steps to persuade and engage colleagues. 'There is a big engagement piece and persuasion job' [Home-based manager, HEI B]. There needs to be an open discussion—at an early stage and with a wide group of stakeholders—about the drivers and goals of the campus (see Lewis 2015), and the risk appetite of the university.

There are often challenges when an institution that is in other ways risk-averse starts having to manage the considerable risks associated with developing a campus in another country.

Theme 2: Cross-boundary Single-Team Ethos

The second theme of actively developing a cross-boundary 'single-team' ethos requires an understanding of the different skills and talents needed on each campus—and how they can best work together.

For certain functions (within the marketing context, these were areas such as design and public relations), the home campus may be in a service delivery relationship to the international campus, especially at the outset—and it is crucial that the expectations of both parties (including timescales) are clarified and agreed.

There needs to be recognition that the skillsets required to start up a new campus locally may be quite different from those needed in a more mature organisation with established processes and familiar context.

In addition to skills and experience, those who will be working in-country must be recruited for attitudes and attributes such as resilience, innovation, cultural intelligence, adaptability and a very special combination of team orientation *and* self-reliance.

Where teams need to collaborate across different locations to achieve a common objective (e.g. building institutional profile and reputation or recruiting students to the new campus), they should be treated as a single distributed team, with a common team culture actively fostered via induction, training, secondments, joint planning, team building, joint celebrations of success and other means of getting to know each other properly (beyond task-focused Skype and conference calls).

While it is important to set up channels and mechanisms for communication so that it runs smoothly across organisational boundaries, it is even more crucial to establish and sustain a *culture* of communicating.

UK-based managers, in particular, highlighted the need to invest time and energy in cross-campus relationship building. 'Apportion time for staff to be involved both at home and overseas, and set aside time to build relationships between… teams at the different campuses' [Home-based manager, HEI A]. It is all too easy for an 'us and them' mentality to take root if insufficient attention is paid to this.

The need to play to respective strengths was also noted. 'The Malaysia team can't and shouldn't be expected to do this on their own. Everyone is now more open to working together' [Home-based manager, HEI B]. While the global strategy tends to be set by the UK campus, it was recognised that local knowledge needs to inform that strategy, its resourcing and its implementation.

It was seen as important to develop an appropriate communications infrastructure. 'There is sometimes a communications vacuum so we need to improve communications mechanisms and infrastructure' [Home-based manager, HEI B]. An overreliance on individuals communicating with other individuals was reported to bring a risk of misunderstanding and confusion.

Theme 3: Responsibility and Accountability

Interviewees stressed the need to allocate responsibility and accountability for tasks as clearly as possible. If there is any lack of clarity, this is only amplified by the distance and time difference. Their advice was to work out which functions and activities are best directed and delivered in which location, recognising that this will change over time and that there needs to be a strategy to develop expertise where there are initial gaps.

Some interviewees said advance consideration was needed of ways in which the new campus can be as agile as possible: 'We started off by saying that we would outsource a lot more than we do in the UK. This gives us greater flexibility, agility and speed' [In-country manager, HEI B].

There was also an appreciation that there would be a migration of responsibilities, devolving them to the new campus as it develops. 'Some things are more centralised where other areas are being delivered very locally. However, we will see greater decentralisation when people are more settled' [Home-based manager, HEI B].

Interviewees emphasised the importance of clarity regarding roles, especially when it comes to final decisions. 'The CEO is ultimately responsible… but there is a lack of clarity on roles' [Home-based manager, HEI A]. The need to bind the international campus into existing home campus structures means that matrix management is common (bringing with it an imperative for clear communication channels and decision-making processes).

Also common are link roles between equivalent functions based on the different campuses. The home campus-based link person provides a single point of contact for colleagues at the overseas campus in order to streamline communications and decision-making.

Transparency was seen as important, especially when distributing resources across the two campuses (in the case under discussion, marketing resources) and being clear about the locus of decision-making and accountability.

Proper scrutiny of processes was also viewed as important. It is tempting to transfer home campus processes directly to the international campus. In some cases, this worked well. In others, there needed to be local adaptations. And in others still, the processes needed to be built up from scratch in a way that works in the local context. It must also be recognised that what starts out as a small institution is likely to grow into a larger one. There will be changes in requirements when a tipping point is reached and processes that work for a small institution (e.g. individual, tailored email responses to each student enquiry) need to be scaled up in order to maintain efficiency.

Golden Thread 1: Willingness to Adapt

In addition to the three themes which emerged from the conversations with senior managers, two golden threads (representing the attributes required of both parties) clearly ran through the interviews.

Flexibility and a willingness to change approach are characteristics required of *all* staff involved with the new campus, whether based at the home campus or overseas.

Most interviewees stressed the need to adapt approaches to the local context. However, it was also seen as necessary to be able to step back and take a global, organisation-wide perspective. 'Context really matters. There should be an effort to work across boundaries and take a global approach' [In-country manager, HEI C].

A deeper level of personal flexibility is also required. This allows individuals to recognise that a firmly held assumption does not hold true in the new context or that an approach which has always worked is no longer effective. As one interviewee put it: 'There is always the danger of assuming that, because something works well in the UK, then it transfers. And the local response feels a bit like a stuck record: "but it's different here...."' [In-country manager, HEI C].

One respondent described the learning curve he experienced (despite being a well-seasoned and well-travelled senior manager) when it came to eliciting feedback from staff used to different cultural norms.

> *One cultural thing I've noticed is that you have to learn how to ask questions. If you are not careful, you will be told what the respondent thinks you want to hear, especially when it comes to feeding back on how things are going. You have to ask the question in a different way in order to get honest evaluative feedback.* [In-country manager, HEI B]

A high degree of self-awareness, reflection and ability to adapt one's own behaviours is needed when setting up a campus which is embedded within a different national culture and assumes a different organisational culture (see Fielden 2011: 50).

This applies not only at the individual level, but also at the institution level. Organisational flexibility and willingness to embrace change is crucial. 'Our initial vision—about providing choice for students, extending access to different groups, being research-active—that all remains. However, there are certain changes as the campus evolves and you learn from this' [In-country manager, HEI C].

The level of input from the home campus may well need to fluctuate over time as both campuses exercise reciprocal influence and contribute to one another's evolution.

> *It wasn't linear. After th[e] initial set-up phase, there was more input from the UK. This was partly also because the UK institution was changing. There was institutional evolution—co-evolution—going on in both places… After a period of increased input from the UK, this then reduced again.* [In-country manager, HEI C]

In-country managers observed a change over time from a purely tactical focus for the international campus during the early days of set-up and implementation, to a more strategic focus once there was space to step back from the fire-fighting.

Golden Thread 2: Willingness to Harness Diverse Perspectives

The second golden thread is the ability to turn differences in perspective into productive and creative collaboration. Diverse perspectives *can* result in an 'us and them' mentality (not helped by physical distance), but, if they are skilfully and actively harnessed, they can generate a more innovative approach that draws on the best of each (see Ng et al. 2012).

One interviewee observed:

> *We need to be prepared to replicate a lot of our UK systems and processes and activities (albeit not on the same scale) in another country, but of course ensuring they are fit for purpose for the local markets and cultures. In some areas, a hybrid approach is needed.* [Home-based manager, HEI B]

Home-based interviewees tended to emphasise the need for strategic planning; in-country interviewees stressed the need to understand local context. However, as one respondent pointed out, as long as all involved have the same ultimate goal—ensuring the campus is a success—apparently divergent perspectives 'may just be different ways of thinking about the same problem' [In-country manager, HEI C].

Practical Applications

One of the drivers for the original study into international campus marketing was the lack of practical guidance for managers contemplating an IBC development, despite the fact that many institutions have already navigated their way to successful overseas campus operations. Those senior managers who have been directly involved on behalf of their institutions have learned lessons, often the hard way, about where to focus effort. However, these lessons are rarely captured in a way that is of practical use for those just about to embark on a similar journey.

This section of the chapter therefore shares a checklist of guiding principles and key questions focused on the topic of collaborating across organisational cultures.

The checklist has been derived from the themes and threads of the interviews. It is designed to facilitate effective collaboration between campuses in different countries. The questions are ones which institutions should ask themselves. They cover different stages in the development of a new international campus.

Guiding Principle 1

Position the international campus as central to the university's mission and encourage early, open discussion of challenging issues.

Questions: What do staff at the home campus think about the plans to develop an international campus? What are their concerns? Do they understand how it will contribute to the university's mission? What mechanisms need to be put in place to initiate and maintain open dialogue? How do we ensure staff at the international campus do not feel like an afterthought?

Guiding Principle 2

Recruit staff who will thrive in a start-up setting; nurture cross-boundary collaboration and sustain effective two-way communication.

Questions: When recruiting staff, are we paying attention to soft skills and personal attributes as well knowledge and experience? Are those involved in staff recruitment and selection well-placed to assess cultural fit? How will new staff be inducted and made to feel part of a wider team? What changes in working practice are needed to facilitate effective cross-campus communication and collaboration?

Guiding Principle 3

Determine the most effective location for different functions and be clear about roles, responsibilities and decision-making.

Questions: What criteria are we using to determine the location of different functions (and the roles within these)? Who is ultimately responsible for different levels of decision? What new mechanisms are needed to ensure key stakeholders on both campuses have the opportunity to feed into those decisions? What changes in working practice are needed to reflect the requirement for greater agility at the new campus?

Guiding Principle 4

Ensure differences in perspective are used constructively and creatively.

Questions: What mechanisms are needed in order to tap into ideas emanating from staff at both campuses? How might national and organisational cultures affect individuals' willingness to contribute—and how will any issues arising from this be addressed? What frameworks might be used to surface differences and initiate discussions about them (see Lewis 2016b)? How will disagreements be resolved?

Guiding Principle 5

Actively review and adapt policy and practice as both institutions mature and evolve.

Questions: What review mechanisms need to be put in place? Have we factored in time and space to step back and reflect on the direction of travel? How do we make the transition from tactical to strategic focus at the international campus? What changes in policy and practice has the international campus generated for the home campus? Have we communicated and explained these effectively?

When one considers these guiding principles and sets of questions, it is clear that their relevance may extend beyond collaboration between two campuses of the same institution. Many of them can be applied to other forms of transnational collaboration between partner institutions operating in different national and organisational contexts.

Conclusion

Research has been undertaken into why TNE *collaborative* partnerships (where 'collaboration exists between local and foreign providers') (Knight 2015: 6) succeed or fail. Some ingredients for success (Emery and Worton 2014; Fielden 2011) and guiding principles (Hoey 2016) have been identified.

Less attention has been paid to the need to prepare the ground for effective collaboration between international campuses of the same institution, although this is as much an exercise in partnership as other forms of more explicitly collaborative TNE.

Certain assumptions may be made about the new international campus being 'related' to the original campus and therefore having similar characteristics. However, even though it may be conceptualised as a child of the original campus, the new campus will have its own culture and way of doing things from the outset.

Over time, as it matures and grows in scale and scope, it may develop similarities and equal status to its parent. One day, a fully grown IBC may even leave the parent, becoming an independent institution embedded within the national context it grew up in. Whatever the final destination, the need to prepare for collaborative partnership working must not be underestimated.

References

Brandenburg, U. (2016) *It must be love: What makes university partnerships tick?* The Guardian Higher Education Network. Available at: https://www.theguardian.com/higher-education-network/2016/may/04/it-must-be-love-what-makes-university-partnerships-tick

British Council (2015) *Transnational education: A guide for creating partnerships in India.* Available at: https://www.britishcouncil.org/education/ihe/knowledge-centre/transnational-education/report-tne-guide-creating-partnerships-india

C-BERT (Cross-Border Education Research Team) (2017) Quick facts. Available at: http://cbert.org/. Last accessed 4 April 2017.

Emery, V. and Worton, M. (2014) *Challenges for the leadership of transnational education in higher education: Balancing risk and innovation.* Leadership Foundation for Higher Education. Stimulus Paper.

Fielden, J. (2011) *Leadership and management of international partnerships.* Leadership Foundation for Higher Education. Research and Development Series 2, Publication 7.

Garrett, R., Kinser, K. and Merola, R. (2016) *International branch campuses: Trends and developments.* [Conference Presentation] OBHE Global Forum: Brain Gain: Charting the Impact and Future of TNE, Kuala Lumpur, 9–11 November.

Healey, N. (2014) When is an international branch campus? *International Higher Education*, 78(Special Issue), 22–23.

Healey, N. (2015) The challenges of leading an international branch campus: The 'lived experience' of in-country senior managers. *Journal of Studies in International Education*. 1-18. Available at: https://doi.org/10.1177/1028315315602928; Last accessed 28 August 2015.

Healey, N. (2016) The future of TNE 'with Chinese characteristics'. Universities UK/HEGlobal. Available at: http://www.universitiesuk.ac.uk/International/heglobal/Pages/the-future-of-tne-with-Chinese-characteristics.aspx

Healey, N. and Bordogna, C. (2014) From transnational to multinational education: Emerging trends in international higher education. *Internationalisation of Higher Education* 3, Article D 3-1, 1–23. Available at: www.handbook-internationalisation.com

HEGlobal (2016) *The scale and scope of UK higher education transnational education*. UUK International Unit/British Council.

Hoey, M. (2016) The internationalisation of higher education: Some ethical implications. *Perspectives: Policy and Practice in Higher Education*, 20(2–3), 37–43.

Knight, J. (2015) Transnational education remodeled: Toward a common TNE framework and definitions. *Journal of Studies in International Education*. 1-14. Available at: https://doi.org/10.1177/1028315315602927; Accessed 22 September 2015.

Kratochvil, D. and Karram, G. (2014) From Protégé to Peer: Measuring maturity at branch campuses. *University World News*. Issue No. 315. Available at: http://www.universityworldnews.com/article.php?story=20140408150224295&query=Protege+peer+Kratochvil

Lawton, W. and Kasomitros, A. (2012) *International branch campuses: Data and developments*. London: Observatory on Borderless Higher Education.

Lewis, V. (2014) Branch campus development: Marketing expertise required. *Forum*. Summer 2014, 14–16.

Lewis, V. (2015) 'A Mission to Learn from the World': How does this play out in international campus development? *Vicky Lewis Consulting*. Weblog. Available at: http://www.vickylewisconsulting.co.uk/a-mission-to-learn-from-the-world.php. Last accessed 4 April 2017.

Lewis, V. (2016a) Embedding marketing in international campus development: Lessons from UK universities. *Perspectives: Policy and Practice in Higher Education*, 20(2–3), 59–66.

Lewis, V. (2016b) Picking a partner for the long term: Setting a collaborative TNE relationship up for success. *Vicky Lewis Consulting*. Weblog. Available at: http://www.vickylewisconsulting.co.uk/picking-a-partner-for-the-long-term.php. Last accessed 4 April 2017.

Lindsay, V. and Antoniou, C. (2016) Applying foreign entry market strategies to UK higher education transnational education models: Finding 50 shades of green. *Perspectives: Policy and Practice in Higher Education*, 20(2–3), 51–58.

Mangan, K. (2015) U.A.E. incident raises questions for colleges that open campuses in restrictive countries. *The Chronicle of Higher Education*. Available at: http://chronicle.com/article/UAE-Incident-Raises/228565/

Maslen, G. (2015) While branch campuses proliferate, many fail. *University World News*. Issue No. 355. Available at: http://www.universityworldnews.com/article.php?story=20150219113033746

McNamara, J. and Knight, J. (2015). *Transnational education data collection systems: Awareness, analysis, action*. British Council/DAAD.

Mellors-Bourne, R., Fielden, J., Middlehurst, R. and Woodfield, S. (2014) *The value of transnational education to the UK*. Department of Business, Innovation and Skills. Research Paper Number: 194.

Morgan, J. (2015) Uclan sets aside £2.8m to cover losses overseas. *Times Higher Education*. Available at: http://www.timeshighereducation.co.uk/news/uclan-sets-aside-28m-to-cover-losses-overseas/2019181.article

Ng, K-Y., Van Dyne, L. and Ang, S. (2012) Cultural intelligence: A review, reflections, and recommendations for future research. In A.M. Ryan, F.T.L. Leong and F.L. Oswald (eds.) *Conducting multinational research: Applying organizational psychology in the workplace*. Washington, DC: American Psychological Association, pp. 29–58.

Redden, E. (2014) Bucking the branch campus. *Inside Higher Ed*. Available at: https://www.insidehighered.com/news/2014/03/12/amid-branch-campus-building-boom-some-universities-reject-model

Redden, E. (2015). Is the international branch campus phenomenon just a fad? *Inside Higher Ed*. Available at: https://www.insidehighered.com/news/2015/03/16/international-branch-campus-phenomenon-just-fad

Wilkins, S. (2013) The future of transnational higher education: What role for international branch campuses? In H. de Wit, F. Hunter, L. Johnson and H. van Liempd (eds.) *Possible futures: The next 25 years of the internationalisation of higher education*. Amsterdam: European Association for International Education, pp. 182–186.

Wilkins, S. and Huisman, J. (2011). International student destination choice: The influence of home campus experience on the decision to consider branch campuses. *Journal of Marketing for Higher Education*, 21(1), 61–83.

Part III

Managing Quality

7

The Challenges of Providing a Truly International Education: The Malaysia Nottingham Doctoral Programme

Christopher Hill

Introduction

Student mobility has been well documented and explored in literature (Wells 2014; Mazzarol and Soutar 2002; Furukawa 2013) and is a key function of many institutions around the world. 'At the country level, mobility is portrayed to enhance international competitiveness, stimulate effective labor markets, and support the interaction between citizens of different countries. This is particularly relevant for degree mobility where students spend a period of their study in another country' (Souto-Otero et al. 2013; De Wit 2008). This chapter will examine the challenges and opportunities inherent in developing an international joint PhD programme and will use The University of Nottingham as a case study. Mazzarol and Soutar (2002) discuss the mobility between distinct universities and provide a clear case for the push and pull factors impacting student mobility in this regard. The University of Nottingham, as a prime

---

C. Hill (✉)
British University in Dubai, Dubai, United Arab Emirates
e-mail: christopher.hill@buid.ac.ae

example of the international branch campus model, has the ability to encourage student exchange between their UK, China and Malaysia campuses. The processes and degree are the same and therefore the 'risk' to the student is reduced. This chapter will examine the development of the Malaysia Nottingham Doctoral Programme (MNDP) and discuss the implications this has for managing the quality of exchange programmes and international degrees, as a key function of transnational education.

There are a considerable number of challenges when creating new and innovative projects. Failure is always a distinct possibility and, at the very least, a significant amount of time and effort will be put into the development and implementation of the idea. The success of any such project rests upon a fundamental understanding of the elements involved, an assessment of the strengths and weaknesses and the ability to adapt and re-brand if necessary. An MNDP Chemical and Environmental Engineering student was quoted in the 2008 annual review meeting, 'Well, I am still slogging in this MNDP. I believe many things were not thought out carefully before implementing this programme. But maybe as a pioneer group, we have to be the guinea pigs that iron out these teething problems.' The absence of a blueprint for activity should not equal the absence of attention to detail or duty of care. Context is crucial here, however, as success and failure should not be measured by pure numbers. The issue should be in ensuring a commitment to quality and student experience throughout and the ability to adapt and improve based on lessons learned.

Rationale and Impetus

The split-site MNDP PhD was introduced in 2007 as a response to the increased demand for international education and as a strategic attempt to further increase Nottingham's presence and degree of partnership in Malaysia. The University of Nottingham Malaysia Campus (UNMC) was established in 2000 and, while UNMC's presence may have been a critical factor in the development of the programme, the agreement was between the UK Nottingham Campus and nine Malaysian public universities. UNMC was responsible for administration but not supervision. This evolved over time but demonstrates a key factor of branch campus development; they cannot initially be considered equivalent to the home campus in terms of capacity and resources and this in turn often means they are not considered equivalent in terms of quality.

While research regarding the transnational education (TNE) student experience may be limited to certain key examples (Humfrey 2009; O'Mahoney 2014), the motivation behind course selection is more clearly documented. Government drive is for numbers and quality indicators, at the student level; however, there is an element of professional development and a desire to develop 'a new identity. These students chose an international education with the hope of expunging provincial outlooks. They wanted new ways of viewing the world, new habits of thinking and new skills and approaches' (Pyvis and Chapman 2007: 235). Programmes like the MNDP provide an opportunity for student exchange and access. The dual nature of the programme provides both outreach and roots. The element of risk is deemed lower as the connection to the 'home' is clear and defined. The fact that students often look to convert the dual degree into a single model abroad does not necessarily detract from the initial design—but should be understood and planned for accordingly.

Numbers

A key driver behind the MNDP was the Malaysian government's interest and push to increase the number of PhD holders at public institutions. The MNDP was designed in response to this and in order to enable existing academics to upscale their qualifications and then return to their academic posts. Government strategy of this nature provides a valuable platform for engagement and funding, but it also brings a significant degree of expectations. The projected and predicted PhD numbers were ambitious, to say the least. When the programme began in 2007–2008 Malaysia had some 8000 PhD holders. The government's initial aim of 100,000 was reduced to the target of 60,000 by 2023. With goals like these, the potential for recruitment is high but so are the expectations. From a quality assurance perspective, it remains critical to ensure that students are only accepted where there is a legitimate pathway to adequate supervision and research completion. It is equally vital that this message is conveyed to all stakeholders and consistently maintained. Failure to do so risks damage to the university brand, the student experience and the nature of the PhD as a research degree of excellence.

The MNDP allowed students to receive a UK education in an international setting, provided opportunities for research collaboration, student movement and promoted integration. The University of Nottingham partnered with nine Malaysian Universities in this endeavour. Not all partners were equally involved but the coalition represented interest and initial engagement. While the number of students registered and graduated is much lower than initial expectations, and as a result, would be a mark of failure of the programme, the outcome is, in fact, better viewed through the lens of lessons learned than pure statistics.

The initial 2008/09 academic year cohort numbered 22 registered students and was split across four of the potential nine partners. Universiti Sains Malaysia had eight students; International Islamic University, five; Universiti Malaya, two; and Universiti Teknologi Mara, seven. The subject range was relatively broad and included Politics and International Relations, Biomedical Sciences, Chemical and Environmental Engineering, Management, Economics, Architecture, Information Technology, Pharmacy, Education, Community Health Sciences, Computer Science, Law, Biosciences, Mathematical Sciences and Geography. The advantage of a programme of this type was in the potential breadth of subject delivery. The University of Nottingham had an extensive offering in place and was therefore able to partner with multiple institutions in Malaysia and tailor the degree scheme to need and interest.

Course Outline

While each PhD programme met the specific requirements of the individual departments, all MNDP students were required to study at The University of Nottingham for a period of up to 18 months in total. A typical pattern would see the student spend the first nine months of study in Nottingham. The student would then return to their home institution for 18 months and complete their PhD with a final nine months in

Nottingham. The nature of the degrees naturally impacted this timeline, and factors such as access to consumables, instruments, training, and so on often dictated the calendar.

Supervision

Students were allocated a supervisor from The University of Nottingham for the duration of their PhD, and he/she had the opportunity to visit Malaysia twice during the period of study. A co-supervisor was also allocated, generally from the student's home institution, who would work closely with the student during their time in Malaysia. On the surface, this is a sound approach. It provides opportunities for support throughout and possible collaboration across borders. In reality, this often led to issues of miscommunication and understanding, essentially rooted in the notion of ownership of the project. As student's travelled, they assumed the connection and identity of their supervisor and, without integrated communication amongst the supervision team, this presented issues of time loss and confusion on the part of the students. Socialisation and a positive supervisor relationship have been shown to drive retention and student success (Ali and Kohun 2007; Barnes 2010; Gardner 2008). Jones (2013) reviewed 995 papers, written between 1971 and 2012, on issues in doctoral studies and found the six main themes discussed, to be: doctoral programme design (29%), student experience (26%), student–supervisor relationship (15%), writing and research (14%), employment (13%) and teaching (3%). The first two, programme design and supervisor relationship, are at the heart of this review of the MNDP and, as such, map onto the pre-existing research and confirm trends and expectations. There were no initial processes in place to enable the co-supervisor to travel to the UK but this became a recurring topic of conversation and request.

Partnership

The University of Nottingham was the dominant partner in the MNDP agreement, securing for the student a UK degree upon completion. All PhDs were co-supervised between Nottingham (primary supervisor) and the local Malaysian partner university (secondary supervisor), thereby securing the connection between the two institutes and providing an avenue for increased research interaction and collaboration. The students were from Malaysian universities, often already employed as academics but without PhDs. They therefore had a connection to a department, and in some cases had already been working in the field of study within which they applied. This provided the opportunity for excellent research students and increased interaction post-PhD. In some cases, Nottingham PhD students in turn become PhD supervisors thus perpetuating the cycle of involvement and attachment.

Application, supervision and examination followed the same structure as would be employed for a full-time student registering at the Nottingham UK Campus. The distance between the UK and Malaysia naturally meant that there were certain differences such as day-to-day supervision or interaction with the primary supervisor but this was ameliorated in several ways that will be discussed below. The consistency of this administrative approach supports efficiency, reduces start-up costs and time and supports the perception of an integrated degree process. The design of the MNDP was very much that of a collaborative effort between two institutions of higher learning. The Malaysian partner universities were chosen based on reputation, research areas and ability to send students to the programme. Acceptance of candidates was based on merit and the ability of the universities in question to provide accurate supervision in the area of application. In this, the MNDP shared internal consistencies and quality assurance oversight with the domestic UK PhD programme.

Student Movement

MNDP students were Malaysians, based in Malaysia, studying for a PhD at a university halfway around the world. Movement and interaction was therefore a critical issue, hence the 18-month period of UK study. While this provided the opportunity for direct supervision, it also served to expose the student to a different research culture, interaction with western colleagues and the advantages and benefits of a cross-cultural educational experience. Students benefited from the travel aspect of the MNDP and forged friendships and research partnerships. The value of student mobility is well documented and discussed but the nature of its impact and reality is open to reconceputatlisation (Gargano 2009; Hoare 2012; Rizvi 2010).

Phelps (2016) argues that, 'universities, while obviously grounded in a national locality, increasingly function as such transnational spaces, as they cultivate highly internationalised student enrolments and multi-national research consortia. As cosmopolitan sojourners, international doctoral students occupy this transnational space where their field of activity consists of simultaneous locations—at minimum their home country and the country in which they are studying, and possibly other locales of research, activism and professional work as well.' The time students spent in Nottingham varied in length and frequency based on their specific needs. It was organised in discussion with both supervisors and connected to particular research needs, equipment training, fieldwork and conference participation. Discussions of this nature serve to begin the process of dialogue between supervisor and student and indeed, between supervisor and supervisor. Decisions of this nature are a result of discussion and combined input with the obvious aim being that which will most accurately benefit the student. The period of 18 months could be broken up into several visits depending, again, on student need and opportunity.

Time spent on the UK campus naturally provided proximity to conferences in the west, of potential interest to the student or the project. Phelps (2016) argues that 'while large scale forces of globalization are profoundly shaping international doctoral student trajectories, these forces are not homogenizing nor fully controlling of student experiences.' Although the MNDP was, by design, homogenous, the experience of the students was anything but. The reality of PhD supervision, particularly across borders, is one of shifting expectations and flexibility (Orellana et al. 2016). The goal should be not to compromise on quality or conistency but to develop awareness of relevant parameters and expectations.

Academic Movement

It was not only the student who travelled during the MNDP process; there was also the supervisor movement. During the three-year PhD, the primary supervisor was eligible to visit the student in Malaysia twice and engage with the co-supervisor and research colleagues at the Malaysian partner university.

This provided the opportunity for dialogue and demonstrated the necessity for interaction and co-operation of this nature. The length of the visit and the dates themselves were also organised in discussion between supervisors and student. Visits of this nature must also take into account the teaching commitments of academics in Nottingham and of activities in Malaysia.

Supervisor visits to Malaysia were, for the most part, successful as they provided face-to-face interaction between academics and allowed the primary supervisor to further cement their relationship with the student. The ability to observe and interact with the students in their own surroundings provided an additional and vital element in the process of academic supervision. There is considerable merit in meeting the colleagues and co-workers of a student, seeing where it is they work, understanding the pressures and factors that influence their work ethic and obtaining an appreciation for the country of Malaysia in general. While discussion in the UK regarding Malaysia provides certain information and insight, until a trip has been taken, there will remain a considerable gap in accurate knowledge and this can impact upon the manner in which supervision is undertaken. A PhD feels long to the student but is in fact a relatively short period of time. When communication and dialogue are not forthcoming, the student can fall between two contrasting approaches and sets of guidance and ultimately lose months or inactivity or uncertainty.

In many ways, this programme operated along similar lines to that of standard student recruitment with the potential that students remain connected to, or even work for, the university from which they have graduated. While the MNDP students go back to employment upon the completion of their PhD, they are still involved with The University of Nottingham and play a role in its future development abroad. International development requires the involvement of international people, in terms of nationality but equally in terms of ethos and the MNDP goes a long way to cultivating this and providing for future co-operation and integration.

Outcomes and Responses

The challenges involved with the MNDP were many and varied in nature from the cosmetic to the integral. Overlooking certain elements and focusing entirely on the 'big picture' can cause problems down the line.

Any development of this nature must only be attempted when the idea and the practice are well thought out in advance and there exists a concrete design for the implementation of the concept and not purely the inception of the idea.

Pre-requisites

It is important to have an established presence and reputation at the home institution, as this provides the platform upon which to base discussions with the universities abroad. These discussions should take place from a position of strength and reputation rather than anything else. In many cultures, and Malaysia in particular, the reputation you gain and the one you perpetuate through action and interaction will become your very identity and it must be protected accordingly.

There must exist the potential for supervision in a variety of areas unless the decision has been made to focus efforts to a limited and specialised area of research. There must exist the mechanism to deal with international interaction and movement of both students and staff and there must be sufficient resources and commitment in terms of personnel, travel and involvement from all sides in order to develop and establish the idea as a working concept rather than an abstract notion. There is of course no guarantee that with all these things in place, success is assured but it will at least provide an opportunity for development rather than merely an arena for failure.

Nature of the Structure

The very design of the programme will have a natural impact upon the relative success or failure rate and must therefore be carefully considered. One of the major challenges with the MNDP was that of the time a student could spend in the UK. The 18-month timeframe was reached in agreement with the Malaysian government and had implications in terms of education spending for fees, tax and residency considerations. While 18 months represent half of the allotted time for completion of the PhD and therefore create a balance between the two countries for the split sight, it was still seen by many as too short a period. A major challenge for the MNDP was that of perception and understanding. There were many who saw the programme as a vehicle for a full-time UK PhD. This was clearly not the impetus behind the programme but nonetheless one that needed to be addressed on a regular basis in order to protect the integrity of the programme, the reputation of the institutions involved and the collaborative link to the government.

There was considerable pressure from both the PhD students and academics, based on the UK campus, for the students to be able to extend their period of study beyond the 18-month agreed upon framework. This was perhaps a natural response and difficult to argue against. There is indeed merit in having a student for the full three years but that was clearly not the objective of a split site PhD where the very involvement of two universities in different countries creates an identity and reality of its own. The challenge therefore was managing the expectations of both students and staff while ensuring that policy was adhered to. A result of this desire for more time in the UK often led to the student switching to a full-time UK-based PhD and leaving the MNDP scheme. While this benefits The University of Nottingham in the long run in terms of funding and direct supervision, it runs counter to the original aim and design of the programme.

Family Matters

The majority of MNDP students were already academics in Malaysia and therefore of an age when family was a consideration. Many of the students took their family with them when they travelled to the UK and this created problems not initially conceptualised. The funding mechanism required adaptation—chiefly on the part of the Ministry; housing requirements during the UK visit changed; access to schooling and health care. While this reality had benefits in terms of recreating the stability of home life, it did have an impact upon the ability to research and work effectively and place a greater strain on the administration and support network required for the MNDP to function. This was not an insurmountable problem as the MNDP did allow for flexible travel dates but the underlying principle exists and cannot be ignored.

PhD students who have spent time both teaching and possibly researching into their area of interest are generally better prepared for the structure and work load required to obtain a PhD, but this time spent developing their professional capabilities creates a different set of circumstances, understanding and expectations than those 'traditional' twenty something students who might join a full-time programme in the UK. From a quality management perspective, the main concern here is in the periphery to the process of studying but the impact of these factors was felt throughout. Future initiatives of this nature must take this into account and ensure that a systematic support network is in place, properly communicated in advance of registration and integrated between the academic and administrative elements of the programme.

Communication and Culture

The very nature of the MNDP is problematic and its concept is perhaps its greatest strength and its greatest weakness. The distance involved between the UK and Malaysia and the eight-hour time difference can cause problems in terms of communication and information flow. There is a legitimate argument for increased supervision and connectivity between academic and student, and despite the existence of video conferencing and Skype, this can never replace the day-to-day interaction that can be enjoyed by a full-time PhD student. The MNDP made great allowances for the distance involved and promoted information flow and dialogue but the relationship between the two supervisors was often fairly distant as they had potentially never met or worked together in the past. The challenge of ensuring a functional working relationship between the two supervisors, thus guaranteeing adequate levels of supervision to the student, is an element of the MNDP that was constantly assessed and developed. Marginalisation of the second supervisor and increased periods of time spent in the UK moved the MNDP ever closer to representing a full-time UK PhD rather than the split sight design of inception. The need for dialogue, in advance of the student beginning their PhD, is vital. The ability to establish a working relationship, at distance, is of benefit to all involved and should be supported by process and practice.

Cultural differences are heightened in projects of this nature where distance magnifies issues. The approach to learning is distinct and the manner in which students are both taught and trained is a significant factor to consider. The Malaysian educational system largely follows the Confucian ethos and does not, by and large, promote the questioning of authority or of established mechanisms of academic delivery. The interactive nature of supervisor and supervisee that is encouraged in the UK model does not exist to any real extent in Malaysia where students are considerably more comfortable following the direction and guidance of their supervisor. This is not to say that Malaysian students are not capable of original thought, far from it, but they often lack the training and confidence required to firmly establish themselves as independent researches. The underlying reality that 'learning styles based on Western measures and ways of understanding that often inappropriately construct approaches to learning in other countries as deficient' (Eaves 2011: 687) must be recognised and addressed accordingly. This is clearly an issue of some import when you factor in the distance and potential lack of working relationship between the supervisors. There exists the very real possibility that the student will be told two different things by their supervisors and, by not questioning either one, can become victim to increased confusion and despair, not to mention the time that can be wasted until this problem is highlighted in an end of year review.

The challenge therefore is to better prepare the students for the PhD experience and to increase the level of communication and discourse between the two supervisors. Increased interaction, even before the PhD has begun will enable supervisors to establish for themselves, and for the student, a clear path of action and a systematic timetable of assessment and monitoring. Training for supervisors is also highly recommended such that awareness of competing expectations can be developed and relevant and timely responses, created.

Expectations

Significant differences exist in the manner in which the UK and Malaysian systems approach education and as a result, their relative expectations and assumptions also differ greatly. Given the cultural factors listed above, there are often issues relating to the very nature of a PhD and what is required to obtain one. Expectations held by the UK academics as to what constitutes a suitable PhD candidate did not always match those held by the Malaysian universities, particularly when operating under the pressures of government aims and expectations. There is a danger in assumptions of learning styles and a real need to ensure a balanced approach and more sophisticated level of understanding of the differences (Starr-Glass and Ali 2012; Chapman and Pyvis 2006). Applications are received based on necessity for the Malaysian academic to receive a PhD in line with their professional job development or government pressure for advancement, rather than from a genuine desire for research development or intellectual curiosity. This naturally affects the quality of applications and has an impact upon the rejection rate, which in turn impacts upon the way the programme is viewed by both Nottingham and Malaysian academics.

The challenge that faced The University of Nottingham in this regard was to protect the brand and reputation of a Nottingham PhD in face of pressure from government and partner university involvement, while still actively recruiting PhD candidates. The MNDP needed a constant influx of students in order to justify the expense and effort involved in maintaining the programme but a higher quality of students ensures reputation is safe guarded and improves future development prospects. The issue here was not to 'educate or re-educate' the Malaysian partner universities, government and education system at large, but to better explain the very nature of the MNDP itself and ensure information dissipation was improved. The fault, if any, lies not with the concept or the idea itself but rather in the way in which it was implemented. Assumptions, by both parties, as to the level of understanding of either side, clearly led to increased confusion and a downturn in the acceptance rate. The task at hand, therefore, was to promote and develop the MNDP concept, in line with the requirements and interests of both parties.

Funding

The issue of mobility and access to research funding arose during the process. Students were provided with research grants of GBP 2000 during their study, but this was only accessible during their time on the UK Campus. A Chemical and Environmental Engineering student from UMS made the very valid point that, 'the School of Chemical and Environmental Engineering, Nottingham U has GBP 1000 or GBP 2000 allocation per student per year but this can only be utilised when I am at Nottingham, not when I am in Malaysia. If MNDP was meant to be flexible, this budget allocation should be flexible too.'

Access to resources and consumables was also raised by another student from Universiti Malaysia Sabah Biosciences, who commented that 'the only facilities available when I am here, in the participating University (UMS) is the online/library services from University of Nottingham with quite limited number of references.' The funding allocation and access to resources must be clearly defined and managed. The mobility and distance elements of the degree require a strong foundation in place to provide support and a level of consistency throughout. In terms of journal access, there are issues of copyright and permission access that must be taken into account when operating across borders. If a student is working on one or more campuses, their access to facilities and internet access must be arranged in advance to reduce confusion and time wasted during the initial period of adjustment.

Interaction

In January 2008, the Graduate School was established at UNMC and over the course of that year demonstrated the importance and relevance of such an initiative. The Graduate School was involved in the co-ordination of the MNDP and therefore spent considerable time in discussion with the MNDP supervisors in the UK, the partner Malaysian universities, the Ministry for Higher Education and the MNDP students themselves. As a result, Nottingham was in a position to better understand the relevant challenges it faced and to more accurately assign resources to the development of the project at large. Given the distance between the UK campus and the partner universities in Malaysia, the presence of a western academic, based at UNMC, went a long way to promoting a working relationship between all partners and to promoting development and interaction. A combination of assistance from colleagues in the UK and direct and structured supervision and observation from the Head of the central Graduate School in Nottingham allowed for a heightened sense of understanding and appreciation to be achieved.

Representatives from the Graduate School in Malaysia delivered presentations at the partner universities in an attempt to better explain the nature of the MNDP, the nature of a western PhD and to increase the intake of students. Presentations of this nature served to provide an arena in which Malaysian academics could ask questions regarding process or procedure and can talk to a Nottingham educated academic first hand. The continued relationship that was built up by these visits was integral to development within the Malaysian field and promoted equality and respect within the split site programme.

In addition to providing an information conduit for the Nottingham campus, the Graduate School provided MNDP students access to research training courses during their time in Malaysia, thus guaranteeing no disruption to this element of their development when away from the UK campus.

Conclusion

The challenges present in establishing a project the magnitude of the MNDP are considerable and should be treated accordingly. The key lies in managing issues as they arise but devoting time and energy to tackling those problems for which there is a potential, and in some cases, immediate solution. Increased dialogue and investigation into the MNDP have enabled discussion as to the relative strengths and weaknesses to take place and have served to better integrate all members of the agreement in a way that will aid research collaboration, intake, reputation and, most importantly, the continued success of the programme itself. The existence of the Graduate School in Malaysia, dedicated to the co-ordination and management of the project, with access to the support base in Nottingham, allowed for the relocation of resources and a more fundamental and accurate understanding of the nature of the problem. This did not solve all issues, far from it, but provided the opportunity to meet the challenges head on, armed with accurate information and to react accordingly. The first MNDP student graduated in 2013 from the School of Biomedical Sciences and, perhaps more telling, a Dual PhD programme with UPM is now in place as a direct result of the MNDP, but following a more targeted approach.

The MNDP was designed to operate in the same manner as a Nottingham PhD and this provided consistency and credibility. The international nature of the scheme ensured that it could not operate in exactly the same manner as a Nottingham PhD. The role of supervisors, funding allocation, resource management, expectations, national agendas, student profiles and distance provided additional challenges. Planning and agenda setting are key but the ability to adapt and respond to issues as they arise is crucial. Clear lines of communication are essential. Institutional reputation, degree value and student experience all rely heavily on this.

References

Ali, A. and Kohun, F. (2007) Dealing with social isolation to minimize doctoral attrition—A four stage framework. *International Journal of Doctoral Studies*, 2, 33–49. Available at: http://www.ijds.org/Volume2/IJDSv2p033-049Ali28.pdf

Barnes, B.J. (2010). The nature of exemplary doctoral advisors' expectations and the ways they may influence doctoral persistence. *Journal of College Student Retention: Research, Theory & Practice*, 11(3), 323–343.

Chapman, A. and Pyvis, D. (2006) Dilemmas in the formation of student identity in offshore higher education: A case study in Hong Kong. *Educational Review*, 58(3), 291–302.

De Wit, H. (2008) Changing dynamics in international student circulation: Meanings, push and pull factors, trends and data. In P. Agarwal, M.E. Said, M. Sehoole, M. Sirozi, and H. De Wit (eds.) *The dynamics of international student circulation in a global context*. Rotterdam, Netherlands: Sense Publishers, pp. 14–48.

Eaves, M. (2011) The relevance of learning styles for international pedagogy in higher education. *Teachers and Teaching: Theory and Practice*, 17(6), 677–691.

Furukawa, T. (2013) An empirical study of graduate student mobility underpinning research universities. *Higher Education*, 66(1), 17–37.

Gardner, S.K. (2008) Fitting the mould of graduate school: A qualitative study of socialization in doctoral education. *Innovative Higher Education*, 33(2), 125–138.

Gargano, T. (2009) (Re)conceptualizing international student mobility: The potential of transnational social fields. *Journal of Studies in International Education*, 13(3), 331–346.

Hoare, L. (2012) Transnational student voices: Reflections on a second chance. *Journal of Studies in International Education*, 16(3), 271–286.

Humfrey, C. (2009) *Transnational education and the student experience: A PMI student experience project report*. UK Council for International Student Affairs.

Jones, M. (2013) Issues in doctoral studies—Forty years of journal discussion: Where have we been and where are we going? *International Journal of Doctoral Studies*, 8, 83–104.

Mazzarol, T. and Soutar, G.N. (2002) 'Push-pull' factors influencing international student destination choice. *International Journal of Education Management*, 16(2), 82–90.

O'Mahoney, J. (2014) Enhancing student learning and teacher development in transnational education. York: Higher Education Academy.

Orellana, M.L., Darder, A., Perez, A., and Salinas, J. (2016) Improving doctoral success by matching PhD students with supervisor. *International Journal of Doctoral Studies*, 11, 87–103.

Phelps, J.M. (2016) International doctoral students' navigations of identity and belonging in a Globalizing University. *International Journal of Doctoral Studies*, 11, 1–14.

Pyvis, D. and Chapman, A. (2007) Why university students choose an international education: A case study in Malaysia. *International Journal of Educational Development*, 27(2), 235–246.

Rizvi, F. (2010) International students and doctoral studies in transnational spaces. In M. Walker and P. Thomson (eds.) *The Routledge doctoral supervisor's companion: Supporting effective research in education and the social sciences*. London: Routledge.

Souto-Otero, M., Huisman, J., Beerkens, M., de Wit, H. and Vujic´, S. (2013) Barriers to international student mobility: Evidence from the Erasmus program. *Educational Researcher*, 42(2), 70–77.

Starr-Glass, D. and Ali, T. (2012) Double standards: When an undergraduate dissertation becomes the object of two different assessment approaches. *Assessment & Evaluation in Higher Education*, 37(2), 179–192.

Wells, A. (2014) International student mobility: Approaches, challenges and suggestions for future research. *Procedia—Social and Behavioral Sciences*, 143, 19–24.

8

Strengthening Cross-border Cooperation in the Quality Assurance of TNE: A QAA Perspective

Fabrizio Trifiro'

Introduction

In order to respond to the growth in scale and spread of UK transnational education (TNE), the Quality Assurance Agency (QAA) over the years has developed processes to ensure that its oversight of UK higher education (HE) delivered overseas remains effective and efficient, continuing to provide assurance to international students and stakeholders. Two ways in which QAA has tried to do so is by adopting a country-based approach and by strengthening cooperation with host countries' QAAs.

This chapter will focus on the latter strategic priority, that of enhancing inter-agency cooperation in the quality assurance of TNE. After having outlined QAA's approach to TNE, and its broader regulatory context, the chapter will turn to look in some detail at a number of recent international initiatives aimed at strengthening cross-border cooperation in

F. Trifiro' (✉)
The Quality Assurance Agency (QAA), Gloucester, UK
e-mail: f.trifiro@qaa.ac.uk

© The Author(s) 2018
V. Tsiligiris, W. Lawton (eds.), *Exporting Transnational Education*,
https://doi.org/10.1007/978-3-319-74739-2_8

quality assurance, in which QAA has played a key role. In particular it will focus on:

- the *Quality Assurance of Cross-Border Higher Education* (QACHE) Erasmus Mundus project led by the European Association for Quality Assurance in Higher Education (ENQA), and the resulting Toolkit for QAAs on inter-agency cooperation
- a study undertaken by QAA, with funding from the International Network for Quality Assurance Agencies in Higher Education (INQAAHE), on the challenges and limits to cross-border cooperation in quality assurance.

The chapter will place particular emphasis on the importance for QAAs to reach out and engage with key stakeholders—especially governments, cross-border providers, and TNE students—in order to develop effective and efficient international approaches that are capable of fully harnessing the potential benefits of TNE to students, providers, and society, while addressing the shortcomings associated with gaps or overlaps in regulation.

The chapter is therefore informed by and contributes to the latest international policy developments and debates regarding the quality assurance of TNE, offering the perspective of the QAA, the quality asurance agency arguably overseeing the largest TNE sector worldwide and with the most experience in quality assuring TNE.

The UK TNE Landscape

TNE is an integral and expanding part of UK HE provision. Over 80% of the approximately 160 UK degree-awarding bodies are engaged in some form or another of TNE, either through distance learning, partnerships, or branch campus arrangements. Significantly this provision is delivered across the continents, as illustrated in Fig. 8.1, taken from the Higher Education Statistics Agency (HESA), the UK national agency collecting HE data.

TNE now also represents the main area of growth in UK HE in terms of student numbers, as illustrated by Fig. 8.2. The latest HESA data for the academic year 2016/17 show that while the total number of students

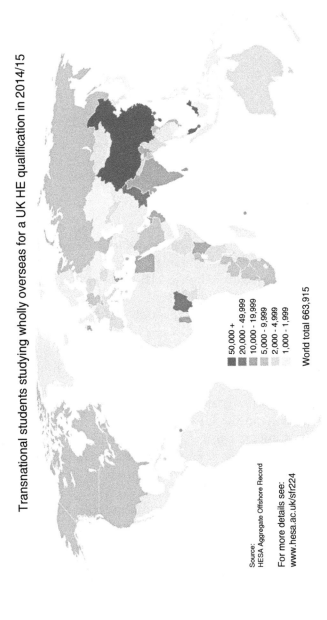

Fig. 8.1 The geographical scope of UK TNE

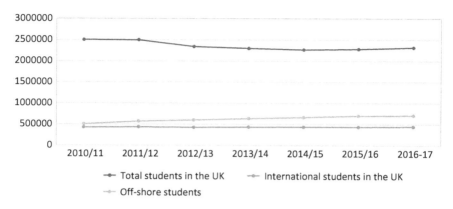

Fig. 8.2 TNE as the main area of growth for UK HE

studying on HE programmes in the UK (2,317,880) has declined by approximately 7% since 2010, and the number of international students studying in the UK has remained roughly constant (442,375), the number of students studying on HE programmes outside of the UK has witnessed more than a 40% increase over the same period (709,323), now largely exceeding the number of international students in the UK.

In terms of host countries of UK TNE, the vast majority of TNE students are located in Asia. As illustrated in Fig. 8.3, China is now the second largest host country, after Malaysia, and growing faster than any other country. China is also by far the main sending country of international students in the UK, and it has been calculated that over 50% of Chinese students coming to study in the UK arrive through TNE arrangements; that is, they start their programme of study in China and then spend a period of their study in the UK (HEFCE 2014).[1]

QAA over the years has had to develop processes that could ensure that its oversight of UK TNE remains effective and efficient in the context of this extended and growing TNE provision. Two ways in which QAA has tried to do so, as I will show in the next section, is by adopting a country-based approach and by strengthening cooperation with host countries' QAAs.

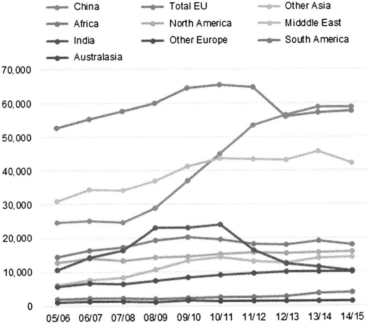

Fig. 8.3 The top 5 host countries for UK TNE

The QAA Approach to TNE

QAA has always looked at UK TNE in two main ways: through its institutional reviews of UK providers and a dedicated in-country TNE review process looking at a number of delivery sites overseas.

QAA's institutional reviews are comprehensive processes looking at the complete range of a provider's HE provision, including its overseas delivery. However, the focus on TNE in the context of institutional reviews can only be limited to the documentation of providers' policies and processes. It would not be viable for review teams to look at TNE delivery sites as part of a provider's institutional review.

For this reason, QAA has traditionally complemented its institutional reviews with a dedicated TNE review process which includes visits to overseas delivery sites of UK providers. This review process is aimed at addressing those aspects that institutional reviews are less suited to meeting, in particular testing the implementation of policies and processes for safeguarding standards and enhancing quality of TNE provision, and getting an understanding of the TNE student experience. It is also aimed at maximising the efficiency and effectiveness of overseeing UK TNE in the context of the volume and spread of UK TNE highlighted above.[2]

QAA has traditionally adopted a country-based approach, whereby, on approximately an annual basis, a country with significant UK TNE or of strategic importance for UK HE is selected, and UK TNE provision there is looked at by a review team, including through visits to a sample of delivery sites. This is more efficient and practical than sending review teams to different parts of the world several times a year to look at different TNE arrangements as part of providers' institutional reviews. Over the past few years, for example, QAA has reviewed UK TNE in India (2009), Malaysia (2010), Singapore (2011), China (2012), United Arab Emirates (UAE) (2013), the Caribbean (2014), Greece and Cyprus (2015), and Ireland (2017).[3]

A country-based approach also allows QAA's review teams to get an in-depth understanding of the specific features and challenges involved in operating in particular countries, since different countries have different policies and systems for HE and TNE which will affect TNE provision in different ways. This is important to ensure an informed assessment of TNE arrangements in the context of their particular operating environments and to gain useful insights that could benefit all providers operating in that country.

In addition, a country-based approach allows QAA to establish stronger links with the host country quality assurance bodies and to explore systematic ways in which to cooperate with them to improve the efficiency and effectiveness of its TNE review process. When undertaking in-country reviews of TNE, QAA regularly seeks to liaise with the local regulatory authorities and QA agencies with a particular view to sharing information, data and intelligence and exploring ways in which it might be possible to coordinate review activity of UK TNE to lessen the burden on TNE providers, and on themselves.

Engaging strategically with partner agencies in UK TNE host countries is indeed a high priority for QAA. The volume and spread of UK

TNE require QAA to seek cooperation with host country agencies to facilitate its quality assurance, focus resources where they are most needed, and enhance international practice.

The following section will provide an overview of two recently concluded projects aimed at strengthening and raising the importance of cross-border cooperation in the quality assurance of TNE, in which QAA has played a leading role. These are the Erasmus Mundus funded project QACHE managed by ENQA, and a short study on the challenges and limits to inter-agency cooperation carried out by QAA with funding from INQAAHE.

Strengthening Inter-agency Cooperation

QACHE Project

QACHE was a two-year project (2013–15) aimed at enhancing the quality assurance of TNE, supported by the Erasmus Mundus Programme of the European Union and undertaken by a project consortium coordinated by ENQA (Ranne et al. 2016). The project consortium included:

- the Asian Pacific Quality Network (APQN) and the Arab Network for Quality Assurance in Higher Education (ANQAHE), representing the national agencies of the two main receiving regions of TNE;
- a number of national European agencies with different experience with TNE, the National Agency for Quality Assessment and Accreditation of Spain (ANECA), the French High Council for the Evaluation of Research and Higher Education (HCERES), the German Accreditation Council (GAC) and QAA;
- the national agency of one of the main TNE provider countries outside Europe, the Australian Tertiary Education Quality and Standards Agency (TEQSA).

The project engaged in a series of activities aimed at gaining a better understanding of the quality assurance challenges posed by TNE and good practice in different national and regional contexts, including producing in-depth country reports outlining the operating environments for TNE of the five national agencies participating in the project, and international policy dialogues. The findings and understanding gained through these activities were pivotal in informing the development of the main output of the project, the Toolkit *Cooperation in Cross-Border Higher Education: A Toolkit for Quality Assurance Agencies* (ENQA 2016).

The QACHE Toolkit, whose development was led by QAA, offers QAAs practical advice on things they might consider doing to strengthen cooperation in the quality assurance of TNE. Four key findings informed the QACHE Toolkit.

- A great diversity of approaches and regulatory frameworks for TNE (in/outbound) both within and across the participating regions.
- General lack of information and knowledge of other countries' and agencies' frameworks and approaches for quality assurance and TNE.
- What can be referred to as a 'trust gap' between home and host countries about the quality and quality assurance of TNE.
- Low levels of cooperation in the quality assurance of TNE.

These four aspects are strictly intertwined, and they can be seen as creating a vicious circle whereby lack of information of other agencies' approaches prevents building reciprocal trust about the quality and quality assurance of TNE, in its turn hindering effective and efficient cooperation in cross-border quality assurance (Trifiro' 2016a, b, c) (Fig. 8.4).

The QACHE Toolkit aims to reverse this vicious circle. It provides practical advice to quality assurance agencies and their networks on how they can set in motion an opposite virtuous circle, whereby by improving the sharing of information, intelligence, data and good practice about TNE and its quality assurance, agencies can start developing a better understanding of each other's systems, building reciprocal trust, and thus pave the way to exploring ways in which they can cooperate in the quality assurance of TNE.

By setting in motion this virtuous circle, agencies will enhance the international quality assurance of TNE in two main ways. They will facilitate the identification of regulatory gaps and therefore help in safeguarding students and stakeholders from low-quality provision, and, conversely, they will facilitate the identification of unnecessary duplication or con-

Strengthening Cross-border Cooperation in the Quality... 137

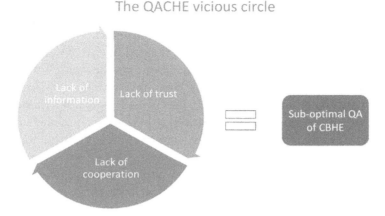

Fig. 8.4 The QACHE vicious circle

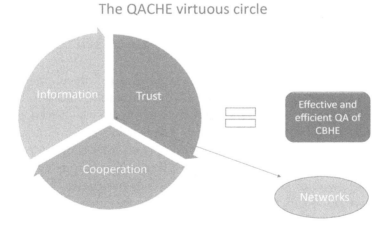

Fig. 8.5 The QACHE virtuous circle

flicts of regulation, therefore lessening the burden on providers and on the agencies themselves (Fig. 8.5).

The QACHE project also highlighted the significant catalyst role that networks such as INQAAHE, ENQA, APQN, and ANQAHE can play in fostering and supporting this virtuous circle, through the facilitation of policy dialogue and information sharing, and other initiatives aimed at improving reciprocal understanding, building mutual trust, and strengthening cooperation between their constituent agencies.

Although the guidance and advice contained in the QACHE Toolkit may seem very simple, its implementation can be complicated. The implementation of the Toolkit not only requires commitment of resources but will also be crucially affected by the broader regulatory frameworks within which agencies operate, which may pose limits and challenges to the extent to which agencies may be able to cooperate across border in quality assuring TNE. Understanding these challenges and the realms of possibility for inter-agency cooperation is therefore crucial for developing viable initiatives for strengthened cooperation in the spirit of the QACHE Toolkit. To this aim, QAA, with the support of a grant from INQAAHE, has undertaken research aimed at exploring the challenges and limits to cross-border cooperation in the quality assurance of TNE.

Developing Viable Strategies for Cross-border Cooperation in the Quality Assurance of TNE

The aim of the INQAAHE-funded research was to help progress inter-agency cooperation, and thus facilitate the implementation of the QACHE Toolkit, by identifying the concrete ways in which agencies may be able to cooperate across borders, and thus help develop strategic and viable approaches to the enhancement of cross-border cooperation.[4]

In undertaking its research QAA was able to draw on its networks of partner agencies in key receiving and sending countries of TNE, which were surveyed to gather their experiences of cooperation in quality assuring TNE, and elicit their perception about the challenges and limits to cooperation as well as facilitating factors and good practice.[5] The participating agencies were asked specifically whether they:

- share data, information, and intelligence about TNE and its quality assurance with other agencies in sending and/or receiving countries of TNE
- have reached agreements with other agencies, in either sending or receiving countries of TNE, for the reciprocal recognition of quality assurance decisions

- engage in any form of joint-review activity of TNE with agencies of either sending or receiving countries.

The following sections report the findings of the survey in aggregate form.

Information Sharing

All surveyed agencies confirmed that they share, to some extent, data, information, and intelligence about TNE and its quality assurance with other agencies in sending and/or receiving countries. Generally, information sharing takes place in the context of formal agreements, such as Memoranda of Understanding, which include commitments to, and protocols for, sharing information, and place terms and conditions on what can be shared. Information about TNE is typically shared as part of, and to inform, TNE review activity undertaken by either the sending or receiving country's agency.

Agencies report a number of limits and challenges to the sharing of information, data, or intelligence. There might be legal restrictions on the type of information to be shared and the rationale for sharing information, often due to issues of ownership of data and confidentiality. Also, some information and intelligence, in particular pertaining to specific providers, might be of a confidential nature or commercially sensitive. More generally, a lack of availability of data and information is also reported as a limit, for instance, where there is no developed data collection system or TNE quality assurance framework. In addition, all agencies have reported the need to build reciprocal trust, and getting to know other agencies better, as a key challenge in information sharing. The key challenge here is that building trust requires time and resources, which calls for a strategic approach and long-term commitment to partnership building.

Regular engagement at different levels of the agency, supported by formal Memoranda of Understanding setting out clear policies about confidentiality, data security, and privacy, is unanimously seen as important to help in enhancing reciprocal understanding and developing reciprocal trust. Clarity on designated communication channels and contact points, and a gradual approach to information sharing, starting with less sensitive issues before diving into more complicated cross-border issues, is also seen as good practices for effective information sharing.

Most agencies stress the role that regional networks can play to facilitate reciprocal understanding and trust building. The need for agencies to move beyond the bilateral level and engage in multi-lateral communication is also highlighted, in order to respond to the growing number of HE providers operating in more than two jurisdictions. In addition, considering that in many jurisdictions different agencies or bodies have different responsibilities with regard to TNE, including data collection, registration, quality assurance, and recognition of qualifications, enhanced cooperation at national level among all bodies with a role in TNE is called for.

Reciprocal Recognition of Quality Assurance Decisions

No surveyed agencies have yet reached agreements with other agencies for the reciprocal recognition of quality assurance decisions. However, a number of agencies in TNE host countries observe how they indirectly recognise quality assurance decisions from sending countries' agencies through their TNE programme registration procedures, which rely on the statement by part of foreign providers that their TNE programmes are recognised and quality assured by the relevant authorities in their home country.

Reaching agreements for the reciprocal recognition of quality assurance decisions is regarded as a desirable goal to work towards by all agencies, but there is general recognition that this is not an easy goal to achieve, and that a number of important challenges might make engagement in this type of cooperation difficult or not possible. These challenges include:

- lack of familiarity with, and understanding of, other countries' and agencies' systems

- differences in quality assurance systems, reference points and processes
- different views of TNE and of how it should be quality assured
- lack of track record of quality assurance activity or of a developed quality assurance system
- limited resources
- legislative or policy barriers to recognising other agencies' decisions.

A key common denominator is once again the expressed need to engage regularly with other agencies so as to enhance understanding of each other's reference points and processes, and build reciprocal trust. Since developing in-depth understanding of each other's systems, including through benchmarking activity, requires time and resources, agencies again stress the need for a strategic, phased, and long-term commitment to partnership building.

In addition to resources and long-term commitment, developed quality assurance systems and the existence of qualification frameworks are considered as important facilitating factors for the reciprocal recognition of other agencies' quality assurance decisions, since they allow for clear and robust benchmarking of reference points and processes. The different focus and nature of reference points and processes, in particular whether they operate at programme or institutional level, or whether they are input or output orientated, are instead perceived as important challenges for benchmarking activity. Nonetheless, agencies still appreciate the utility of being able to rely on other agencies' views on these complementary and related aspects of quality assurance.

A number of agencies expressed the importance for the recognition of quality assurance decisions to be linked with, and conducive to, the recognition of TNE qualifications. This link is not always easy and possible to establish, as in a number of countries the quality assurance and qualification recognition functions are separate. This calls again for strengthened cooperation at national level between the relevant bodies. Proactively engaging with government is also seen as needed, in particular when a change to restrictive policy or legislation impeding the recognition of other quality assurance agencies' decisions is required.

Joint-Review Activity

Most respondents have had some form of experience of joint review of cross-border provision. Those agencies who have not yet engaged in this type of cooperation are, however, willing to do so, and actively considering ways in which they can engage in joint-review activity in the future, including by developing appropriate policies.

Compliance with national laws and regulation, and limited resources, are the most often quoted obstacles to undertaking joint-review activity, with a number of agencies stressing the high costs and the amount of preparatory work involved. Other major challenges most commonly identified by the respondents include:

- differences in reference points and review processes, and the need to safeguard their legitimacy and integrity within the respective local quality assurance frameworks
- different views of the purpose and expected outcome of the review process
- different preset review schedules
- different criteria for selecting reviewers and different views about their role
- language and cultural issues.

In order to be able to overcome these challenges, agencies regard it as crucial to dedicate resources to undertaking preliminary work, in order to reach an adequate understanding of the respective quality assurance frameworks and approaches. This will enable agencies to develop a shared understanding of the purpose and expected outcome of the joint-review exercise and agree on processes for the conduction of the review, including criteria for selecting reviewers, data sharing and follow-up activities. Training and briefing review teams is essential to enable reviewers, used to operating within different quality assurance systems, cultures and languages, to work together effectively. Agencies also agree on the need to make sure that the reference points and procedures used are well understood and received by providers. Significantly undertaking joint-review activity is seen as a possible instrumental step towards facilitating the reciprocal recognition of review decisions, generally regarded as a more efficient way of cooperating in the quality assurance of TNE.

Lessons Learned

On the basis of the findings of the QACHE project and the INQAAHE-funded QAA project, it is possible to extract a key strategic recommendation to agencies to help them in their efforts to implement the advice contained in the QACHE Toolkit, and ultimately to support the achievement of the original purpose of the UNESCO/OECD Guidelines for Quality Provision in Cross-Border Higher Education (OECD 2005):

> to protect students and other stakeholders from low-quality provision and disreputable providers as well as to encourage the development of quality cross-border higher education that meets human, social, economic and cultural needs (p. 7).

This general strategic advice is to recognise that quality assurance agencies do not operate in isolation, but within broader regulatory systems involving a variety of other stakeholders, and that therefore it is crucial for agencies to engage with these stakeholders in order to be able to develop more efficient and effective ways to quality assure TNE.

In particular, it will be crucial to engage closely with government, HE providers, students, and employers.

- Engaging with government is crucial in order to induce and drive policy or legislative change needed to facilitate cross-border cooperation among quality assurance agencies, both at national and international level.
- Cross-border providers, being at the receiving end of the quality assurance and regulatory requirements of sending and receiving countries' agencies, are ideally placed to help agencies identify areas where there is unnecessary duplication of regulation, and where possible synergy and cooperation across borders are viable and desirable.

- Engaging with TNE students and employers further enables agencies (as well as providers and governments) to avoid setting unnecessary obstacles to the development of TNE programmes that meet the needs of students living and working in different countries.

In conclusion, it is safe to say that the agencies contributing to the QACHE project through its different phases, and those responding to the QAA survey, seem to share the common view that it is essential to cooperate across borders to address the quality assurance challenges posed by TNE, with an ultimate view to enabling providers, students, and governments to fully harness the opportunities that TNE offers for meeting unmet demands for quality and relevant HE provision. All agencies seemed to share the same view of their role as facilitators of quality and relevant TNE provision, and the same willingness to avoid posing unnecessary obstacles. Since trust is also built through the realisation that we share a common ground together with others, the realisation that agencies share such common views about the value of TNE and their role with regard to TNE is in itself an important facilitating factor for enhancing inter-agency cooperation.

Notes

1. 'Directions of Travel: Transnational Pathways into English Higher Education' (HESA), available at: www.hefce.ac.uk/pubs/year/2014/201429/. This report draws on data from the Higher Education Funding Council for England, and refers to England only. However, the findings can be regarded as representative of patterns of Chinese students' mobility to the UK.
2. A handbook for TNE Review can be found at: http://www.qaa.ac.uk/publications/information-and-guidance/publication?PubID=3146#.WjJHSsncu70. Last accessed on 14/12/2017.
3. Detailed information of QAA's latest TNE review exercises can be found here http://www.qaa.ac.uk/reviews-and-reports/how-we-review-higher-education/review-of-overseas-provision. Last accessed on 07/03/2017.
4. See Trifiro' (2016d) for an overview of the project and its outcomes.

5. The following agencies were surveyed:

- China Academic Degrees and Graduate Academic Information (CDGDC), China
- China Education Association for International Exchange (CEAIE), China
- Council for Private Education (CPE), Singapore
- Knowledge and Human Development Authority (KHDA), Dubai, UAE
- Hong Kong Council for Accreditation of Academic and Vocational Qualifications (HKCAAVQ), Hong Kong
- Malaysia Qualifications Agency (MQA), Malaysia
- National Institute for Academic Degree and University Evaluation (NIAD-UE), Japan
- Quality and Qualifications Ireland (QQI), Ireland
- Tertiary Education Quality and Standards Agency (TEQSA), Australia
- Western Association of Schools and Colleges, Senior College and University Commission (WSCUC), USA

Considering that the UK, Australia, and the USA are the three main TNE sending countries and that Malaysia, China, Singapore, Hong Kong, and Dubai are among the main host countries, the findings of the research can be regarded as capturing the experience and perceptions of the agencies overseeing most of the currently existing global TNE, and include some of the agencies with most experience in quality assuring inbound or outbound TNE.

Although there is no comprehensive data available on the global landscape and extent of programme and institution mobility, it is possible to obtain a reliable picture from the few national statistics agencies or regulatory bodies collecting regular data about outbound or inbound TNE. Among the sending countries, the UK and Australia have established databases for outbound TNE provision, while China, Hong Kong, Singapore, and Dubai collect comprehensive data about inbound TNE. By triangulating the information gathered from these countries, it is possible to establish with some confidence that the UK and Australia are the main TNE sending countries, followed by the USA, and that China, Hong Kong, Malaysia, Singapore, and Dubai (for branch campuses) are the leading host countries (see HESA 2018; DET 2015; McNamara and Knight 2015; ENQA 2014).

References

Department for Education and Trade (DET) (2015) Higher Education Statistics, Department for Education and Training, Australian Government. Available at: www.education.gov.au/higher-education-statistics. Last accessed 7 March 2017.

ENQA (2014) QACHE country reports. Available at: https://qache.wordpress.com/outputs. Last accessed 7 March 2017.

ENQA (2016) Cooperation in cross border higher education: A toolkit for Quality Assurance Agencies. Available at: www.enqa.eu/wp-content/uploads/2015/11/QACHE-toolkit.pdf. Last accessed 7 March 2017.

HEFCE (2014) Directions of travel: Transnational pathways into English higher education. Available at: http://www.hefce.ac.uk/pubs/year/2014/201429/. Last accessed 7 March 2017.

HESA (2018) Aggregate offshore record. Higher Education Statistics Agency. Available at: www.hesa.ac.uk. Last accessed 7 March 2017.

McNamara, J. and Knight, J. (2015) Transnational education data collection systems: Awareness, analysis, action. British Council and DAAD. Available at: www.britishcouncil.org/education/ihe/knowledge-centre/transnational-education/tne-education-data-collection-systems

OECD (2005) UNESCO/OECD guidelines for quality provision in cross-border higher education. Available at: http://www.oecd.org/general/unescooecdguidelinesforqualityprovisionincross-borderhighereducation.htm. Last accessed 7 March 2017.

Ranne, P., et al. (2016) Final report of the QACHE project: Quality assurance of cross-border higher education, ENQA 2016. Available at: http://www.enqa.eu/indirme/QACHE%20final%20report.pdf. Last accessed 7 March 2017.

Trifiro', F. (2016a) Strengthening cooperation in the quality assurance of cross-border higher education: An introduction to the QACHE project. Observatory for Borderless Higher Education (OBHE), 20-10-2015. Available at: http://www.obhe.ac.uk/what_we_do/news_articles_reports/news_analysis/na_2015/news_analysis_ga10_20oct15. Last accessed 7 March 2017.

Trifiro', F. (2016b) The QACHE toolkit: Strengthening and enhancing interagency cooperation in the quality assurance of TNE. HE Global 20-11-2015. Available at: http://heglobal.international.ac.uk/join-the-debate/comments/the-qache-toolkit.aspx. Last accessed 7 March 2017.

Trifiro', F. (2016c) The QACHE toolkit for quality assurance agencies: Cooperation in cross-border higher education. OBHE 9/12/2015. Available at: http://www.obhe.ac.uk/what_we_do/news_articles_reports/news_analysis/na_2015/news_analysis_ga11_9dec15. Last accessed 7 March 2017.

Trifiro', F. (2016d) Inter-agency cooperation in the quality assurance of transnational education: Challenges and opportunities. *Quality in Higher Education* (forthcoming).

Part IV

Student Experience

9

Chalk and Talk? Teaching Practice and Innovation in Transnational Education

David Cockayne and Heather Cockayne

Introduction

In this chapter, our aim is to explore the nature and effect of teaching innovation in transnational education (TNE). Drawing from the idea of "performativity" and elements of "actor-network-theory" (ANT), we utilise a practice-based approach (PBA) and propose that teaching innovation evolves not directly from formalised education management, but from the everyday, sometimes spontaneous, and often mundane practices of human actors (i.e. teaching staff) and their interaction with non-human devices (i.e. physical environment). Practices are not synonymous with activities. Indeed, what we refer to as a practice can be formed by numerous micro-level activities. This is not to say that activity is in itself

D. Cockayne (✉)
University of Liverpool, Liverpool, UK
e-mail: David.Cockayne@liverpool.ac.uk

H. Cockayne
University of Manchester, Manchester, UK
e-mail: heather.cockayne@manchester.ac.uk

innovation, but rather that activities may provide evidence of invention that if captured and developed more broadly may eventually become an example of teaching innovation. By exploring the root of TNE teaching innovation, rather than assessing the outcome, we envisage our contribution as providing policymakers and education management with valuable insights beneficial to the better organisation, management, and practice of teaching in TNE.

The Nature of Innovation

Innovation often manifests in the form of new products, services, or processes of operations. Innovations can be defined as radical, or alternatively they might be seen as incremental improvements to an existing entity or process. At the core of these definitions however is the understanding that innovation is not synonymous with invention and that any form of innovation ultimately derives from a process of discovery.

The term "discovery" refers to processes of recognising or observing a particular natural phenomenon or object for the first time. Discovery in this sense is the starting point of invention. As a simple example, humans "discovered" electricity; however, the process of producing and distributing it has been "invented". Discovery is therefore the result of a specific purposeful activity that involves a continuous process of searching for a solution to a preconceived problem.

Inspired by Schumpeter (1939) it is common for authors in the innovation literature to distinguish between invention and innovation. Rothwell and Zegveld (1985: 47) define invention as "the creation of an idea and its reduction to practice". When referring to "reduction to practice", they are referring to laboratory tests to confirm or reject the concept value or principle. Although this is a useful definition, like many other definitions in the innovation literature, it is biased towards technological products, largely ignoring services such as education or organisational processes such as teaching. Both the innovation and invention literature refer to the concepts of "idea creation" and "newness" in their definitions. A key distinction however is that definitions of "invention" do not necessarily embrace the bringing into common use of a new idea, whereas innovation does. Ultimately, the difference between invention and innovation is the extent to which an invention becomes commonly used, or diffused through the organisation, market, and so on. In essence, we understand innovation as a process of discovery, invention, and social diffusion.

Performativity and the "Practice-Based Approach"

The concept of "performativity" offers an alternative conceptualisation of innovation. Here innovation is continuously made, shaped, and changed through the actions of actors (i.e. students and teachers) and their interaction with each other, and various technical devices (i.e. the Internet and facilities). Innovation is therefore a continuous process of interaction rather than a definitive outcome. These interactions involve dimensions of discovery and invention and ultimately lead to innovation in the sense described above. The actions of actors, and the devices that influence their interactions, can be understood as practices.

The PBA offers an epistemological means of identifying and understanding organisational and social phenomena (Bourdieu 1990). Here the unit of analysis is the field of practices that joins the individual and the collective, orchestrated through material and technical devices. A practice is a way of doing, embedded in a context of interlinked elements (Schau, Muñiz, and Arnould 2009), rather than simply a process. Actions and processes help to shape practices.

As noted earlier, by emphasising practices it is possible to conceptualise innovation differently. A practice-inspired perspective moves innovation away from its traditional definition as the product of a company's processes (Schatzki et al. 2001). The benefit of this is that researchers and practitioners alike can focus on understanding the social connections amongst individuals and organisations.

> *Practices as linked and implicit ways of understanding, saying and doing things. They comprise a … nexus of behaviours that include practical activities, performances and representations or talk.* (Schau, Muñiz, and Arnould 2009: 31)

Activities associated with innovation are accomplished by actors who rely on practical–evaluative agency (Emirbayer and Mische 1998) to understand and assess how practices can be altered or tailored in order to accomplish specific tasks or to cater to different audiences. Taken in context, the practices of staff working in TNE are composed of essential job-specific tasks, for instance, delivering a lecture or seminar, as well as variations inspired by the individual staff member. Such variations may be encouraged by a desire to modify existing practices to address localised concerns. This could be the inclusion of additional language support, team-teaching, or enabling the availability of additional learning resources to help meet the specific needs of the TNE market.

The aim of this chapter is to explore the day-to-day activities used by staff working in UK-led TNE to create variance, and to modify the teaching and learning practices in order to address localised concerns.

Context and Design

Driven by numerous factors including globalisation, restricted access to education, technological development, branding, and political motive, the TNE market continues to grow and mature. While we acknowledge a wide variety of definitions used to describe TNE depending on the type of international programme, location, and provider mobility (Knight and McNamara 2017: 1), our chapter adopts a definition of TNE which refers to "the provision of education for students based in a country other than the one in which the awarding body is located" (HE Global 2016: 9).

Irrespective of definition, the TNE market is undoubtedly unique compared with traditional education markets. In the first instance, students are relatively unbounded by geographical location. For example, a student from Europe is today able to enrol and study for a degree from New York University (NYU), delivered in Shanghai, China, or Dubai, UAE. On paper, the perceived value and formal learning outcomes of the NYU degree are the same irrespective of geographical location. However, the dynamic fusion of host, home, and local cultures; unique learning environment; and locally available resources foster an innovatively different lived learning experience for the student. The same is also true for the staff tasked with delivering TNE programmes. Hybrid departments of local employees, adjunct faculty, and staff flown in from the "home" institution naturally alter the delivery dynamic and ultimate learning experience of the student.

Since 2008, the supply of UK higher education (HE) TNE provisions has risen sharply, and the majority of these are located outside of the European Union (O'Mahony 2014). Indeed, UK-led TNE in HE is now being delivered in all but 15 countries globally (HE Global 2016). HE Global (2016) highlighted that 28% of all UK HE TNE programmes in 2014–15 were being delivered in Asia, with Malaysia, Singapore, Hong Kong, and China being the top four regions recorded as having the highest number of UK HE TNE students (HE Global 2016: 26). In China alone, there were more than 38,000 students studying through UK HE TNE in China in 2011–12 (QAA 2013a), and this is likely to have increased since then.

TNE provisions have been seen as conduits for nations to develop global trade and investment links (Mellors-Bourne et al. 2014: 59). In this sense, education becomes a *lingua franca* for engagement and mutually beneficial political alignment. According to Yang (2008), it was in the mid-1980s that TNE provisions first appeared in China. However, it was following China's accession to the WTO (in 2001) that resulted in significant changes to educational policies which helped the growth of Sino-foreign educational partnerships.

The types of TNE partnerships often differ by activity, whether this be distance learning, an international branch campus (IBC), franchise or validation (Healey 2015), but the motivations behind these foreign partnerships in China are usually quite simple: to break into the Chinese market, to attract Chinese students to the foreign side, or to make profit. There are many for-profit institutions, or there are those institutions that may need extra revenue sources that will undoubtedly look towards international projects as a source of financial gain (Altbach and Knight 2007). Brand building, a heightened international profile, and the enablement of student mobility in locations with restricted access to HE are often cited as the key drivers behind this rapidly expanding market.

This increase in UK-led TNE provisions in recent years has prompted a greater focus on the quality of delivery, background and qualifications of employees, and whether or not the transnationally delivered programme is able to offer a comparably valuable learner experience to that of the domestic offering. This has led to the Quality Assurance Agency (QAA) reviewing TNE programmes (QAA 2013b), while the British Council has initiated a research agenda focused on determining the scale and scope of UK TNE (HE Global 2016) and supported research to outline a framework for classification and data gathering within this area (Knight and McNamara 2017).

The strategic context of provisions, along with some of the key drivers for UK HE providers to become engaged in TNE, was considered in HE Global's (2016) report, which also included information relating to the responsibility of various aspects of a TNE programme. The report's survey received responses from 22 different institutions concerning 910 programmes and found that curriculum development and quality assurance rested with the UK institutions in two-thirds of cases. However, where there was a local delivery partnership model, responsibilities for teaching, academic support, pastoral support, and buildings and infrastructure were with the host institutions, whereas assessment, learning resources and staff development were the combined responsibility of the awarding and host institutions (HE Global 2016: 73). With these varying responsibilities of content and quality between the differing partnerships, coupled with localised regulations, it is important that the staff actually delivering these programmes are given the recognition and consideration required in order for the students' experience to be positive, but also for partnership motivations and drivers to be realised.

Research Design

The data collected from this study occurred during two phases, throughout the academic year 2015–16 and semester one of 2016–17: (1) a series of informal discussions and loosely structured interviews with 11 staff members based across multiple UK-TNE provisions in China and (2) open-ended questionnaires exchanged by email with respondents. This was to help clarify and expand upon key themes identified in the previous stage. Participant observation would have ideally been used initially as we acknowledge that respondents may not be explicitly aware of some day-to-day activities. Unfortunately, both time and funding constraints limited the potential for this. We were however able to conduct multiple interviews and/or discussions with each respondent longitudinally. This involved narratives of example teaching days or specific periods of the academic year. Some respondents also voluntarily shared photos, extracts from teaching plans, and links to online content and social media pages as a way of illustrating certain points made during the interview. These contributed to our interpretations of activities and identification of practices; however, they were not directly used in our analysis.

As the unit of our analysis is the activities and practices of teaching staff, rather than the staff or institution itself, our sample consists of staff working at a variety of TNE institutions in China. We also allowed respondents to refer back to past examples at previous TNE institutions if they felt there was a particular example or activity that they engaged with. It should also be noted that both authors of this chapter also formally worked at a China-based TNE provision. We see this as a strength to our research given that we were able to use our own past experiences to dig deeper into responses that a researcher unfamiliar with the day-to-day working life of a TNE institution in China may not have been aware of.

Findings

The interviews and discussions with teaching staff at TNE institutions in China were insightful. A thematic review of our discussions identified a wide range of activities performed by staff on a day-to-day basis. It was interesting to see how various social contexts sought to (re)frame traditional perceptions of time and space in teaching. Further, the absence of resources commonly found in home institutions inspired creativity amongst staff and required them to deeper embed approaches in broader localised practices.

It is important to note that the aim of our research is to identify and document activities and micro-level processes as a means of identifying innovation in teaching practice. It is not our aim to try and evaluate, or assign a value to such practices. The activities and practices that we discuss in the forthcoming section cannot be defined as "right" or "wrong". They simply exist. This is an important aspect of our research.

Following the thematic review, we identified numerous examples of activities performed by teaching staff on a day-to-day basis that ultimately shape and influence the standard and quality of education taking place in the Chinese TNE market. We clustered these activities into three broad categories of practices: (1) interacting, (2) exploring, and (3) extracting. Each practice enables resource exchange and integration within the TNE institution.

We also identified performative relations between each practice. The practices of extracting and discovering often overlap and act as the core of teaching innovation. These practices only however lead to innovation in the presence of the "Interacting" practice. The practice of interacting helps to facilitate moments of discovery and invention. This is a cyclical process which over time leads to the normalisation of certain practices framed with the TNE teaching environment.

The Practice of Interacting

Our findings revealed that staff at TNE institutions would often create scenarios that would help to identify new opportunities for them as individuals and to the benefit of their teaching. The practice of interacting was also seen as essential for the sharing and dissemination of new ideas, information, and knowledge in relation to teaching and other personal matters. Interaction was performed through three core networking activities: (1) socialising, (2) diversifying actions, and (3) exploring practices.

Socialising

Socialising activities relate to situations where staff engaged together in an informal setting. The goal of such action was simply to nurture, build, and extend relationships with colleagues, although it also enabled ideas and information to be shared (this will be covered in "the practice of exploring").

One key example of "socialising" actions was going to a venue outside of the work environment. These included bars, pubs, and restaurants. Staff felt that this was necessary as facilities provided at the teaching institution did not encourage informal social interaction. Shared offices often resulted in people being disturbed or interrupted and as such *it was actually quite rare to go into others' offices to discuss things.*

With the limited spaces provided, more informal, but arguably more available spaces were sought. One location that was evidently popular, particularly with expatriate staff, was *the local [bar]*:

> *A large portion of discussion and reflection with others actually happened over a drink in the bar after work—the more informal setting maybe facilitating more open-minded and honest comments.*

> *…we'd call a few places 'our local'… and we'd also go out for tea together quite a lot. I never did that in England, go for tea with people from work that is… working abroad pushes you to make new friends—even with the people you work with!*

The "bar" was often seen as *the location* for interaction amongst expatriate staff working at TNE institutions. The theme continued when staff from home institutions visited TNE locations. In relation to local staff however, restaurants were the location of choice. This was also the case when local staff and expatriate staff sought to interact:

> *…well this is our home so we have families but for the foreigner staff its different. I don't like to drinking in bar[s] but sometimes we'd all go for Chinese food. It's good to get to know people and learn about new culture and thinking.*

Pubs, bars, and restaurants all helped to provide an informal setting for socialisation amongst teaching staff. Sharing ideas and creating new spaces for collaboration are key to teaching innovation and require socialising actions to take place. The outside-of-work environment and organic organisation of actors create an open-team dynamic and enable unrestricted communication. Although interactions are brief, staff not only become more familiar with each other individually, but they have the potential to share examples of best practice, and stories of failure and success. Individual ideas and views can become transformed into collective perspectives. This process is cyclical and as collective perspectives become more common, further socialising is required.

One such example of this was the use of extra-curricular activities, in particular—sport. Interestingly, in some situations this particular form of socialisation also included students. Participants believed that a sports environment, such as a basketball or football team, provided a safe environment for good relationships to be built. It was also noted that the context of "the game" would temporarily ignite rare informal conversations between staff and students within the teaching institution—that is, in offices, along the corridor, outside classrooms, inside classrooms—immediately after the event. Staff also commented that the setting was a useful mechanism to gain informal feedback from students about their learning experience.

> *…the first time we played, we mixed the teams with staff and students. I was a bit uncomfortable at first as it blurred that barrier between us staff and the students, and probably because I couldn't play football to save my life! … what I found interesting was how other students would come to watch and cheer both teams on. It was just a bit of fun but we all became equals on the pitch and that helped in the classroom—definitely. Suppose you'd say it humanised us.*

A clear benefit for interaction through sports activities was the decoupling effect. The staff–student relationship temporarily subsided, although did not disappear. A more equal relationship in terms of authority allowed freedom of expression. Staff spoke about being able to access informal feedback, gage student morale, and learn of their interests, strengths, and weaknesses. Staff also said it was interesting to learn of different friendship groups between student clusters and identify power hierarchies. This was seen as being extremely useful in classroom management, creation of groups for particular assessments, seating arrangements (if necessary).

More broadly than sport, staff recognised that frequent extra-curricular activities and events allowed staff to gain a *live insight* into student morale and experience. Staff commented on how this enabled them to modify examples, *mix up lecture delivery*, or review topics.

> *I think for me just being able to chat to the students informally was important…every conversation helped add something to my teaching plan. I quickly learned what examples would fly and which ones would fall on deaf ears. This didn't necessarily change the content specified in the learning descriptors, but it did change the way I delivered it.*

There was however evidence that socialising activities might create tension relative to formalised institutions of practice specified by management:

> *I also used to be much more involved in students' activities such as the football team or the singing competition and it definitely had a positive impact on my relationship with them in the classroom. But considering the fact that there is very little rewards from the management side for our time spent outside the classroom with the students the majority of the teachers and including myself now do try to limit these extracurricular activities as much as possible.*

This example was a common theme. Extra-curricular activities that helped to facilitate interaction between staff, and staff and students ultimately became the first casualty when changes were made to the formal management of teaching. Increased teaching hours, timetable changes, increases in marking, and additional administrative responsibilities all negatively affected the level of socialisation through this medium. The absence of recognition or *reward* from management consolidated the view that despite the perceived benefits, extra-curricular socialisation was precisely that—extra.

Diversifying Actions

Socialising actions represent opportunities for interactive practice in a physical context. When considering the physicality of practice however, it is impossible to ignore technology-enabled mediums such as the Internet. Our findings suggest that recently social media applications such as WeChat (in China) have been essential in facilitating interaction between staff, and again between staff and students. We refer to these as "diversifying actions" in the sense that they alter and diversify the medium and scope for interaction.

> *Every class has its own WeChat group. They're all on it, and so am I. I use it to post reminders, links to interesting and relevant material and to discuss questions with students individually. They seem to feel more comfortable with that than coming to my office…I've also used it in class to get their attention. If I notice too many on their phone I send a message mid-lecture reminding them to pay attention. I know they will read it!*

Staff mentioned numerous examples of how social media was useful to help create classroom participation and engagement amongst students. This was an interesting finding as in our experience the use of mobile technology in classes was not openly encouraged. Staff also commented that being "connected" to other staff members made them feel more comfortable when lesson planning, or marking as this often took place at home or in offsite locations due to restricted suitable space on campus.

Exploring Practices

Teaching staff often showed evidence of practices that were largely explorative. In this sense, staff sought to extend and develop knowledge that existed within their network. The core aim here was to improve the students' learning experience, but also to improve assessment performance as this was often seen as performance measure by home institutions. Interestingly, "problem-recognition" followed by explorative practice was a common theme.

We identified two central activities that constituted explorative practice: (1) idea generation and (2) experimentation.

Idea Generation

> *chalk and talk, that's all you need in this job, chalk and talk, and dictation. That was another one. We had a 2-hour in-house training session that was supposed to show us how to be better teachers. Our teaching and learning director delivered the session. He hated technology. Chalk and talk. That's all we had to do to get the students through the exam… but what could we say? He was the expert. Nobody else in the room had the same qualification… many of us had other teaching qualifications but at our place the PGCHE made him the expert. We were told to follow.*

The above response highlighted several of the problems consistently identified through our other discussions. In-house training designed to advance teaching practice was often delivered by *experts*. Many had qualifications in the area, but had rarely refreshed and developed those qualifications for a number of years. The notion of *chalk and talk* and *dictation* was referred to several times in different forms.

There was also the problem of direction. TNE staff, both expatriate but especially local, often felt they had no choice but to follow the direction of the expert. In this sense, training ceased to be about reflective learning and more about establishing a uniformed process of delivery to standardise teaching, rather than improving standards of teaching. Respondents also mentioned how home institutions would often deliver in-house training across one or two days and sometimes conduct peer observations. In contradiction to the *chalk and talk* approach, training would encourage student-centred learning, creative delivery methods, engagement with online content and independent student research. This was however rarely reinforced by local management once the home institution had left. New practices and ideas would often take years to *trickle into existence*.

Legitimisation was another common problem. Many staff spoke of teaching qualifications from previous employers, having attended training courses, viewed material online or attended online workshops. Despite this if the qualification or training was not personally known by senior management, the knowledge lacked legitimacy.

> *I'm a lecturer in business, but I have a certificate and diploma in English language education (CELTA, DELTA). These are level 6 and level 7 teaching qualifications accredited by Cambridge but my institution doesn't recognize them as valid teaching qualifications.*

Despite some negative experiences, idea generation was derived from some formalised events, conferences, and teacher training sessions organised by TNE institutions.

> *[our] annual conference did include some topics about Transnational Education [that consisted of] talks delivered from academics at other local institutions… and [there was an expectation that] teachers within departments [would] share materials and ideas on an informal basis*

In addition to formal events, regular meetings between small groups of staff across departments were also fairly common:

Teachers are in teams and we discuss issues that we personally have with any aspect of the job. The teams are cross departmental in an effort to spread ideas as far as possible.

It was noted that this was a new type of activity and something which was considered unusual as, *usually in China, management only pay lip service to such things at best.* Questions of direction, control, expertise, and legitimacy inspired a range of organic responses from staff that we spoke with. Despite the lack of recognition of informal, free, and/or non-HE-specific qualifications, staff ultimately were passionate about creating an outstanding learning experience for their students. They also accepted a responsibility to disseminate knowledge from formal events amongst each other as a collective:

…at the end of the day, we all left 'chalk and talk 101' laughing. Really it said more about the people running these places than the standard of teaching… to get ideas I watch others, listen to others, and talk with other teachers. I download lectures from ITunesU and watch how people at the best Universities in the world deliver sessions.

The use of online content was particularly prominent, although it required access to a virtual private network (VPN). *Without them (a VPN), you are basically [relying] on China's intranet…almost nothing useful can be acquired without one.* The struggles relating to the Internet services in China seemed to be an obstacle for many:

Many UK institutions seem oblivious to the plight of people here in China. Particularly for students or staff needing to access journals and other online libraries. VPNs are sometimes too slow or unable to access such resources. I do not know what transnational education providers can do but raising awareness among them of this issue is important.

Despite this barrier, for those with access to a VPN, downloading sessions from various sites and watching how others taught was a major source of idea generation. This mimicked gains from watching colleagues from the TNE institution or home partner. Formalised activities also sparked idea generation, although not all staff were able to attend such events and so there was a collective understanding that those who attended would frame and disseminate understanding to other team members at a later date.

Experimenting

Experimentation refers to micro-level changes to teaching material, delivery, and support implemented by staff following a particular phase of idea generation. Many staff saw experimentation as a necessary activity given the unique nature of TNE provisions.

When considering academic guidance, out of class support and pastoral support, it was evident to staff that there were students who could benefit from extra support. Many of the institutions where our participants work insist that teachers have dedicated office hours available for such support. One of the TNE provisions insisted that all teachers had *two office hour sessions…. designated each week*; however, this did not seem to be helpful as *virtually no students ever showed up*. It seemed that *the vast majority of the students did not feel comfortable coming to [the] office to ask for help*. By way of contrast, the few students who did attend office hours would often monopolise the time allocation, and *most of the students that attended had exactly the same questions, it was like it was planned so they could compare and triangulate notes afterwards*. Additionally, students would request support through email, often at night, and *demand responses by the early morning*. Some teachers would therefore spend quite a large amount of time answering student emails. In order to try and provide the additional support, it is likely that there could have been cultural issues at play here as students in China often expect the teacher to initiate the discussions and students will speak only when invited to do so (Chang and Chin 1999).

In order to overcome this issue and ensure students received the additional support required, two teachers recalled how they worked together to set up a timetabled workshops in lieu of formal office hours. There would be two workshops of two hours each arranged and facilitated by both teachers. Although this technically doubled the time management specified to be available for office hours, the two staff concerned felt that this was a better use of time for student support. To their surprise, the sessions attracted about 11 students to each two-hour block, double the usual number of office hour attendees. Staff encouraged students to talk through their questions with each other, while the staff acted as mediators, and of course to provide insight if the group could not advance understanding themselves. These workshops provided a space where students could work on their own, or in groups, but with academic support on hand. *The workshops proved to be really popular with students bringing their textbooks and working on understanding the materials from the previous class, which then helped them for the upcoming classes.*

Experimenting in classrooms was not always easy as *the size of the classroom (70+ per lecture) and the time of the lectures (40 min all together as it would take a good 10 min for them to get ready to take notes and for me to do the attendance) was a real obstacle when trying to come up with more original and creative way to deliver knowledge.* However, using various e-learning materials such as ParticiPoll (audience polling for PowerPoint) was attempted *as a way to bring more interactivity within the classroom.* Due to *the lack of IT support [at the host institution] and the fact that there was insufficient Wi-Fi* this unfortunately had to be abandoned.

However, the use of other e-learning materials, such as video podcasts, was considered a great success as these could be streamed by students in their dormitories or downloaded to their mobile devices. *Students told me they really liked the video podcasts and they would like more.* The short videos would generally be a recap or overview of a particular topic and included audio and interactive diagrams, *one student even produced transcripts for the podcasts.*

> …*the podcast idea was something that came from the economics team. We would get the same questions over and over again, student after student. To try and make better use of time we used our experience of past cohorts to design 're-caps' on topics commonly found difficult. We then made a simple PPT and voice over. These usually lasted about 5–8 minutes. Students loved them, office hours became more about reviewing work, and discussing economic theories and application instead of recapping the basics.*

The use of technology and reorganisation of learning space and time by staff in the above examples happened organically, without the direction of management. Unfortunately, despite student feedback, management brought an end to the creation of podcasts, arguing that it was an unnecessary use of time with no clear measurable benefits. This led to staff reverting back to past practices, including usual office hours.

Other organic, experimental activities included gamification of in-class quizzes and formative assessment; field trips; outdoor team-building activities; creation of module booklets summarising key concepts, theories, and language support; non-subject-specific weekly podcasts on current affairs; culture evenings; language drop-in classes; film nights; and reading groups. These activities were not initiated by management; however, their longevity depended on the extent to which management saw them as worthwhile. Teaching experimentation occured frequently, often as a result of limited resources and absense of student support mechanisms available locally. Interestingly, respondents highlighted excessive micro-management, and *a need to make everyone teach the same way* even if this was not how teaching took place at home institutions.

Extracting Practices

The practice of extracting involves actions that enable staff to move across a range of different contexts to discover how available knowledge in one context can be used, combined, and re-defined in new ways. There is overlap here with the previous practice of exploring; however, this particular practice is specifically about discussing and appropriating knowledge so that it can be reframed in different contexts. Through our discussions, we found that this practice is deployed through two key types of actions: (1) discussing and (2) disseminating.

Discussing

Here the creativity of staff, how they express that personal creativity, and the extent to which they are inspired by other people's ideas and experiences help to shape teaching innovation through processes of modification and diversification.

Often, when working on a TNE provision, the teaching materials and/or the syllabus is provided by the UK institution, but it is down to the staff at the host institution to deliver the content. Often the content may have been suitable for a class in the UK, but the same class would require adaptation when being used in the host institution.

> …*delivering a new module would require quite a lot of work as the lectures were video based but needed to be condensed and adapted in order to fit our delivery format (45 min in China compared to 70-80 min in the UK).*

It is often not only the format that differs, but due to the context it is often necessary to *adapt the examples used* to allow for more global or perhaps country-specific comparisons to be drawn. Using more familiar, locally contextualized examples, such as the Shanghai Stock Exchange crash, can help to provide a deeper understanding of subjects.

Creativity and expertise were also required when delivering the materials to a monolingual group (Mandarin speakers) who are working in their second language (English).

> *Considering the 'mixed' level of English … quite a lot of work was also done in order to adapt the content and change the delivery. Most of this work was done on Sunday* afternoon, both at home and in the office.

Activities and assessments, which were considered suitable for the students in the UK, were often not playing to the strengths of the learners based in China. For example, a 60-minute reading task and then a written analysis would be a very difficult and much more time-consuming exercise for those working in their second language. As such the seminar was reorganised in three separate sequences emphasising different objectives: review (and reinforce knowledge) of the previous lecture, a small group research activity where the students were expected to produce a short presentation on their application of the day's learning outcome to any specific interest/country/events, followed by a short group presentation.

It was important that when participants talked about actions of discussion they were often contextualised in socialised and/or diversified contexts (see earlier section). There was therefore a clear link between the two actions which implies that for fruitful discussion to take place, socialising and diversifying practices need to be enabled.

Disseminating

To build idea acceptance and begin to formalise ideas amongst peers, a series of disseminating activities were identified, for example, staff-organised meetings; brief discussions in offices during lunch and break time; and impromptu meetings in photocopier rooms, corridors, and through social media. Peer-to-peer dissemination of ideas allowed participants to act as a sounding board or reflective agent.

Again the context was important. Informal social and diversifying contexts allowed discussion and dissemination of ideas; however, the latter tended to take place on campus over a much shorter period of time, and sometimes right before a class.

Following individualised changes to teaching materials and/or lesson plans, there were sometimes informal meetings arranged. *Every Thursday after my last seminar I would spend at least an hour reporting in detail to the collaborative course leader.* Both the *challenges and success met by the students during the week* were raised and any *adaptations ... made to the module guide* were also disseminated. This allowed an ongoing improvement plan to be in place and reflections could easily be considered and acted on if required.

> *I was fortunate enough to be in a team which made materials available to students incrementally throughout the year. We were also able to use the VLE as a way to provide MCQ progress tests, great for students as they could anonymously check their progress and understanding; and great for teachers as we could see overall scores and areas where student may require further assistance. Sadly, in my experience access to such contemporary software is not [always] possible and even worse, when it is available most teachers are not willing to try*

to learn how to use it and sadly I've found management to be unsupportive and in some cases hostile towards teachers trying to use it to benefit the learning environment.

In this above example, staff ability and willingness to engage in professional development played a crucial role in the extent to which knowledge was able to transform. The classic multiple choice test, through integration with technology, showed the potential be transformed into a support mechanism for student progress and reflection on learning. Unfortunately, the idea that *technology can inspire some and instil a fear of the unknown in others* was evident and ultimately significant in terms of the extent to which the technology was adopted, or allowed for the dissemination of knowledge and change in teaching practice.

Discussion

Our study has sought to shed light on the activities, sources, and applications of knowledge—or everyday practices—demonstrated by teaching staff at TNE institutions in China. The aim here has been to shift the unit of analysis away from the outcome of social phenomena and towards the practices of key actors—in this case teaching staff. We have done this to try and encourage fresh and alternative conceptualisations of the nature and effect of organisational and market innovation in the TNE environment. We hope that in doing so our findings and discussion can enable future research trajectories in the field, and also have positively impactful results for practitioners working in both the teaching and administration of TNE. Our contribution seeks not to be a prescription for future practice, nor a criticism of current trends.

Practice Field

Our study identified three key types of practices: integrating, exploring, and extracting. The practices of exploring and exploiting are interconnected, and often help to reveal opportunities and risks associated with routine teaching on a day-to-day basis. For example, they may help uncover a particular problem in assessment and delivery, or a trend, such as the use of social media to enable or support learning. These practices also help to develop ideas and experiments that help to modify existing practices, or "invent" new ways of delivery or types of teaching materials. These two practices are however shaped by the practice of interaction. Interaction enables the diversification and socialisation of staff interaction. Without this practice, it would be difficult for activities such as discussion, idea generation, and experimentation to take place. The social context in many cases acts as both a conduit for engagement and a lubricant to the nature of the exchange. The more informal the setting, the freer staff felt about sharing ideas, ambitions, examples of teaching practice, and so on. Likewise, the introduction of new technology and mobile applications created a new digital dimension that helped staff development, knowledge exchange, and more frequent interaction.

We have visualised this synergy as a "practice field" (see Fig. 9.1):

The practice field offers a simple visualisation of the interconnection between different practices. It is however important to understand in our performativity-inspired view of innovation, it is not the outcome of these

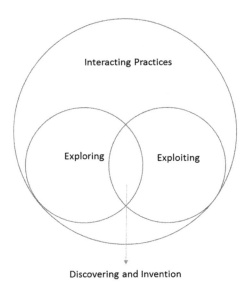

Fig. 9.1 Practice field of teaching in TNE institutions in China

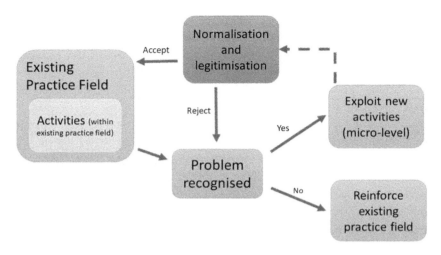

Fig. 9.2 Practice-based process model of innovation in teaching

practices that creates innovation, but the continual interaction between them. In this sense, innovation is a process performed, shaped, and changed by its constituent social, material, and technological actors (i.e. staff, technology, and culture).

Figure 9.2 offers our conceptualisation of how these practices interact and manifest at an organisational level. From our study, we have found that most efforts to initiate change or to alter a current practice stem from a form of problem recognition. This could be personal—that is, in terms of professional development—or institutional—that is, management interference or (limited) resource allocation. Whatever the particular issue, this acts as a driver for change.

Through the existing practice field, discussion, and socialisation, new ideas generated, and some experimentation or sampling may take place. The concentration, impact, and perceived success of these activities result in a decision as to whether the new incarceration of a particular activity is indeed suitable. If the problem subsides, or is not deemed resolved, staff often revert to original practices and their inherent activities. If, however, there is an element of success, the new activity is exploited and becomes a temporary new feature of teaching practice. Over time, these new activities normalise and invite attention. Evidence at internal conferences, management-directed emails, publication, and public endorsement all help to legitimise the activity formally; however, peer acceptance and use amongst peers also helps to normalise the activity. The combination of normalisation and legitimisation acts as the point of diffusion throughout the organisation. Rejection of the activity does not mean the end; however, it may be reformulated or altered. Acceptance through formal or informal channels results in it being re-absorbed into the existing practice field. This is a cyclical process; however, in our conceptualisation this process presents the nature of teaching innovation in TNE. Innovation ceases to be a product of management decision-making, and instead it is a composite outcome of staff members' practices and their interaction with other social, material, and technological actors.

Conclusion and Implications

The aim of this chapter has been to explore the day-to-day activities used by staff working in UK-led TNE in order to modify the teaching and learning practices to address localised concerns. We identified the existence of a practice field consisting of three interlinked practices: interacting, exploring, and extracting. As mentioned, the activities and practices discussed cannot be defined as "right" or "wrong". They simply exist. Collectively, it is the synergy of these practices that helps to realise teaching innovation. We feel this understanding contributes positively to TNE providers, policymakers, and education management to assist with better organisation, management, and practice of teaching in TNE.

Clearly social interaction enables staff to communicate, and develop and share ideas. This is something that is worth encouraging particularly for new staff who may not originate from the TNE institution's country of origin. At the same time, it seems obvious that providing staff with a formal platform to showcase, discuss, and be proud of their teaching may help develop certain activities further to the benefit of institutional morale and positive student experience.

Much of what we have discussed has been centred on the host element of the TNE partnership. There are also clear responsibilities for the home or awarding institution. Staff development opportunities and investment in local facilities and curriculum activation should be a shared responsibility. Teaching innovation is ultimately a co-created process involving multiple actors through a dynamic integration of resources and practices. Home and host institutions broadly represent this network, and thus have an equal role to play.

Finally, our study has drawn attention to the performative role of not only social but also material and technical devices. The role of technology, facilities, location, and cultural systems are significant agents of the overall teaching innovation process. This helps to diversify and expand integrative potential, disseminate ideas, support experimentation, and add real value from a learning perspective, without driving up costs for the TNE institution. Indeed, much of the technology referred to in our study is provided by the students themselves, or as a standard attribute of either/or both home and host institution. The key is to understand its importance and potential, rather than to see it as a distraction or worse.

It is not our aim to prescribe a toolkit of management practice from the above findings. We would hope that readers are able to draw conclusions from the interpretation of our work. The few points noted above represent our general feelings for the future development of teaching in TNE institutions. More broadly, the above findings may be transferable in part of a wider range of education institutions. We would encourage fellow scholars to pursue such avenues.

References

Altbach, P.G. and Knight, J. (2007) The internationalization of higher education: Motivations and realities. *Journal of Studies in International Education*, 11(3–4), 290–305.

Bourdieu, P. (1990) *The logic of practice*. Cambridge: Polity Press.

Chang, V. and Chin, K.L. (1999) Cultural issues in teaching and learning. *Journal of the Australian and New Zealand Student Services Association*, 14, 3–16.

Emirbayer, M. and Mische, A. (1998) What is agency? *American Journal of Sociology*, 103(4), 962–1023.

HE Global (2016) *The scale and scope of UK higher education transnational education*. Available at: http://heglobal.international.ac.uk/media/3780659/Scale-and-Scope-of-UK-HE-TNE-Report.pdf

Healey, N.M. (2015) Towards a risk-based typology for transnational education. *Higher Education*, 69(1), 1–18.

Knight, J. and McNamara, J. (2017) *Transnational education: A classification framework and data collection guidelines for International Programme and Provider Mobility (IPPM)*. British Council and DAAD. Available at: www.britishcouncil.org/sites/default/files/tne_classification_framework-final.pdf.

Mellors-Bourne, R., et al. (2014) The value of transnational education to the UK. Department for Business, Innovation and Skills. *BIS Research Paper 194*. Available at: www.gov.uk/government/uploads/system/uploads/attachment_data/file/387910/bis-14-1202-the-value-of-transnational-education-to-the-uk.pdf.

O'Mahony, J. (2014) Enhancing student learning and teacher development in transnational education. The Higher Education Academy. Available at: www.heacademy.ac.uk/system/files/resources/enhancingtne_final_080414.pdf.

QAA (2013a) Review of UK transnational education in China 2012: Overview, May.

QAA (2013b) Review of UK transnational education in China 2012. *Case studies: Setting and maintaining academic standards*, May.

Rothwell, R., & Zegveld, W. (1985). *Reindustrialization and technology*. ME Sharpe.

Schatzki, T., Knoor Cetina, K. and Von Savigny, E., eds. (2001) *The practice turn in contemporary theory*. New York: Routledge.

Schau, H. J., Muñiz, A. M., Jr., & Arnould, E. J. (2009). How brand community practices create value. *Journal of Marketing, 73*(5), 30–51.

Schumpeter, J.A. (1939) *Business cycles* (Vol. 1, pp. 161–174). New York: McGraw-Hill.

Yang, R. (2008) Transnational higher education in china: Contexts, characteristics and concerns. *Australian Journal of Education*, 52(3), 272–286. Available at: http://aed.sagepub.com/lookup/doi/10.1177/000494410805200305

10

Designing a Successful International Course: What Can We Learn from Students' Experiences on an Erasmus Intensive Programme?

Gill Richards, Simoni Symeonidou, and Eleni Livaniou

Introduction

The European Region Action Scheme for the Mobility of University Students (Erasmus) Programme is a well-established European scheme for university students, staff and institutions to exchange ideas and develop mutual respect for different cultures, languages and beliefs. The Programme was introduced in 1987 with the aim of increasing mobility within the European community, and through this, developing cooperation between higher education institutions to increase compatibility and quality of qualifications, and facilitate innovative practice (Zylkiewicz-Plonska 2013).

G. Richards (✉)
Nottingham Trent University, Nottingham, UK
e-mail: gill.richards@ntu.ac.uk

S. Symeonidou
University of Cyprus, Nicosia, Cyprus

E. Livaniou
Multidisciplinary Diagnostic, Research and Treatment Unit "Spyros Doxiadis", Athens, Greece

More recent developments produced the Erasmus+ Programme (2014–2020); the European Union programme for education, training, youth and sport that aims to change lives and open minds (Erasmus+ 2016). Although this programme has several new features, it continues to maintain the original focus of offering opportunities for over four million students and staff from over 125,000 organisations to study, train and gain work experience abroad, through strategic partnerships and alliances.

This chapter explores the experiences of a group of students who participated in an Erasmus Intensive Programme (EIP). It focuses on their views of learning in a transnational education context and the challenges they encountered. These perspectives are drawn upon to identify student-centred issues for universities to consider when planning and delivering international courses.

The "Erasmus" Context

Erasmus Programmes provide significant benefits for universities, students and societies (Ekti 2013). Universities are able to increase their international experience and respect within the academic community and in particular provide students with educational opportunities through a multi-cultural lens; a key aspect of global employability (Mellors-Bourne et al. 2015; Turkan 2013; Zylkiewicz-Plonska 2013; Mitchell 2012). Individual staff can learn from exchanging ideas with international colleagues and access new partners for research activity (Van Swet et al. 2013). Similarly, students also benefit from interacting with peers from other cultures who can introduce them to different ways of working and offer new friendships and networks. Where these benefits are achieved most successfully, Erasmus Programmes can contribute towards improvements in societies where transnational interactions reduce prejudice and attitudinal barriers (Ekti 2013; Yücelsin-Tas 2013; Kreber 2009).

Literature about Erasmus Programmes mostly emphasises the benefits for students. One recurring theme is the contribution of Erasmus exchanges to foreign language acquisition and increased self-confidence (Ekti 2013; Yücelsin-Tas 2013; Llanes et al. 2012). Another important benefit can be students' individual growth. Zylkiewicz-Plonska (2013) argued that students were able to build their individual identity and "expand" themselves through interacting with the ideas and values held by students from other countries. This personal development came from their acquisition of professional skills and wider skills (like self-reliance and self-awareness) that increased their capacity to participate in European societies and other new environments. A study by Mitchell (2012) also suggested that the importance of Erasmus Programmes went beyond learning about the host culture and language. She described them as "transformative" experiences for participants, where they developed their awareness of European countries, and through this gained a deeper understanding of "Europe", leading them to self-identify as "European" (2012: 493).

The UK HE International Unit/British Council's report on students' experiences of Erasmus Programmes (Mellors-Bourne et al. 2015) identified similar benefits to those described by other researchers, but claimed these were secondary to a principal motivation of seeking "interesting" experiences that broadened horizons and enhanced employability. This report also identified student priorities affecting participation, which included "the availability of funding and total cost of the experience, personal safety and security, reputation or perceived quality of host and location" (p. 5). Specific barriers to participation centred on concerns of isolation, insufficient funding and lack of language skills. Institutional support with applying for Erasmus Programmes was particularly valued by students from disadvantaged backgrounds. Interestingly, longer-term benefits were experienced irrespective of length of course, suggesting that it was the quality of the international experience that was important, rather than how long the activity took.

The Study Context

The research study presented in this chapter took place after the completion of an EIP on 'behaviour management' in Athens, Greece. An EIP is defined by the European Commission as "a short programme of study which brings together students and teaching staff from higher education institutions of at least three participating countries. It can last from ten continuous full days to six weeks of subject related work" (European Commission 2015a). All participating universities must hold an Erasmus University Charter and the students must be enrolled on a programme of study at one of the universities. EIPs are required to be innovative in design and content, and delivered through participatory learning experiences. Most focus on undergraduate student activity (European Commission 2015b), and although the European Commission apportions a significant share of its resources on approximately 250 IPs each year, there appears to be little research addressing their effect as a distinct phenomenon (James 2013). What differentiates IPs from other Erasmus exchanges is that students engage with a short intensive period of international learning, without extending their degree length. This key benefit of the programme is supported by the requirement for EIP participants to have access to joint social networks and online course learning rooms, thus offering opportunities for continuing contact outside of course attendance and establishing a "community of learners" beyond the course (James 2013: 81).

The uniqueness of EIPs can not only lead to innovative developments but also set distinct challenges. Successful cross-national courses need to take account of "the importance of the local, social, cultural and indeed political contexts" in which participants' practice takes place (Lloyd 2013: 332): genuine equal engagement can only happen where all participants are valued equally, engage proactively and share responsibility for their learning. This approach can raise tensions in a collaborative programme. Different institutions may be bound by their own ways of working, regulations and quality assurance procedures that affect student expectations and staff behaviour (Siska et al. 2013). Tutors in particular may be concerned about intellectual property rights to their academic work and question what limits should be placed on knowledge sharing, so overcoming such concerns requires a collaborative approach with an embedded trust of each other's institutional practices and academic professionalism. Students may be used to culturally specific expectations of their behaviour in learning situations and engagement etiquette with tutors. In EIPs where students are jointly taught by tutors from different institutional contexts (including sometimes, different disciplines), this may create stress as they struggle to cope with demands for new learning behaviours, in addition to acquiring new knowledge intensively presented in a less familiar language. Achieving all of this within the limited timeframe of an EIP requires an exceptionally co-operative approach by all participants, an approach that was fundamental to our own EIP success.

Our EIP involved 21 postgraduate students from universities based in the UK, Greece and Cyprus. It was a unique programme, even for an EIP, because it was delivered during a summer vacation with an additional (optional) qualification for all participants, a Postgraduate Certificate in Behaviour Management. This was awarded by the EIP UK host university, who was responsible for all assessment, some of which took place during the course, with the rest completed after students' return home. Teaching for the EIP took place in Athens, Greece, as it was the most accessible country for all students, with assignment support provided after the course through distance learning activities delivered by the UK host university.

The EIP evolved from previously successful working relationships. The UK university had delivered an MA in Special and Inclusive Education in Athens for several years in collaboration with one of the Greek university tutors. This provided links with other academics in Greece and Cyprus who specialised in Special and Inclusive Education and also had experience of working in both Greek and UK universities. Decisions about the course programme were made jointly during planning meetings in Greece and through email contact.

Selection of the student group was a key aspect of ensuring a successful outcome for our EIP. The language of the course was English, so students were required to demonstrate oral and written skills commensurate with postgraduate level study. All participants were studying on a range of MA or PhD courses in Special and Inclusive Education within their own institutions, either as full-time students or part-time while working full-time. They were mature students, most of whom had significant professional experience as school teachers. The course was delivered over 11 consecutive days during the summer vacation to enable working teachers and those already studying full-time to attend.

Selection of the course accommodation presented early challenges for our planning. Programme funding for this reflected the usual undergraduate participant group, where low-budget multiple-shared living accommodation was expected and teaching took place in university classrooms already allocated for the taught modules. Our EIP participants were mature students who did not necessarily know other attendees from their own university. They were not enthusiastic about sharing rooms with 'strangers', so the selection of living accommodation required significant research and negotiating skills with local small hotels to bring this within budget. We were unable to use the local partner university teaching accommodation due to constraints evolving from the Greek recession. Again, tutors' local links proved key to creating a partnership with an English Teaching School that had well-equipped classrooms available throughout the summer vacation.

The aim of the EIP course was to offer challenging insight into managing pupil behaviour through inclusive teaching and learning approaches. Each university within the partnership had its own stance on this, strongly influencing the students and tutors' viewpoints. This provided both challenge and opportunity for innovative teaching and learning activities. Two of the universities favoured a psychological perspective in understanding and managing children's behaviour, contrasting with the other two, who took a sociological view. Presenting both approaches enabled students to challenge their own understanding and synthesise aspects of each that were most appropriate for their professional needs. Tutors were careful to demonstrate respect for alternative viewpoints and model positive approaches to academic debate. The course activities were jointly designed by partnership tutors, who then delivered specialist topics in their usual university teaching style. This provided students with sessions that covered the latest subject knowledge through presentation styles which were familiar on occasions, but at other times placed new demands on them. Mindful of this, student groups were carefully organised for each session, requiring them to work in internationally mixed groups or with their home university peers, depending on the learning activities.

Methods

The research question guiding our study asked: "What are student experiences of learning and challenge on an international course?" This aimed to gain a rich, detailed understanding of our students' experiences of attending a unique EIP. The sample comprised all 21 students who had attended the EIP: six students were from Greek universities, five Greek-Cypriot students from a university in Cyprus, and ten students were from the UK university (five of whom were Greek nationals from the University's MA Special and Inclusive Education in Greece). Data were collected from semi-structured individual interviews after completion of the course and individual student coursework reflections on their learning experiences. In accordance with the ethical guidelines set by BERA (2011), students were not approached until after completion of the course to avoid engendering any perception of coercion. They gave informed consent to contribute to all aspects of the study and responses were anonymised, although where relevant, the country they came from was named.

The interviews were jointly designed and conducted by three EIP tutors in students' home language and then transcribed, where necessary, into English. They focused on three key aspects: (1) why students wanted to attend the EIP course, and their views before and after attending it; (2) students' experiences of the course and completing coursework; and (3) advice students would give to others considering attending a similar course. Further student perspectives were collated from analysing coursework which required a reflective account of their learning from the EIP. Cross-examination of data was used to identify themes that contributed towards planning and delivering a successful, student-centred international course.

Findings

Analysis of the findings from the interviews, coursework and student feedback on the EIP identified five main themes: (1) motivating factors for attending the EIP; (2) views about the EIP, before and after attending the course; (3) experiences of working with tutors and students from other countries; (4) experiences of learning from the EIP and course assessment; and (5) advice to other students.

Motivating Factors for Attending the EIP

All of the students stated that they had wanted to attend the EIP because of their interest in the course topic of 'Behaviour Management'. This is an area in which many teachers lack confidence, especially newly qualified teachers (Carter 2015; Mintz et al. 2015), while alternatively, more experienced teachers may wish to specialise in behaviour management. The EIP course offered an opportunity to develop skills and knowledge about managing pupil behaviour, irrespective of individual participants' experience and levels of confidence. It focused on inclusive approaches to behaviour management, a current priority for many schools with an increasingly diverse population, and of particular relevance for Greek teachers who were coping with many new problems created by the effects of the national recession. It was also of interest to the student group because the topic complemented their own university studies:

> *It was a unique chance to acquire knowledge from a different European university, it was important for my work.* (Greek student)

> *I wanted to attend because it was the behaviour side I was interested in. I'd done other SEN [special educational needs] modules and I want to be a SENCO [Special Educational Needs Co-ordinator], so it fitted with my career plans.* (UK student)

> *Challenging behaviour and bullying are important issues and we need to know how to deal with them. Since I am an educator, I thought it was important to receive training on this issue.* (Cypriot student)

Most of the students (18) also said that they were motivated by the opportunity to study with peers and tutors from other countries:

> *I attended the EIP in order to expand my knowledge and understanding on the subject. Also to be exposed to tutors from other countries and to advance my knowledge professionally.* (Greek student)

The primary reason was that I wanted to have the experience of other countries. I consider this a great challenge: meeting people from other countries and finding out what they think. (Cypriot student)

For the amazing experience of working alongside other countries—I wanted to open my eyes to the wider perspective of education and be able to get first-hand experience of discussing important parts of education and see it from another angle—from the mix of people taking the lectures and the mix of people giving the lectures. (UK student)

Several also described other individual motivating factors such as the opportunity to live away from home for a few days, work with like-minded people and cover topics not addressed on their own university course. Some of the Greek and Cypriot students specifically mentioned their interest in discovering more about UK education practice and developing their skills in English.

Views About the EIP, Before and After Attending the Course

Students had mixed feelings before embarking on the EIP. Pre-course activities had included tutors from each university organising meetings to enable their own students to get to know each other and the UK host university making regular direct contact with each student through online activities that prepared them for the EIP. These activities were described by some students as reassuring, although several were also anxious about attending the course for a wide range of personal reasons:

It's always nervous travelling to an unknown place … but our minds were put at rest and it was organised well. I was nervous personally that I wouldn't be able to keep up because of my dyslexia, but [tutor] supported me and made me feel comfortable and capable. (UK student)

I was nervous and felt rather apprehensive whether I could cope because I am not so fluent in English and didn't have any experience with foreign students. (Greek student)

A little apprehensive, also wary about the other students—would we understand each other, what will it be like? I was also excited. (UK student)

I was excited to meet new colleagues and professionals but nervous because it was an intensive course. (Greek student)

My big worry was the language … it was the first time I had visited another country not for holidays, but for work. Of course I was excited that I was going to meet people from other countries, but I was stressed because of the language. (Cypriot student)

Reflecting back on the course after completing it, student responses showed that any early concerns had been dispelled. They described the EIP as a *"fantastic"* and *"very positive"* experience, with several stating that it had exceeded their expectations and wished it could have been longer. They particularly commented on their enjoyment of "pacey" sessions, approaching topics from different disciplines and the mix of academic and social activities. One student who had been anxious about her level of English explained the effect the course had on her:

We were a good team, we became closer, we could talk over the breaks and at the hotel, we exchanged ideas. The most important thing for me was that I managed to speak, write and interact in English! At the beginning, I didn't think I would make it. It was a very positive experience and it was something that I will remember for a long time. (Greek student)

Experiences of Working with Tutors and Students from Other Countries

Tutors from each country shared the teaching and learning activities on the EIP course. They organised sessions based on their own subject and discipline specialisms, delivering these in their usual teaching style. This provided every student with new experiences of different discipline approaches to course topics and different tutor expectations of learning behaviour, which they found both *"inspiring"* and *"challenging"*. Students were positive about the new insights that they had gained from different tutors, especially where these were supported by practice-based examples from tutors' own discipline specific experiences. This, several explained, had challenged their thinking, especially where tutors had been open to discuss differences of opinion through respectful academic debate, despite an obvious passion for their own perspective. Some did struggle with teaching styles that were different to their usual experience:

It was a very challenging experience because we couldn't understand the way they wanted us to work. In the end however, everything worked OK. (Greek student)

I definitely had preferences about sessions. Some tutors were very much about us listening. Others were more 'hands on'—looking at case studies, discussing, getting stuck in. We [students] were all quite different. When we had to listen for a long time, we [UK group] got fidgety. The Greek students were used to it. (UK student)

It was interesting to see how different education systems formed people and the way they responded to tutors—we just called you [UK tutor] by your first name, but the others didn't do that. (UK student)

Session activities involved mainly group work, with students organised either in internationally mixed groups or with their own university peers. This approach was praised by all students, describing this as "*the best part of the course*" because it involved learning from shared experiences and had led to new friendships that were maintained after the course. Communication had proved difficult at times, especially at the start of the EIP, but this was resolved through induction activities and peer support:

At the beginning, you didn't know how you will behave and how you will speak. Slowly-slowly the ice broke. I remember we did the ice-breaking games at the beginning and they were helpful. Later we had to speak with people we didn't know in our groups. At the beginning, I was not sure if they understood what I said ... I talked with the students from the UK who were teachers. They had interesting ideas to share about how they work with parents. So, I liked the fact that they were experienced and I could learn from them. (Cypriot student)

I found it nice that they had different experiences to us, they had done different courses—theirs was more about theory and essays and ours was more about practice. Communication was difficult at times—they could understand us but … we didn't know any Greek. (UK student)

I feel that the tutors did their best to make us feel comfortable, to meet each other and break the ice. I admit that I did not feel comfortable right away because of my personality, but after we worked together, we became closer. We 'clicked' easily with the students from Greece because we share a similar culture. I felt uncomfortable to approach the students from England because of my insecurity with the English language I didn't have the opportunity to practice it in ten years. (Cypriot student)

I loved working in mixed groups but also having the 'comfort' of being able to sit next to people you knew, sometimes too. I admired how talented they [Greek and Cyprus students] were, speaking often more than two languages and felt it was kind of them to translate sometimes! It was fantastic hearing their experiences and views, and we could socially see each other out of lesson times. (UK student)

Experiences of Learning from the EIP and Course Assessment

All of the students spoke positively, about their learning from the EIP experience. This learning fell into two categories, subject knowledge that enhanced professional practice and new approaches to learning. Most of the students had studied 'behaviour' in previous university courses, but not in the depth provided on the EIP, nor from an 'inclusive' education perspective. This new knowledge had provided them with increased confidence and a deeper understanding of their own impact on classroom behaviour. The emphasis on developing critical thinking and challenging traditional perceptions about managing behaviour was also viewed as a key learning experience, with students commenting:

Through the EIP course, new insights and possibilities for better relationships with the students and a happier classroom have been opened up, which enriched and reinforced my 24-year teaching experience. In this way, I have already started self-reflecting, so as to better understand my personal beliefs, ideas and intentions. (Cypriot student)

I deepened my knowledge about the value of exchanging ideas and new experiences, as well as gaining new information. Therefore, the participation in this program made me more mindful, conscious and open-minded, in order to manage difficult behaviour more appropriately and effectively. (Greek student)

The EIP has led me to think in dramatically different ways about behaviour management. Being critical and honest in my reflections of the role I play in behavioural issues will be a significant consideration in my future teaching career. (UK student)

This Erasmus Intensive Programme has had a profound impact on my professional development. As it bridged the worlds of education from England, Cyprus and Greece in order to understand behavioural issues and respond to them, I have come to listen and respect all different perspectives. (Greek student)

Observing academics discussing issues modelled constructive debates and encouraged me to be critical about my own views. (Cypriot student)

Assessment for the EIP's Postgraduate Certificate in Behaviour Management included presentations, essays, seminar papers and an individually selected study of behaviour. Two presentations were completed during the EIP and students found these manageable because time was given within course sessions to work on these. Other assignment tasks were completed after the EIP, with students receiving support from their own university tutors and formative feedback given on draft work by the UK university lead tutor.

Students from Greece and Cyprus were unfamiliar with the UK university's style of postgraduate assessment, finding the explicit assignment briefs and assessment criteria, alongside expectations of independent study, to be both stimulating and challenging:

At first it seemed very difficult, mainly because it was very different in style from which I was used to in my own university … nevertheless, the experience was positive, the assessment criteria were transparent and the feedback was on time. (Greek student)

The fact that we had the criteria in advance and had feedback was important. (Cypriot student)

> *This type of assessment gave me ideas to improve assessment in my own work with students.* (Cypriot student)

> *It was very difficult and exhausting experience and also very demanding. I would have liked more specific assignments.* (Greek student)

Several found the expectation to be 'critical' difficult and were wary of being seen to 'criticise' tutors' views or published authors' perspectives. Accessible tutor support was praised, especially in providing formative feedback on draft work. The flexible submission of assignments after the EIP was also seen positively, as this enabled students to manage this in conjunction with their own university coursework and work commitments.

Advice to Other Students

All of the students strongly recommended that other students should attend an international course, describing it as "*a fantastic opportunity*", "*a must for any educationalist!*" and a "*fruitful experience which would improve them as professionals as well as persons*". Their advice demonstrated the impact of very individual "journeys" that included social as well as educational experiences:

> *Don't be held back by fears of language barriers, not understanding different systems. Have a genuine interest, don't go for a holiday!* (UK student)

> *To have a personal goal as to why you are attending, relevant to yourself and above all, to your own students.* (Greek student)

> *Language is a barrier you can overcome. You learn new things, meet people from other cultures … it's good to get out of your shell.* (Cypriot student)

> *Take all the opportunities you can when you are there. I managed to tick something off my 'bucket list' (watching an opera outside) and it was a memory I'll never forget.* (UK student)

Be yourselves and express your opinions. Maintain contacts with students from other countries. (Cypriot student)

One newly qualified UK teacher explained that the timing of the EIP was important, that it was "*such a nice way to go into your start of teaching. Great timing after university and something to talk about in school, sharing anecdotes. If I was teaching and just had a difficult year in school, I'd be thinking 'can I cope with it and lose my holidays?'*". This reflected our original concerns when deciding to hold the EIP during a summer vacation to maximise attendance from students who either had term-time course commitments at their own universities or were teaching in schools.

Lessons Learned

Analysis of students' responses indicated clearly that they had embraced the Erasmus aims of using the EIP experience to exchange ideas with peers from other countries and through this develop mutual respect for different ways of working. They had gained new friendships and made professional networks that continued after the completion of the EIP. Their primary motivation for attending the course was the subject topic, which either complemented their current university studies or provided insight into something they considered lacking from previous courses. Most students were also motivated by the opportunity to learn from an international experience, with some Greek and Cypriot participants specifically identifying the importance of improving their English skills.

With this level of motivation, it was perhaps surprising that so many mature and experienced students had felt really anxious before attending the EIP. Most had been concerned about factors that any traveller might have expressed about travelling to a new place and using a less familiar language, despite competing feelings of excitement for a new challenge. They were worried about coping with language differences, the intensive mode of study, working with strangers, being young inexperienced teachers and requiring support for additional learning needs. These responses highlight the importance of knowing students well, because their individual concerns can escalate when they are removed from familiar support networks. Several students mentioned that the pre-course activities and induction had helped them overcome their initial feelings of anxiety. These had been carefully selected to model the 'inclusive' course topic ethos and respect for the maturity of the participant group. One activity contributed effectively to this. Students were asked at the end of each day to use two sets of coloured post-it notes to identify "What worked well today" and "What didn't work so well/this concerned me", and leave them on a desk. These were reviewed by the tutors, who then made adjustments, if necessary, to plans for the following day. This enabled an immediate response to matters of concern and maintenance of what was working well. It also provided tutors with the opportunity to reflect on their own practice and develop this in response to international differences in learning experiences (Daniels 2013; Van Swet et al. 2013).

Despite this daily development of the course, students still found the experience "challenging" as well as "inspiring". While 'challenge' should be an integral part of postgraduate study, tutors were mindful of the impact of too many challenges within an IP taught in a language that for most students was not their first language. The subject matter and learning activities were intended to be stimulating, in accordance with the primary aims of EIPs. This was achieved by alternating sessions delivered by tutors from different disciplines and countries, so students experienced a daily mix of teaching and learning that was familiar and new.

Some students struggled with the different demands made on them during sessions because of previous experiences in their own universities. Generally, Greek students were more comfortable listening to a lecture, wishing to glean every detail presented by a tutor. The UK students preferred a more interactive approach with activities where they had to seek their own answers and could question tutors' ideas. This led to anxiety: Greek students were unsure of exhibiting behaviour that might be seen to be criticising and disrespectful, while UK students were uncertain of how their questioning might be received during a lecture-style session. Individual tutor's attempts to reassure the group had some success, but this situation was returned to on several occasions, especially to support students produce the critically reflective assignments required for postgraduate assessment. These student concerns mirrored to some extent the wider issues of behaviour management studied on the course. Enabling the group to reflect critically on their own individual values about behaviour led to students identifying that a key learning experience had been how to become more critical about their own views and how this impacted on their professional practice (Armstrong 2013; Keogh and Russel-Roberts 2009).

Students enjoyed working in internationally mixed groups and learning from each other's practice. This was enhanced by spending time together in social activities, organised by course tutors or themselves. The maturity of the group contributed to this, as most had significant prior experience of coping in new academic and professional situations. They were at ease spending evenings in restaurants taking leisurely meals or arranging visits to cultural events. The first evening in Greece, prior to the course start, was spent in internationally mixed group induction activities which culminated in a meal at a local restaurant. This established an early ethos of intermixing, that students used as a platform for further social networking, moving them beyond superficial relationships (Robson 2014; Bilecen 2013).

Students found the demands of completing EIP coursework in addition to their own university course commitments, challenging. They reported that completing two presentation assignments during the EIP was difficult, but also recognised that this experience of the UK university's assessment regime gave them confidence to complete the rest of the assignments after the course. Several of the Greek and Cypriot students found the expectation of independent study challenging, especially when they could select their own assignment topics to meet the assessment outcomes. Some struggled with this, stating that they would have preferred specific assignment titles, but others enjoyed the freedom to focus on individual interests. They all appreciated the detailed assignment briefs and assessment criteria, and the opportunity to receive formative feedback on draft work, with some expressing an intention to replicate this style of working with their own pupils in school.

Whatever the challenges and initial anxieties, all of the students stated that they would advise peers to take up a similar opportunity. They gave many positive reasons for this, identifying the benefits for professional and personal development. In particular, they argued that a fear of language barriers should not prevent participation on an international course, giving examples of how sessions delivered in a less familiar language were supported by tutors and native speakers. The intensity of an EIP was acknowledged by several students, who were clear that these courses were for professional and academic development, not a holiday. Most also identified benefits from the EIP's social aspects; meeting new people, exchanging ideas and using this opportunity to attain personal goals. This concurs with Llane et al.'s study (2012) where individual differences were found to be more important than group differences, reinforcing the impact of individual variables as an important factor to consider when analysing international learning experiences.

Conclusions

Findings from this study identified factors that had motivated participation in the EIP and learning from it. Despite the EIP offering a different experience to other types of international study, there were several transferable elements that students viewed as key to achieving a successful course. Irrespective of age, experience and current level of study, participants had similar experiences to other researched groups. What differed in this study was the 'intensive programme' context, which intensified anxieties and created pressure to manage student development within the course at a faster rate. This situation exacerbated some situations that would normally have taken longer to surface and involve longer term strategies to resolve. It did however offer a micro-focus on student well-being and learning experiences which can serve as a platform for future international course development.

References

Armstrong, C. (2013) Collaboration, partnerships and alliances: Perspectives on Erasmus Mundus MA/Magistri in special educational needs. *International Journal of Inclusive Education*, 17(4), 364–376.

BERA (2011) *Ethical guidelines for educational research.* London: BERA.

Bilecen, B. (2013) Negotiating differences: Cosmopolitan experiences of international doctoral students. *Compare: A Journal of Comparative and International Education,* 43(5), 667–688.

Carter, A. (2015) *Carter review of Initial Teacher Training (ITT).* Manchester: DfE

Daniels, J. (2013) Internationalisation, higher education and educators' perceptions of their practices. *Teaching in Higher Education,* 18(3), 236–248.

Ekti, M. (2013) An evaluation regarding to the gains of Erasmus program in terms of language and science. *Procedia—Social and Behavioral Sciences,* 70, 1800–1809.

Erasmus+ (2016) *Erasmus plus programme.* Available at: www.erasmus.org.uk

European Commission (2015a) Supporting education and training in Europe and beyond. Available at: www.ec.europa.eu/education/erasmus/doc900 en.htm. Last accessed 8 June 2016.

European Commission (2015b) *Erasmus facts, figures and trends.* Available at: www.ec.europa.eu/erasmusplus. Last accessed 14 September 2016.

James, C. (2013) Problems encountered by students who went abroad as part of the Erasmus programme and suggestions for solutions. *Journal of Instructional Psychology,* 40(1), 81–87.

Keogh, J. and Russel-Roberts, E. (2009) Exchange programmes and student mobility: Meeting student's expectations or an expensive holiday? *Nurse Education Today,* 29, 108–116.

Kreber, C. (2009) Different perspectives on internationalisation in higher education. *New Directions for Teaching and Learning,* 118, 1–14

Llanes, A., Tragant, E. and Serrano, R. (2012) The role of individual differences in a study abroad experience: The case of Erasmus students. *International Journal of Multilingualism,* 9(3), 318–342.

Lloyd, C. (2013) The Erasmus Mundus programme: Providing opportunities to develop better understanding about inclusion and inclusive practice through an international collaborative programme of study. *International Journal of Inclusive Education,* 17(4), 329–335.

Mellors-Bourne, R., Jones, E., Lawton, W. and Woodfield, S. (2015) *Student perspectives on going international.* London: UK HE International Unit and British Council. Available at: www.britishcouncil.org/sites/default/files/iu_bc_outwd_mblty_student_perception_sept_15.pdf.

Mintz, J., Mulholland, M. and Peacey, N. (2015) *Towards a new reality for teacher education for SEND. DfE SEND in ITT project report and roadmap for SEND.* London: UCL Institute of Education.

Mitchell, K. (2012) Student mobility and European identity: Erasmus study as a civic experience? *Journal of Contemporary European Research*, 8(4), 490–518.

Robson, S. (2014) Internationalization: A transformative agenda for higher education? *Teachers and Teaching: Theory and Practice*, 17(6), 619–630.

Siska, J., van Swet, J., Pather, S. and Rose, D. (2013) From vision to reality: Managing tensions in the development and implementation of an international collaborative partnership programme for institutional change and sustainable development in inclusive education. *International Journal of Inclusive Education*, 17(4), 336–348.

Turkan, Y. (2013) Problems encountered by students who went abroad as part of the Erasmus programme and suggestions of solutions. *Journal of Instructional Psychology*, 40(1–4), 81–87.

Van Swet, J., Brown, K. and Tedla, P. (2013) Learning together: An international master programme in inclusive education, *International Journal of Inclusive Education*, 17(4), 377–392.

Yücelsin-Tas, Y. (2013) Problems encountered by students who went abroad as part of the Erasmus programme and suggestions for solutions. *Journal of Instructional Psychology*, 40(1–4), 81–87.

Zylkiewicz-Plonska (2013) The importance of socio-cultural context of learning, specificity of working with culturally diverse groups of students. *TILTAI*, 3, 103–113

11

Images of Student Experiences on Social Media: The Case of International Branch Campuses in Dubai

Ummesalma Mujtaba Husein

One of the central purposes of higher education is student development (SD). This chapter will assess how far SD remains the drive of transnational education (TNE), via analysing the elements of student experiences (SE) influencing SD at international branch campuses (IBC) in the UAE. The underlying notion is that occurrence of experiences of any kind during a student's term at a higher education institution provides an indication towards SD. For this purpose, instances of SE are gathered as demonstrated and brandished on social media, as it is the place to discuss experiences today. And in a competitive environment offers the easy probability of connecting existing and potential customers (Kang et al. 2007). The methodology adapted to sieve information is generalizable and findings are intended to provide useful information to institutional managers, who can in turn identify elements of SE to be posted on social media such that would reflect on the branch campus's reputation for SD.

U. Mujtaba Husein (✉)
University of Birmingham, Dubai, United Arab Emirates

© The Author(s) 2018
V. Tsiligiris, W. Lawton (eds.), *Exporting Transnational Education*,
https://doi.org/10.1007/978-3-319-74739-2_11

The chapter is structured as follows. First, the concept of SD is discussed. This is followed by an elaboration on the seven dimensions of SE that impact SD. Each of the seven dimensions were discussed for key branch campuses in the UAE, for this purpose their official facebook accounts were studied.

Seven Dimensions of Student Experience

SD can be possible only if students involve themselves in educational practices. Astin (1984) defines student involvement as physical and psychological energy that the student devotes to the academic experience. Rodgers (1990) defined SD as 'the ways that a student grows, progresses, or increases his or her developmental capacities because of enrolment in an institution of higher education' (p. 27). Walker (2008) posited that SD was less like a dynamic body and more like a conceptual and theoretical foundation which forms the basis for collaborating efforts and envisaging a better comprehension with students in college. He further added that SD implementation aims at providing every possible facility and service which may foster student's progress and growth. This chapter will make use of Wilkins et al. (2012) and Ahmad's (2015) study, who consider seven primary aspects, to present the determinants of students' perceptions of quality and experience of study at IBC as part of overall SD:

1. Learning resources (LR)
2. Programme effectiveness (PE)
3. The quality of lecturers and teaching (QLT)
4. Student learning environment (SLE)
5. Use of technology (UoT)
6. Assessment and feedback (A&F)
7. Facilities and qualities of social life (FQSL)

The next section familiarizes readers with the conceptual understanding of the seven dimensions.

LR

Researchers proclaim that for effective learning, students should be sincerely involved with attractive and challenging learning sources (Daradoumis et al. 2013). Maloney et al. (2013) stated that along with many substantial resources present in educational institutes, there is a broader resource, that is, Web-based learning, which provides a wider scope of knowledge. Web-based learning makes it simpler for students as it allows easy access, storage, and instant retrieval of data. The material can be stored in a variety of formats and easily shared across diverse user groups. Internet-based learning is continuously supplementing and substituting the hard copy LR (Cook et al. 2008). Students not only learn but seem to enjoy and incorporate this source of active learning.

McBurnie and Pollock (2000) identify that resources (such as library, laboratory, IT, and classroom facilities), academic staff, administrative staff, and systems may be areas of potential inadequacy when creating a resource base in other locations, that is, branch campuses. A decade later, Wilkins (2010) underlines that in the wake of significant increases in supply and competition in the internationalized scenario in UAE, branch campus institutions should also invest more in their physical and human resources. He emphasizes the point as students will increasingly expect to have learning, social, and cultural experiences that are closer to that of the parent campus.

PE

The usefulness of a taught programme is simply a two-stage process, inclusive of the knowledge gained from the content delivered and its future utility. Within the specific context of IBC, PE encompasses the belief that local employers would eventually prefer graduates of an IBC over other local institutions or the feel of certainty that an international education and a foreign qualification will better prepare graduates for a career in the international labour market (Zimitat 2008). With reference to this facet, scholarly debate tends to comprise of localizing the curriculum and therefore the associated PE (Hughes 2011), and the one-sided thought of simply studying a programme due to its affiliation to an international name (Pyvis and Chapman 2004).

QLT

The earlier days of the lecture format of teaching do not successfully deliver the learning objectives as it is a passive intake of the information already available to the students. Teaching approaches have undergone a tremendous change of late, encouraging and promoting student motivation, autonomy, and overall development (Fernandes et al. 2012).

Teacher-centred approach or surface delivery approach is a traditional phenomenon which needs to be actively replaced with student-centred approach or active learning approaches which promote critical thinking approach along with problem-solving and independent learning (O'Neill and McMahon 2005). Due to such transformational shift in the pedagogy approaches and the introduction of new diverse methods of teaching, the need to eliminate the traditional approaches of teaching is emerging (Moulding 2010; Meyer and Land 2005).

Quality teaching promotes the application of knowledge in a way that provides equitable access and opportunities that build upon learners' present knowledge and extends facilitating the ability to acquire, construct, and create new knowledge (Hollins 2011).

Within the context of IBCs, the value of lecturers and subsequently their delivery is deliberated under varied themes. On the one side, there is this simplistic debate on what quality teaching entails; however, from the internationalized perspective the deliberations bring new discussions. Some examples of these discussions include themes such as; the employment of local staff from the existing expatriate workforce (Wilkins et al. 2012) the relatively high proportions of locally contracted part-time teaching staff (Mujtaba 2007) and its implications on the quality of teaching. Much of this seems to be out of scope of this chapter; nonetheless, it forms an interesting debate to consider whilst deliberating on the issue of QLT at IBC.

SLE

In *Learning Reconsidered 2*, Borrego (2006) propounds that the 'entire campus is a learning community' (p. 11). Borrego significantly pointed out that professors and academic resources alone are not responsible for underpinning student's learning but each component of educational surrounding/circle supplements for a firm student learning foundation. Studies also point out at collaborative assignments as a greater openness towards diversity (Cabrera et al. 2002) and growth in personal development (Umbach and Wawrzynski 2005). One of the effective learning approaches is STEM. STEM education is an interdisciplinary approach to learning where rigorous academic concepts are coupled with real-world lessons as students apply science, technology, engineering, and mathematics in contexts that make connections between school, community, work, and the global enterprise enabling the development of STEM literacy and with it the ability to compete in the new economy (Tsupros 2009).

In the context of IBC, the SLE is to a considerable extent linked to the QLT. Gopal (2011) argues that to be able to provide an equitable educational environment for students, it is the lecturers who need to be prepared to teach in a cross-cultural, globally diverse setting. Additionally, it is straightforward to envisage that a fruitful SLE should encourage critical discussions regarding beliefs, and cross-cultural teaching should take place during professional development seminars. Furthermore, student's involvement in local academic and industry competitions is also seen to be of added value to SLE.

UoT

Henrie et al. (2015) mention that UoT-mediated learning experiences has become a common source and means of learning for students today. Numerous one-to-one tablet and laptop initiatives are promoted by schools and governments around the world.

HOTL or high-order technological learning is a gaining and scoring process where learning and growth of students are promoted through the application of communication and information technologies. HOTL, which may also be called as technology-enhanced learning (TEL), adds to the wider scope of education by practicing and interacting with the perspectives which happen to exist in an individual's surroundings.

Whilst deliberating the UoT in branch campuses, the significant advancement of educational technologies becomes clear and relevant. The development of technology has borne its fruits and has led to the subsequent ease in coordinating operations associated with TNE and allowing institutions to effortlessly synchronize operations in different countries (Ziguras 2001).

Branch campuses are expected to utilize a range of technology facilities both in-class and in form of dedicated web emails, access to university e-libraries, and adequate subscription to academic journals.

A&F

Assessment is a systematic process for making inferences about the learning and development of students (Swan et al. 2006). Feedback is defined as 'specific information about the comparison between a student's observed performance and a standard, given with the intent to improve the student's performance' (Van de Ridder et al. 2008: 193). Bergh et al. (2014) clarify this standard as something which is contrived in the learning goals which students should be knowing so that they can figure out how the gap between learning goals and their current performance could be bridged. Also to bridge this gap, it is mandatory that students be directed, motivated, and rightly led to achieve better comprehension and improve performance.

According to Bergh et al. (2014), various studies on feedback highlight the unfortunate fact that learning goals (standards) and feedback are not given much importance due to which metacognitive processes of a student are not enhanced. Since feedback can be a very powerful tool for enhancing student learning (Hattie 2009), it is important that teachers give their students qualitatively valuable feedback. Therefore, teachers should guide students with constructive feedback on how to improve and perform better to attain the set standards, that is, learning goals. This feedback activity could make learning easy and result in positive learning outcomes.

Within TNE, assessment moderation is treated under quality assurance (Coleman 2003) and the scholarly debate surrounds issues of comparability and consistency with the parent campus. Wallace et al. (2010) note the views of staff who felt strongly that curriculum and assessment should be identical to ensure that there was equity between students and that standards could more visibly be assured. In the same vein, some critics have warned that requiring IBCs to conform to the curriculum and assessment requirements of the home campus leads to a stifling degree of homogenization (Egege and Kutieleh 2009; Liston 1998)

Additional matters under discussion have been identified by Dobos (2011), who notes the issue of control and subsequently identifies that assessment and moderation are two tasks strictly controlled by the parent university and counterpart staff at branch campuses whine the inability of any major structural change to the assessment tasks.

FQSL

Studies show that campus climate, student-centredness, campus social life, and institutional effectiveness are strong factors to impact upon the SE (Elliott and Healy 2001; Wilkins et al. 2012; Ahmad 2015). According to Çelik and Akyol (2015), the extracurricular activities which are said to improve the FQSF are widely beneficial; for example, it promotes experiences of competency, creativity and self-expression, self-improvement, self-fulfilment, and personal meaning. Haines (2010) submitted that campus recreation centres now aimed to attract diligent students as this is viewed as an essential element to provide better programmes, services, facilities, and equipment to the campus community.

Gibson (2010) also confirmed that the quality of campus services affects student satisfaction. Consequently, literature also suggests that FQSF at campus should be valued and successfully designed to improve SE and satisfaction.

Padlee et al. (2010) underline that facilities or infrastructure dimensions are among the potential dimensions of choices of criteria, with special reference to the environment surrounding students such as campus life, campus design, and social life whilst deciding on an IBC.

Having understood what each of these dimensions signifies, we would now like to locate these dimensions within the social media (specifically official Facebook pages) of a selection of four IBC in Dubai. The natural question that could arise here is why mind social media? And straightforwardly the response is expressed in the data collected and clear message therein.

People spend more than one third of their waking day consuming social media (Lang 2010). It is not an uncommon sight to find social media used by both individuals and organizations equally to share their experiences. For organizations in a competitive environment today, social media offers the easy probability of connecting existing and potential customers. The wide adoption of social media tools has generated a wealth of textual data, which contain hidden knowledge for businesses to leverage for a competitive edge. There are varied tools available that are used for text mining to help organizations stay abreast on how to drive potential customers via using positive experiences of existing customers. In the context of this case, the right portrayal of SD via positive SE ought to initiate the potential student's intention to study with the IBC.

For the sake of this study, the official Facebook pages of several branch campuses in the UAE were studied. The decision to explore Facebook rests with its undeniable popularity, as of March 2017, Facebook has 1.94 billion monthly active users. This style of research may be largely categorized as a netnographic study and is conducted to signpost the power of web-based content. Readers must be guided here that institutions may not even be consciously releasing and posting the content to emphasize SD. Such a study can inform decision makers to make informed strategic and operational decisions. Lau et al. (2005) make an interesting note that competitive intelligence can help organizations to realize strengths and weaknesses, enhance business effectiveness, and improve customer satisfaction. Hence the exercise: 'whether student experience as portrayed on social media indicative of student development?', can assist IBC to appreciate their fortes, understand their feebleness in areas that are underrepresented (it may be the case that the aspect under represented is merely not embodied in the right fashion and simply requires accentuation in its presence). Nonetheless, the exercise is a useful one.

The following section will reproduce instances of actual content from official Facebook pages of few branch campuses in the UAE. The content is selected based on ongoing activities during the academic year. This criterion was particularly needed to ensure that current SE is captured, as opposed to marketing activities outside academic year that are specifically designed to attract potential students.

UK branch campus 1: A
UK branch campus 2: B
Indian branch campus: C
American branch campus: D

LR

LR seems to be an area of concern for potential students; all the three branch campuses sieved contained queries from 'students to be'. For example:

<B>*hello everyone, just want to know more about the mechanical engineering program, is there any problem with the staff, the program, etc. Do the professors teach well, and is the **lab well-equipped with materials** and is there **enough research**, etc., please let me know and thanks*

Samples of posts related to LR on Facebook pages of the under-study IBCs.

<A> *The Centre of Innovation & Excellence at <A> links industry and academia to advance education, research, corporate training and outreach in key areas.*

<C> *Advantage 700,000 Sq. ft Campus*
<C> *World-Class Infrastructure*
<C> *High-tech Laboratories*
<C> *Video postings of 'ground breaking ceremonies'*
<D> *Video postings illustrating resources and university's history including parent campus information.*

<D> Preparing to study abroad at <University's name> This blog post could come in handy—it'll help you to navigate the campus and give you the history behind some of RIT's most well-known buildings.

Branch campuses from the UK, the USA, and India showcase the role of facilities in building the SE and hence prove the associated link to SD as poised by McBurnie and Pollock (2000) and Wilkins (2010). All branch campuses apart from <B> tend to include posts with explicit information on LR. It is interesting that in reality <B> is housed in a purpose-built campus and can make use of existing facilities to represent SE.

PE

Samples of posts related to PE on Facebook pages

<A> The Department of Computer Engineering and Informatics at <A> Dubai covers computer technology and includes system design, programming concepts, application development for modern web and mobile systems, network design and management and skills to apply this learning to real-world problems. Find out how you can study with us this September: <Webpage link>.

<A> Careers and Employability Service has launched a Summer Internship Programme for all current students. Find out more:<Webpage link>.

<B> With advances in technology and the move towards omni-channel retailing globally and in the UAE, there is an increasing importance placed on the logistics and supply chain efficiency aspect of organizations. Learn more about our <Programme Title> and improve your employment opportunities!: <Webpage link>.

<B> is the only university in the UAE to offer maximum exemptions from <Professional qualification> Find out more about our program and choose from our September or January intakes. Enquire today! <Webpage link>.

<D> We're delighted to have recently signed an Memorandum of Understanding with Smart Dubai's Dubai Data Establishment to develop a Master's program specializing in <Programme Name>. As one of the first of its kind in the world, the program will teach students how to use big data to innovate new ways to live, learn and do business <Webpage link>.

From the social media content analysis, it is evident that UK and US branch campuses are explicit about usefulness of their taught offerings. There are unambiguous particulars on the programme, its affiliations, and its further utility from careers perspective. One of the branch campuses prides in its Careers and Employability Services, emphasizing that the programme taught yields tangible results in form of future job prospects. The Indian branch campus,<C> however, does not detail the programme expediency. It is evident that <C>'s Facebook presence is unable to illustrate PE and this would imply that those relying on Facebook page would have an information gap.

QLT

<A> *The curricula for the disciplines offered in <Programme name>, are informed by cutting-edge research and are developed and delivered by scholars and teachers who have engaged in strong synergies and enjoy world class reputations. Understanding the underpinning sociological, socio-economic, legal and socio-political realities within society, is crucial to engaging, diagnosing and improving society. Find out more: <Webpage link>.*

<A> *<teacher's name and designation>, publishes his research on Swarm Robotics. <Webpage link>*

<A> *<teacher's name and designation> speaks to Gulf Marketing Review about Blogging being a real threat to traditional advertising.*

<D> *Congratulations to <teacher's name and designation>, whose article on "modelling coupled conduction-convection ice formation on a horizontal axially finned and un-finned tubes" has been accepted for publication by ASME (American Society of Mechanical Engineers)'s Journal of Fluids Engineering.*

<D> *It might be summer and fairly quiet around campus, but our faculty and students are still busy around the world. Here's <teacher's name and designation>, at the 3rd International Conference on Mechanics of Composites (MECHCOMP3) hosted by School of Engineering and Architecture, University of Bologna, Italy. His paper on 'Strain Rate effects on Sandwich Panel's Core Shear properties via Beam Flexure' was well received.*

One of the UK branch campuses <B> and the Indian branch campus <C> do not illustrate any material on the QLT. Hence, they provide a vague picture of staff competitiveness. For a potential student, this could very well raise question marks, as to whether, full-time staff, research active staff is employed by their university of choice.

SLE

<A> *student research is one of the cornerstones of our academic community. Many of our students have excelled at research including winning numerous national and international research awards and presenting at academic conferences. Find out more:<Webpage link>*

<A> *Dubai student <name of the student is advertised> gains first place in the Management Category at the Fifth Annual Undergraduate Student Research Competition. Congratulations <name of the student is advertised>*

<A> *<name of the student is advertised> wins first prize at the Sci-Fi Dubai Science Fiction Writing Competition!*

<A> *<names of the students are advertised> attended the Persuasive Communication for the Workplace, 4-Day workshop led by Cornell University at SAE Dubai. The workshop is designed to sharpen the soft skills valued by employers combined with an online, self-paced Career Progression Series designed to set the participant apart for potential employers.*

<B> *We're very happy to announce the completion of our joint project with <Organization's name. Great work by our Architectural Engineering students! <Webpage link>.*

<B> *We are proud to announce that our students, <names of the students is advertised>, have won 1st and 2nd prizes in the 5th UAE undergraduate research competition and the UAE ICE Emerging engineers award! Congrats to both on all their hard work.*

<C> *Hear the experts take on the challenges and opportunities in the Islamic Economy on <date> from 4pm onwards.*

<C> *Videos and posters of conferences held on campus*

<C> *<Name of the club> (Aerospace Engineering) Students in Hamburg, Germany for an industrial visit.*

<C> hosts a competition for young engineers of UAE with 'Robotech and Technoscience'.
<C> Civil Engineering won Second position at <Name of local university competition>s Tower Crane Competition.
<D>Speakers from <Organization's name>, shared their knowledge of trading with BS Finance students at the university recently. Media Coverage: <Webpage link>.
<D> A big congratulations <University's name> MS Service Leadership & Innovation <Student's name> for winning the Fikra award for Youth Engagement from <Organization's name>.

Interestingly, one of the most vibrant entries for all four branch campuses was found in demonstrating the scope of SLE. Posts included industry and academic competitions alike. Winners' names and pictures were put up, depicting active student participation and student involvement at the campus.

UoT

<C> Livestreaming conferences held on campus
<D> Videos uploaded of seminars held at the campus

Although it is common knowledge that all branch campuses offer some sort of a virtual learning platform, the Facebook pages did not reflect 'use of technology' to be of any significance. Students generally use these platforms to check their emails. Nonetheless advanced systems allow students to view recorded lectures, post their work, and engage in discussion groups. However, the Facebook page entries only provided livestreaming of conference activities and videos uploaded of previous events and that too of only two IBCs.

A&F

Although the heart of studying is being assessed, more so the fact that A&F is related to 'quality assurance'—the most significant aspect of TNE—it was inauspicious to observe that none of the branch campuses under study posted even subtle mention related to assessments. And certainly, it stood out to be an area that was utterly ignored. Since feedback follows assessments, it was only natural to have no reference to feedback.

Nonetheless, coming from the same industry, the author fully appreciates that both elements are well addressed by most IBCs. And just like A&F forms the backbone of any higher education system, it does for IBCs in Dubai.

Facilities and Qualities of Social Life (FQSF)

Team <A> offer a variety of non-sporting social clubs including Dance Club, Debate Club, Music Club and Photography Club…find out more, <Webpage link>.

Team <A> Football is excelling in its game, consistently winning competitions and performing in leagues outside of the University. Find out more: <Webpage link>.

<A> Transportation is a fundamental part of the student experience and we understand getting from your home to campus is a priority for many of our students. Find out more about the transportation services we offer: <Webpage link>.

<B> 2 days and counting! Join us on campus this <Event day and date> for activities, competitions and much, much more!

<C> Indoor and Outdoor Sports facilities (Explicated via posters)

<C> Videos depicting the social life.

<C> Celebrating Halloween's at the exciting new campus!

<D> Our Student Government just don't stop putting on great events for <University Name> Dubai Tigers! Want to know more about what's going on? Be sure to check out their Facebook page<link to university's webpage>

<D> GO TIGERS! Our team recently took home the bronze medal during this year's <Competition's name>. Just look at them go!

On the one hand, quality of social life is overwhelmingly well depicted within Facebook posts of all branch campuses, aligning well with the general usage of Facebook which is a medium used to share fun updates and achievements. And, on the other hand, facilities are not well-represented by at-least one UK branch campus that potentially could use more photographic illustration as used by the other competitors.

Lessons Learnt

It is evident from the above that there is an opportunity for all IBCs to evaluate their social media postings against the SE criteria. For IBCs, it is of utmost significance to understand that SE is the value-added component that a student anticipates receiving on enrolling in a particular institution. And institutions that focus on the wholesome SE strengthen the concept of higher education institutions as establishments that are diligently work towards SD (Mujtaba 2012: 154).

Results from the evaluation above indicate an utter lack of mention related to assessment. Nonetheless, examination dates, related preparations, the assessment process, and finally the results and feedback are a happening part of a student's study life. It also has a substantial impact on how a student shapes his/her future. It is common knowledge that some essential information of these processes resides on the institution's official webpage. Nonetheless, it is equally important to have some facts available on the formal social media outlets; as a matter of fact, it is prudent to synchronize activities on various official social media platforms to offer a

Table 11.1 Evaluating the seven dimensions

Dimensions of student experience that impact student development	UK university branch campus <A>	UK university branch campus <B>	Indian university branch campus <C>	American university branch campus <D>	
LR	✓		✓	✓	3
PE	✓	✓		✓	3
QLT	✓			✓	2
SLE	✓	✓	✓	✓	4
UoT			✓	✓	2
A&F					0
Facilities and qualities of social life	✓	✓	✓	✓	4
Total score	5	3	4	6	

homogenous message to those browsing the web. This is of utmost significance as new applicants look for overall SE.

On a final note: as relatively non-experts in the field, one can still appreciate the notion that depth of information will differ on all different platforms. Twitter will only allow a few words worth of information, Snapchat will encourage stories, institution's official webpage is a jungle of information, and our oldie Facebook will offer a mix of all.

References

Ahmad, S.Z. (2015) Evaluating student satisfaction of quality at international branch campuses. *Assessment & Evaluation in Higher Education*, 40(4), 488–507.

Astin, A.W. (1984) Student involvement: A developmental theory for higher education. *Journal of College Student Personnel*, 25(4), 297–308.

Cabrera, A.F., Nora, A., Crissman, J.L. and Terenzini, P.T. (2002) Collaborative learning: Its impact on college students' development and diversity. *Journal of College Student Development*, 43(1), 20.

Çelik, A.K. and Akyol, K. (2015) Predicting student satisfaction with an emphasis on campus recreational sports and cultural facilities in a Turkish university. *International Education Studies*, 8(4), 7.

Coleman, D. (2003) Quality assurance in transnational education. *Journal of Studies in International Education*, 7, 354–378.

Cook, D.A., Levinson, A.J., Garside, S., Dupras, D.M., Erwin, P.J. and Montori, V.M. (2008) Internet-based learning in the health professions: A meta-analysis. *JAMA*, 300(10), 1181–1196.

Daradoumis, T., Bassi, R., Xhafa, F. and Caballé, S. (2013, October) A review on massive e-learning (MOOC) design, delivery and assessment. In *2013 Eighth International Conference on P2P, Parallel, Grid, Cloud and Internet Computing (3PGCIC)* (pp. 208–213). IEEE.

Dobos, K. (2011) "Serving two masters"—Academics' perspectives on working at an offshore campus in Malaysia. *Educational Review*, 63(1), 19–35.

Egege, S. and Kutieleh, S. (2009) Dimming down difference. In L. Dunn and M. Wallace (eds.) *Teaching in transnational higher education: Enhancing learning for offshore international students* (pp. 67–76). London, UK: Routledge.

Elliott, K.M. and Healy, M.A. (2001) Key factors influencing student satisfaction related to recruitment and retention. *Journal of Marketing for Higher Education*, 10(4), 1–11.

Fernandes, S., Flores, M.A. and Lima, R.M. (2012) Students' views of assessment in project-led engineering education: Findings from a case study in Portugal. *Assessment & Evaluation in Higher Education*, 37(2), 163–178.

Gibson, A. (2010) Measuring business student satisfaction: A review and summary of the major predictors. *Journal of Higher Education Policy and Management*, 32(3), 251–259.

Gopal, A. (2011) Internationalization of higher education: Preparing faculty to teach cross-culturally. *International Journal of Teaching and Learning in Higher Education*, 23(3), 373–381.

Haines, D.J. (2010) The campus recreation assessment model. *Recreational Sports Journal*, 34(2), 130–137.

Hattie, J. (2009) *Visible learning: A synthesis of over 800 meta-analyses relating to achievement.* London, UK: Routledge.

Henrie, C.R., Halverson, L.R. and Graham, C.R. (2015) Measuring student engagement in technology-mediated learning: A review. *Computers & Education*, 90, 36–53.

Hollins, E.R. (2011) Teacher preparation for quality teaching. *Journal of Teacher Education*, 62(4), 395–407. Available at: https://newsroom.fb.com/company-info/. Last accessed 7 July 2017.

Hughes, R. (2011) Strategies for managing and leading an academic staff in multiple countries. *New Directions for Higher Education*, 2011(155), 19–28.

Kang, I, Lee, K.C., Lee, S. and Choi, J. (2007) Investigation of online community voluntary behaviour using cognitive map. *Computers in Human Behavior*, 23, 111–126.

Lang, B. (2010, September 20) Ipsos OTX study: People spend more than half their day consuming media. Available at: http://www.thewrap.com/node/21005

Lau, K., Lee, K. and Ho, Y. (2005) Text mining for the hotel industry. *Cornell Hotel and Restaurant Administration Quarterly*, 46(3), 344–362.

Liston, C. (1998) Effects of transnational tertiary education on students: Proposing an assessment model. Available at: http://www.aair.org.au/app/webroot/media/pdf/AAIR%20Fora/Forum1998/Liston.pdf

Maloney, S., Storr, M., Paynter, S., Morgan, P. and Ilic, D. (2013) Investigating the efficacy of practical skill teaching: A pilot-study comparing three educational methods. *Advances in Health Sciences Education*, 18(1), 71–80.

McBurnie, G. and Pollock, A. (2000) Opportunity and risk in transnational education—Issues in planning for international campus development: An Australian perspective. *Higher Education in Europe*, 25(3), 333–343.

Meyer, J.H. and Land, R. (2005) Threshold concepts and troublesome knowledge (2): Epistemological considerations and a conceptual framework for teaching and learning. *Higher Education*, 49(3), 373–388.

Moulding, N.T. (2010) Intelligent design: Student perceptions of teaching and learning in large social work classes. *Higher Education Research & Development*, 29(2), 151–165.

Mujtaba, U. (2007) Part-time faculty training and development. Paper presented at the *Middle East Forum for Academic Research and Reflection*, GETEX, Dubai, UAE.

Mujtaba, U. (2012) Higher education management and operational research. In G. Bell, J. Warwick and P. Galbraith (Eds.), *Enhancing the student experience: Setting up the student experience unit*. The Netherlands: Sense Publishers, pp. 153–166.

Padlee, S.F., Kamaruddin, A.R. and Baharun, R. (2010) International students' choice behavior for higher education at Malaysian private universities. *International Journal of Marketing Studies*, 2(2), 202.

Pyvis, D. and Chapman, A. (2004) *Student experiences of offshore higher education: Issues for quality*. Australian Universities' Quality Agency Occasional Publication. Melbourne: AUQA.

Swan, K., Shen, J. and Hiltz, S.R. (2006) Assessment and collaboration in online learning. *Journal of Asynchronous Learning Networks*, 10(1), 45–62.

Tsupros (2009). STEM: Defying a simple definition. [Blog] *NSTA News*. Available at: http://www.nsta.org/publications/news/story.aspx?id=59305. Last accessed 26 July 2017.

Umbach, P.D. and Wawrzynski, M.R. (2005) Faculty do matter: The role of college faculty in student learning and engagement. *Research in Higher Education*, 46(2), 153–184.

Van de Ridder, J.M., Stokking, K.M., McGaghie, W.C. and Ten Cate, O.T.J. (2008) What is feedback in clinical education? *Medical Education*, 42(2), 189–197.

Van den Bergh, L., Ros, A. and Beijaard, D. (2014) Improving teacher feedback during active learning: Effects of a professional development program. *American Educational Research Journal*, 51(4), 772–809.

Walker, M. (2008) Working with college students & student development theory primer. Available from University of North Carolina Wilmington Student Affairs Professional Development Committee: http://uncw.edustudentaffairs/pdc/documents/StudentDevelopmentTheorybyM.Walker.pdf

Wallace, M., Mahmud, S., Sanderson, G., Yeo, S., Briguglio, C. and Hukam-Singh, P. (2010) Moderation of assessment in transnational higher education. In *IEEA 2010* (pp. 1–11). Australian International Education Conference 2010.

Wilkins, S. (2010) Higher education in the United Arab Emirates: An analysis of the outcomes of significant increases in supply and competition. *Journal of Higher Education Policy and Management*, 32(4), 389–400.

Wilkins, S., Stephens Balakrishnan, M. and Huisman, J. (2012) Student satisfaction and student perceptions of quality at international branch campuses in the United Arab Emirates. *Journal of Higher Education Policy and Management*, 34(5), 543–556.

Ziguras, C. (2001) Educational technology in transnational higher education in South East Asia: The cultural politics of flexible learning. *Educational Technology & Society*, 4(4), 8–18.

Zimitat, C. (2008) Student perceptions of the internationalisation of the undergraduate curriculum. In L. Dunn and M. Wallace (eds.) *Teaching in transnational higher education: Enhancing learning for offshore international students*. New York: Routledge.

12

The Future of TNE

William Lawton and Vangelis Tsiligiris

In summer 2017, the British Council published a research report entitled "The Shape of Global Higher Education" that measured and compared governmental support for international mobility, transnational education (TNE) and international research collaboration. It noted that there was, within countries, "a strong positive relationship" between having supportive policies for international student mobility and for TNE, and suggested that this is in part because student mobility "is an integral part of many types of TNE" (Ilieva et al. 2017: 25).

This seemingly simple statement on the relationship between TNE and mobility shows the extent to which TNE has been reconceptualised in very recent years. In fact, much of the activities that institutions now call TNE are outside its traditional definition: education leading to a

---

W. Lawton (✉)
Higher Education Consultant, London, UK

V. Tsiligiris
Nottingham Trent University, Nottingham, UK
e-mail: vangelis.tsiligiris@ntu.ac.uk

© The Author(s) 2018
V. Tsiligiris, W. Lawton (eds.), *Exporting Transnational Education*,
https://doi.org/10.1007/978-3-319-74739-2_12

degree that is delivered in a country other than the country in which the awarding institution is based.

The traditional concept of TNE refers to programme mobility rather than person mobility. TNE in this sense has been brought into operation within institutions as a strategic alternative to international student recruitment—that is, an alternative to person mobility. At institutional level, this has been, therefore, consistent with the development of TNE export precisely as a hedge against volatility in international student recruitment markets.

TNE has been a rational response to such risk—and it remains so today. At the time of writing (September 2017), onshore recruitment of international students to the UK is stagnant but TNE is experiencing a boom. In fact, TNE growth was five times greater than international student recruitment to the UK in 2014–15 (HEGlobal 2016; see also Chap. 8). The downturn in inward mobility was a consequence of two factors identified in the Introduction: the rise of new players in the global higher education (HE) market and the UK government's political decision in 2012 to stem the number of incoming students. Brexit is a further self-imposed reason for the slowdown in recruitment.

But there is a problem—one that is frequently alluded to at TNE seminars and conferences. It is that the traditional concept of TNE implies a "neo-colonialist" mindset. This was discussed briefly in Chap. 4. The essence of this mindset is twofold: first, that degree provision developed over a long period of time in one location can be transplanted and reproduced in another; and second, that the principle behind the traditional definition is mercantilist and unidirectional: we produce, they consume.

This export-led approach to international HE remains an enduring part of the UK mindset, but many within the HE sector at least are aware that it is no longer consistent with the aspirations of prospective partners in other countries. The UK government's view of HE internationalisation, however, remains firmly instrumental and mercantilist. This is illustrated by the arbitrary targets for export revenue placed by the government upon the sector. The most recent target, articulated in 2015, was earnings of £30 billion by 2020 (Government of UK 2015). This is not what the "importing countries" want to hear, but their perceptions and aspirations are evidently not a concern.

From One-Way to Partnership Models

Some TNE delivery models do fit well into the traditional import/export definition, with one-way programme provision and no student mobility. Distance learning delivered online to students in other countries represents more than half of UK TNE in terms of student numbers, and is mostly one-sided. The same goes for franchising and validation, in which an exporting institution's programme is delivered by a partner institution overseas for a series of fees (franchising) or in which an exporting institution awards a degree for a programme designed largely by the overseas partner (validation). Given that these are also large delivery modes in terms of student numbers, export-led TNE remains dominant.

Chapter 5 discussed the dynamics of managing the relationship between home and branch campuses. The evolution of international branch campuses is interesting. They appear to epitomise the traditional definition of one-way programme mobility but there are as many different models as there are campuses. As has been argued elsewhere (e.g., Hiles 2016), the "take-it-or leave-it" neo-colonial picture is really no longer accurate: UK branch campuses are increasingly integrated into local environments and many have local partners (they are often required to).

Two big developments in branch campuses illustrate the departure from the export-led programme mobility concept. The first is inter-campus mobility programmes: Nottingham and Heriot-Watt universities, for example, have well-developed programmes for their students to transfer freely between campuses in the UK, China, Dubai and Malaysia, and this includes mobility back to the UK. In a similar vein, New York University insists that there is no hierarchy of home-versus-satellite operations across its integrated network of three full campuses and 11 other sites around the world. This network-type model of TNE could be considered as a precursor of what Hawawini (2016) defines as the "metanational institution"—that is, an open and fluid network of campuses that has no home-campus bias (Hawawini 2016). Overall, we observe bidirectional person mobility, and less hierarchical organisational structures are quickly becoming part of the branch campus collaborative offer.

The second development, which takes years to come to fruition, is the implementation of distinct research agendas relevant to the host countries and regions—the University of Nottingham's Centres for Islamic Finance and Tropical Environmental Studies in Malaysia are good examples. On a similar line, the American campuses at Qatar Education City, such as Texas A&M, have developed collaborative research on water reclamation and solar energy with local industry and with Qatar University itself.

Branch campuses are prestige projects for exporting universities and the governments of importing countries, and they consequently receive more media attention than their relatively modest student numbers warrant (see also Brexit, below). But the gradual trend in TNE is towards explicitly partnership models that include student mobility. These include articulation (or progression or pathway) arrangements, by which students typically do a foundation course with a partner institution abroad and progress to degree study in, for example, the UK. A report for Higher Education Funding Council for England in 2014 found that 34% of international students arriving in the UK did so via an articulation programme—and much higher percentages of students from China and Malaysia in particular (Ilieva 2014). On a practical level, it is becoming increasingly difficult to distinguish between "at home" and "abroad" provision—this observation is developed below.

But the most egalitarian partnership model for TNE is that of international dual degree programmes. In Chap. 4, it was pointed out that such programmes—many of which are at postgraduate level—are marginal in terms of both student numbers and income generated (data from HEGlobal 2016). It is very likely that online delivery (with or without local partners) and franchising and validation will continue to dominate TNE delivery at undergraduate level and in terms of overall student numbers.

Even so, the direction of travel matters. A British Council TNE project in Thailand that commenced in 2015 drove home the point strongly that the future of TNE—for research-intensive universities especially—will be built on equal international partnerships. The priorities of the participating Thai universities were, and continue to be, dual degrees (including at postgraduate level), student and staff mobility in both directions, and developing existing research expertise and new research collaborations (Lawton 2016).

Their prioritising of mobility as a core rationale for TNE challenges our traditional definition of TNE, but the recent British Council report mentioned above ("The Shape of Global Higher Education") demonstrates that our thinking is already changing. Although the Thai Ministry of Education is a very recent (in 2017) convert to the presumed benefits of enticing foreign universities to establish campuses in Thailand, Thai universities see TNE as part of a wider international partnerships strategy. They do not want to "import" anything and do not see foreign involvement primarily as a matter of "capacity-building"—they believe they are past that stage of development. Chapters 2 and 3 demonstrate, incidentally, that this collaborative view of TNE is much closer in ideal to the non-commercial and institutional partnership approach assumed by the German and Dutch governments from the start.

Brexit and TNE

There is currently (2017) little respite from the Brexit debate in the UK and this concluding chapter offers none either. The Brexit vote in 2016 was strongly but unsuccessfully opposed by the UK university sector. The debate and its aftermath triggered media excitement over how the sector would respond; perhaps predictably, this focused on the possibility of new UK campuses on the continent as a means of securing continued access to both EU students and EU research funding.

Europe has historically been more important to the more research-intensive universities in the UK. Sixty per cent of the UK's internationally co-authored papers are with EU partners, and German and UK researchers co-author more papers with each other than with any other country except the USA. In 2015, TU Dresden alone had 132 research projects with 57 UK universities (and 15 more under negotiation).

But the teaching-led universities that compete with each other for international students have tended to look *beyond* Europe to the bigger student markets in Asia—although this historical distinction is changing.

UK TNE in Europe involved about 75,000 students in 2015–16—about a tenth of the worldwide total for UK TNE. Most is delivered by a partner or by distance education, and there are only a handful of UK campuses in the EU (including Middlesex in Malta, Central Lancashire in Cyprus, Sheffield in Thessaloniki—and University of London in Paris, depending on the definition used).

The Brexit-led speculation was that a campus presence in Europe would both offset the recruitment risk once free movement of people was terminated, as well as facilitate access to funding from the European Research Council and Horizon 2020.

But branch campuses are not part of the internationalisation strategies of most universities; in this case, leaders at universities such as Manchester said they did not see the value or logic of a European campus. Branch campuses may work best where there is under-capacity in HE, and UK campuses would be competing in markets where quality is generally high and tuition is free or subsidised. Perhaps the risk to recruitment was overestimated because thousands of EU students come to England already and take out substantial student loans when they can study at home for free. In the event, the decline in recruitment from other EU countries for autumn 2017 entry was about 4%—less than feared.

For many UK universities, the biggest threats posed by Brexit are to the maintenance of collaborative research links with Europe and to the ability to attract top researchers from the continent. The UK government may wish to have the "associated country" status of non-EU members such as Switzerland, Norway and Turkey in order to participate fully in EU research programmes. But the European Commission might see that as incompatible with the ending of free movement of people. A clear implication of Brexit, for which there is already anecdotal evidence, is the exclusion of UK scholars from big collaborative research bids.

In regard to TNE, perhaps a more rational concern is the manner in which Brexit will impact on *existing* UK TNE provision in the rest of Europe. This includes consideration of cross-border degree recognition. In Greece, for example, where the UK has a substantial amount of franchised and validated TNE provision, the government defied EU directives for years and did not effectively recognise any TNE qualifications until 2015. Brexit means the potential loss of the EU legislative protective net for TNE students and local providers.

Conclusions

As HE provision internationalises and traditionally importing countries develop their own capacity, it can be asked whether TNE is an idea whose time has already come and gone. The answer depends on what exactly is meant by TNE. The example from Thailand suggests at least that when a HE sector reaches a certain level of maturity, the producer-consumer model of TNE is inconsistent with their institutional and national aspirations.

TNE models are evolving in conjunction with this development of capacity in education-importing countries. The direction of travel is towards bidirectional partnerships with mutual benefits for all parties. As the HE sectors of countries that import HE develop and mature, it seems inevitable that, at both governmental and institutional levels, they will seek bidirectional partnerships with universities in the traditionally exporting countries. In an echo of the Uppsala internationalisation business model for companies (Johanson and Vahlne 1977), this might be seen as an entirely predictable trajectory for the internationalisation of HE: from domestic provision, to export-led, then franchising, and finally mutuality.

The preferred partnership models require that academic ownership must consequently shift to them. Students in the traditionally importing countries have more options to choose from and competition between foreign and domestic providers can increase (Tsiligiris 2014). The current situation in Qatar shows also that initial competition can give way to collaboration. TNE providers seek to develop differentiating attributes for comparative advantage but in all cases these must demonstrate relevance to the host environment—not least through establishing research and skills links with local industry and institutions.

As the provision of TNE matures, the boundaries between at-home and offshore provision blur. The amalgamation or convergence of TNE with traditional at-home activities is exemplified by the increasing difficulty to develop a fixed definition for TNE that captures the full range of existing activities.

It would appear in fact that the future of TNE is secure. It remains a work in progress. Its continuing expansion follows from the adaptability of its business models, the expectation that global demand for HE will continue to grow and on the risks inherent in international student recruitment—or even the perception of those risks. Predictions that the growth of TNE would be greater in student numbers than the growth of international student mobility have been borne out over the past few years.

There will be a mass market for HE globally for the foreseeable future. Where mass HE exists, technology-assisted education is the norm and it provides the scale. Online and distance learning is a growth industry from Latin America to North Africa. In South Asia, it is taking hold, slowly.

Online education is expanding as a preferred model of TNE for most Western universities. Fifty-two per cent of UK TNE is delivered through distance or online learning, and more than 80% of these students are with the Open University and University of London International Programmes. Top research universities in the UK offer fully online versions of their master's degrees—using very different models but often at the same price as the campus version. For all the unrealised hype attached to MOOCs (massive open online courses), one of their undisputable effects was to raise the profile of online HE and to legitimise it in the eyes of students, universities and governments. Online provision can be cost-effective and it is a delivery mode that carries relatively low reputational risk because control of academic quality and operations is maintained.

At the same time, it appears that blended learning is becoming the "new normal". For example, 70% of University of London International Programmes TNE students are undergraduates and almost all of them have a blended option through which partner institutions worldwide provide either full-time or part-time provision face-to-face. Some German universities such as the Free University of Berlin also offer blended master's degrees. In the Netherlands, as we saw in Chap. 3, online learning is characterised as a supplement to the traditional face-to-face forms of HE and learning.

Franchising and validation are also relatively easy modes of delivery for institutions prepared to invest in monitoring and overcoming the potential reputational risks posed by local partners.

However, one-way producer-consumer relationships are increasingly seen as insufficient and unsustainable by importing countries. Sending your students abroad, receiving a very few students from other countries, and importing HE through TNE are not a pathway to realising the goals of developing quality HE at home, with excellence in research and relevance to regional, national and local economies. Instead, the models of TNE that interest like-minded and research-driven prospective international partners are egalitarian in formal structure, even if the partner institutions occupy vastly different pegs on the international reputation hierarchies. For example, double degrees at master's and doctoral levels, with student mobility in both directions and the promise of research collaboration, meet these strategic requirements. This "mutual mobility" model of TNE is seen as qualitatively distinct from the programme mobility model and is increasingly preferred by major TNE importing countries.

TNE has been a driving force behind emerging forms of global HE delivery. A very nascent one is the use of virtual reality technology that facilitates synchronous online delivery so that the physical locations of providers and students become irrelevant. At the bricks and mortar level, TNE was the genesis and driving force behind the evolving transition from the campus model to the "metanational" university.

The relevance of TNE is apparent and its value to prospective partners is shifting. Traditional views are being challenged and new ones adopted. TNE as a delivery mechanism for education and as a subject of research in its own right deserves consideration and discussion. This book has demonstrated some distinct approaches and programmes and highlighted key thematic concerns within the theory and practice of TNE. TNE is no silver bullet to educational reform and success. It is increasingly delivered within distinct contexts and being leveraged accordingly. The balance of power is shifting towards the "receiving" countries. The understanding of opportunities and challenges changes also.

References

Government of UK (2015). International higher education, speech by Jo Johnson, Minister of State for Universities and Science, 15 June 2015. Available at: www.gov.uk/government/speeches/international-higher-education

Hawawini, G. (2016) *The internationalization of higher education and business schools*. Springer. Available at: www.springer.com/gp/book/9789811017551

HEGlobal (2016) *The scale and scope of UK higher education transnational education*. UK Higher Education International Unit and British Council, June 2016. Available at: www.britishcouncil.org/sites/default/files/scale-and-scope-of-uk-he-tne-report.pdf

Hiles, R. (2016) The rise of TNE: If you can't import students, export degrees instead. *Wonkhe blog*, 12 October 2016. Available at: http://wonkhe.com/blogs/analysis-rise-of-tne-cant-import-students-export-degrees

Ilieva, J. (2014) Directions of travel: Transnational pathways into English higher education. *HEFCE Report*, 27 November 2014. Available at: www.hefce.ac.uk/pubs/year/2014/201429/

Ilieva, J., Killingley, P., Tsiligiris, V. and Peak, M. (2017) The shape of global higher education: International mobility of students, research and education provision, Vol. 2, *British Council Report*, July 2017. Available at: www.britishcouncil.org/sites/default/files/h002_transnational_education_tne_ihe_report_final_web_2.pdf

Johanson, J. and Vahlne, J.-E. (1977) The internationalization process of the firm—A model of knowledge development and increasing foreign market commitments. *Journal of International Business Studies*, 8(1), 23–32.

Lawton, W. (2016) Lessons from Thailand: Conceptualising TNE. *HEGlobal blog*, 3 February 2016. Available at: www.universitiesuk.ac.uk/International/heglobal/Pages/Lessons_from_Thailand_Conceptualising_TNE.aspx

Tsiligiris, V. (2014) *Transnational education vs international student mobility: Substitutes or distinct markets?* Observatory on Borderless Higher Education. Available at: www.obhe.ac.uk/documents/view_details?id=952 (available for purchase and to OBHE members)

Index[1]

A

Academic freedom, 24, 29, 35, 39, 40
Academic imperialism, 46
Accountability, 90, 97, 100–101
Actor-network-theory (ANT), 151
Arab Network for Quality Assurance in Higher Education (ANQAHE), 135, 137
Articulation, 34, 220
ASEAN Student Mobility Forum, 74
Asian Pacific Quality Network (APQN), 135, 137
Assessment and Feedback (A&F), 198, 202–203, 209–211
Association of Dutch Universities (VSNU), 30–32
Australia, 1, 74, 145n5
Australian Tertiary Education Quality and Standards Agency (TEQSA), 135, 145n5

B

Bachelor, 15, 29
Behaviour management, 179, 184, 189, 193
Bidirectional partnerships, 223
Branch campus, 6, 11, 29, 35, 40, 91, 113, 130, 145n5, 197–199, 202–211, 219, 220, 222
Brexit, 2, 6, 218, 220–222
British Council, 11, 71, 72, 74, 92, 93, 156, 179, 217, 220, 221

C

Caribbean, 134
China, 1–3, 13, 15, 29, 91, 112, 132, 134, 145n5, 154–157, 161, 164, 165, 168, 170, 171, 219, 220

---

[1] Note: Page numbers followed by 'n' refer to notes.

Index

Chinese-German College for Postgraduate Studies (CDHK), 15, 17
Chinese-German Technology College (CDTF), 15
Chinese-German University of Applied Sciences (CDHAW), 15
Code of conduct for German Higher Education Projects abroad, 24
Collaborative, 11, 22, 24, 29, 46, 52, 75, 79, 81, 82, 92, 116, 120, 180, 201, 219, 220, 222
Collaborative forms of TNE, 11, 24, 93, 105, 106, 221
Collaborative partnership, 28, 89, 94
Collaborative TNE provision, 12
Community of learners, 180
Completion requirements, 49, 52, 60–61, 64
Confucian ethos, 122
Cooperation agreement, 20
Coventry University, 4, 70, 74, 78, 79, 81, 83
Cross-boundary 'single-team' ethos, 90, 97–100
Cultural differences, 80, 93, 94, 122
Curricula, 16, 17, 20, 45, 61
Cyprus, 134, 181, 183, 188, 189, 222

D

Day-to-day interaction, 121
Degree-awarding bodies (DABs), 130
Distance learning, 9, 11, 130, 155, 181, 219, 224
Diversifying actions, 158, 161–162

Doctoral programme, 115
Domestic academic staff, 16
Dual-way knowledge transfer, 46
Dutch-Indonesian joint degree programme, 31
Dutch institutions, 28, 29, 33–37, 39, 41, 42
Dutch legislation, 31
Dutch national TNE policy debate, 28

E

Egalitarian partnership model, 220
Egypt, 13
England, 144n1, 159, 188, 189, 222
Erasmus, 73, 178–180, 191
Erasmus+, 178
Erasmus programme, 74, 178, 179
Established presence, 119
Europe, 74, 78, 135, 154, 179, 221, 222
European Approach for Quality Assurance of Joint Programmes, 31
European Association for Quality Assurance in Higher Education (ENQA), 130, 135–137, 145n5
European Research Council, 222
European Union (EU), 6, 135, 155, 178, 221, 222
Evidence-based approach, 3
Experimenting, 95, 98, 165–167, 171
Exploring practices, 158, 162–167
Export-led approach, 218
Extracting practices, 167–169

F

Facilities and Qualities of Social Life (FQSF), 198, 203–205, 210–211
Family matters, 120–121
Federal Ministry for Economic Cooperation and Development (BMZ), 23
Financial planning, 19, 20
Financial risk, 35, 39
Franchise models, 11
Franchising, 46, 219, 220, 223, 225
Free University of Berlin, 224
French High Council for the Evaluation of Research and Higher Education (HCERES), 135
Full Dutch degree programmes abroad, 33, 35, 37, 39–42
Future Initiative for Knowledge, 17

G

German Academic Exchange Service (DAAD), 4, 10–14, 16–18, 20, 22–24, 71, 72, 74, 92
German Accreditation Council (GAC), 135
German binational universities, 12
German higher education institutions, 9
German Jordanian University (GJU), 13
German-Mongolian Institute of Resources and Technology (GMIT), 23
German Rectors' Conference (HRK), 15, 24
German TNE, 4, 10–15, 18–25
German universities, 9, 10, 12, 15–18, 22, 24, 224
German University in Cairo (GUC), 13, 17
German University of Technology (GUtech), 13
Germany, 1, 4, 9–25, 61, 208
Global employability, 178
Greece, 134, 179, 181, 183, 188, 189, 193, 222

H

Higher Education Funding Council for England (HEFCE), 132, 144n1, 220
Higher Education Statistics Agency (HESA), 70, 130, 132, 133, 145n5
High order technological learning (HOTL), 201, 202
Home campus, 29, 70, 76, 77, 79, 89, 92, 93, 95–102, 104, 105, 113, 203, 219
Hong Kong, 1, 145n5, 155
Horizon 2020, 222
Host countries, 5, 10, 11, 17, 35, 36, 39–43, 91, 92, 98, 129, 132, 134–136, 140, 145n5, 220

I

Idea generation, 162–165, 171
Impact of TNE on host countries, 71
Importing countries, 1–3, 218, 220, 223, 225

Independent, 6, 11, 12, 20, 22, 89, 92–94, 97, 106, 122, 163, 189, 193, 200
India, 2, 3, 134, 206
Indonesia, 18, 29, 31
Information sharing, 138–140
Institutional governance, 60
Institutional reviews, 133, 134
Intellectual property rights, 20, 180
Inter-agency cooperation, 129, 130, 138–144
Inter-campus collaboration, 94
Inter-campus mobility programmes, 219
Intercultural competence, 4, 15, 69–84
International branch campuses (IBC), 2, 4, 6, 29, 39, 75, 89–106, 112, 155, 197–212, 219
International Dual Degree (IDD) programmes, 45–64, 220
Internationalisation, 4, 10, 15, 16, 19, 23, 24, 30, 32, 39, 43n1, 69–74, 76–83, 218, 222, 223
Internationalisation at Home (IaH), 70, 74, 76, 77, 79
Internationalisation of the Curriculum, 29, 32, 41, 69, 70, 74
International Islamic University, 114
International Network for Quality Assurance Agencies in Higher Education (INQAAHE), 130, 135, 137, 138
Issues in doctoral studies, 115

J

Joint degree, 15, 17, 28, 30–33, 35, 47, 54, 61
Joint PhD programme, 111
Joint-review activity, 139, 142–143
Joint study courses, 11
Joint university, 11
Jordan, 13

K

Kazakhstan, 81–82
Kenya, 18

L

Language skills, 15, 17, 22, 179
Learning resources (LR), 56, 154, 156, 199, 205–206

M

Malaysia, 1, 90, 91, 93, 94, 96, 112–122, 124–126, 132, 134, 145n5, 155, 219, 220
Malaysian, 5, 94, 112–114, 116, 117, 119, 122, 123, 125
Malaysia Nottingham Doctoral Programme (MNDP), 5, 111–126
Managing organisational culture difference, 93
Marketing, 4, 23, 46, 89–91, 94, 99, 100, 103, 205
Massive Online Open Courses (MOOCs), 28, 224
Metanational, 6, 219, 225

Misalignment of expectations, 48
Mongolia, 18
Motivations of universities, 22
Multiple-degree programmes, 28, 30, 34, 37, 42

N

National Agency for Quality Assessment and Accreditation of Spain (ANECA), 135
National strategy, 4, 10, 11, 22
Netherlands, 1, 4, 27–43, 224
New TNE legislation, 28, 33, 34
New York University (NYU), 154, 219
Non-EU student recruitment, 41

O

Online education, 34, 224
Online programmes, 34
Open University, 224
Operating contex, 4, 90
Organisational cultures, 3, 4, 89–106

P

Parent-child analogy, 96
Pathway arrangements, 220
Performativity, 5, 151, 153–154
Postgraduate programmes, 15
Practice-based approach (PBA), 5, 151, 153–154
Primary supervisor, 115–118
Programme effectiveness (PE), 199–200, 206–207
Progression arrangements, 54, 220

Pull factors, 111
Push factors, 111

Q

Qatar, 29, 91, 223
Qatar Education City, 220
Qatar University, 220
Quality assurance, 19–21, 39, 40, 46, 50, 59–60, 64, 93, 96, 113, 116, 130, 134–136, 138–144, 156, 203, 209
Quality Assurance Agency (QAA), 5, 129–144, 155, 156
Quality Assurance of Cross-Border Higher Education (QACHE), 130, 135–138, 143, 144
Quality assurance of TNE, 129–144
Quality assurance procedures, 60, 180
The Quality of Lecturers and Teaching (QLT), 200, 201, 207–208
Quality of the TNE programme, 20–21

R

Reasons for TNE development, 28
Reciprocal recognition of quality assurance decisions, 138, 140–141
Recognition of degrees, 21
Reputation, 16, 27, 32, 33, 43, 48, 63, 98, 99, 116, 119, 120, 123, 126, 179, 197, 207, 225
Research completion, 114
Retention, 115

S

Secondary supervisor, 116
Sending countries, 9, 11, 132, 138, 140, 145n5
Singapore, 1, 91, 134, 145n5, 155
Sino-foreign educational partnerships, 155
Skype, 80, 82, 99, 121
Socialisation, 115, 159–161, 171, 172
Socialising, 158–161, 169
Social media, 6, 157, 161, 162, 169, 171, 197–212
Stenden University of Applied Sciences, 29
Strategy for internationalisation, 19
Student development (SD), 6, 194, 197, 198, 204, 206
Student exchange, 15, 18, 28, 39, 48, 54, 57, 62, 112, 113
Student expectations, 72, 180
Student experience, 3, 5, 6, 46, 51, 55, 79, 82, 112–115, 117, 126, 134, 173, 182, 197–212
Student Learning Environment (SLE), 201, 208–209
Student mobility, 15, 32, 33, 41, 111, 217, 219, 220, 224, 225
Student success, 115
Supervisor movement, 117
Supervisor relationship, 115
Sustainable staffing, 21–22

T

Teaching innovation, 5, 151, 152, 158, 159, 167, 173, 174
Teaching practices, 151–174
Technical University Sofia (FDIBA), 17
Texas A&M, 220
TNE provision, 6, 12–15, 22, 23, 70, 83, 92, 132, 134, 144, 145n5, 155–157, 165, 168, 222
Tongji University, 15, 17
Traditional HEIs, 4
Traditional international partnership, 90
Transformative internationalisation, 82
Transnationale Bildung, 11
Transnational pedagogy, 75
Tunisia, 18
Turkey, 18, 222

U

UK, 1, 2, 4–6, 48, 70, 75, 77, 78, 81–83, 90, 91, 94, 96, 99, 101–103, 112, 114–125, 129, 130, 132–134, 144n1, 145n5, 155, 156, 168, 181, 183–193, 206–208, 211, 218–222, 224
UK Quality Code, *Chapter B10*, 133
UK Quality Code for Higher Education, 133
UK TNE, 5, 70, 91, 130–135, 156, 219, 221, 224
United Arab Emirates (UAE), 91, 134, 154, 197–199, 204–206
United States (USA), 1, 10, 78, 91, 145n5, 206, 207, 221
Universiti Malaya, 114
Universiti Sains Malaysia, 114
Universiti Teknologi Mara, 114
University of Groningen, 29
University of London International Programmes, 224

The University of Nottingham, 111, 112, 114, 115, 118, 120, 123, 124, 220
University of Ulm, 17
Use of Technology (UoT), 167, 201–202, 209

V

Validation, 34, 46, 155, 219, 220, 225

Video conferencing, 121
Vietnam, 18
Vietnamese German University (VGU), 13, 18
Virtual mobility, 70, 78–81, 83

W

WHEEL framework, 49–54, 59, 63, 64
Work-based learning experience, 50

CPSIA information can be obtained
at www.ICGtesting.com
Printed in the USA
LVHW02*2219080718
583087LV00008B/385/P